the complete gui

VISUAL
BASIC 5

the complete guide to
VISUAL BASIC 5

STEVE BROWN

Computer Step
Southfield Road . Southam
Warwickshire CV33 OFB . England
http://www.computerstep.com

Tel: 01926 817999 Fax: 01926 817005

Notice of Liability
Every effort has been made to ensure that this book contains
accurate and current information. However, the publishers and
the author shall not be liable for any loss or damage suffered
by readers as a result of any information contained herein.

Trademarks
Microsoft, Windows, Windows NT, Visual Basic are either
registered trademarks or trademarks of Microsoft Corporation.
All other trademarks are acknowledged as belonging to their
respective companies.

Printed and bound in the United Kingdom

ISBN 1 874029 64 4

For Sale in United Kingdom and Ireland Only

This book is dedicated to my wife Susan, who encouraged me to go for it on my own. You can have your husband back now. Thanks to "Brownie" for giving me the motivation to undertake this venture and especially to God for loaning me the talent to actually do it. I would also like to thank my family and friends for their constant support and encouragement throughout the years.

ACKNOWLEDGEMENTS

Many thanks go out to many people for the production of this book. To Scott Calamar and Kristine Plachy: Thanks for hooking me up with the job. Thanks to Arthur Tennick for writing the book which served as this book's predecessor. Peter Kuhns: Thanks for helping me get the feel for this book-writing thing. Kim Wimpsett: Thanks for your patience and helpful comments during the editing process. John Piraino: Thank you for the nice tech editing and "good saves." Finally, thank you to the many others at Sybex who put in numerous hours to make the intangible tangible—most notable are Amy Eoff and Dina Quan.

CONTENTS AT A GLANCE

Introduction 1

Skills 1 Mastering the Integrated Development
Environment (IDE) 5

2 Working with Forms 39

3 Selecting and Using Controls 75

4 Working within Modules and Classes 145

5 Creating and Using Menus and Toolbars 167

6 Using Variables, Arrays, and Constants 183

7 Storing and Retrieving Data 205

8 Printing 255

9 Using Dialog Boxes 273

10 Working with the Mouse 287

11 Creating and Using Help Files 299

12 Compiling and Distributing Your Application 323

13 Learning and Using Object-Oriented
Programming (OOP) 345

14 Using ActiveX 363

15 Using DLLs and the Windows API 385

Index 403

TABLE OF CONTENTS

Introduction 1

Skill 1.   **Mastering the Integrated Development**
                 Environment (IDE) 5

Introducing Visual Basic 5

Learning the IDE Features 8

    The Toolbar 10
    The Project Explorer 12
    The Properties Window 14
    The Form Layout Window 20
    The Toolbox 21
    The Form Designer 23

Know Your Visual Basic Editor, and Know it Well 24

Working with Multiple Projects 25

Customizing the IDE 26

    The Editor Tab 27
    The Editor Format Tab 29
    The General Tab 29
    The Docking Tab 30
    The Environment Tab 30
    The Advanced Tab 31

Creating Your First Applet 32

    Hello World! 32

Summary of Skills Acquired 37

Skill 2.   **Working with Forms** 39

The Anatomy of a Form 39

    The Border 40
    The Caption 40
    The Title Bar 41
    The Control Menu 41
    The Minimize Button 41
    The Maximize/Restore Button 41
    The Close Button 42

Working with Form Properties 42
    The *BackColor* Property 44
    The *BorderStyle* Property 44
    The *Caption* Property 45
    The *ControlBox* Property 45
    The *ForeColor* Property 46
    The *Height* Property 47
    The *Icon* Property 48
    The *Left* Property 48
    The *MaxButton* Property 49
    The *MinButton* Property 49
    The *Name* Property 50
    The *ScaleMode* Property 50
    The *ShowInTaskbar* Property 50
    The *Width* Property 51
    The *WindowState* Property 51
Tweaking a Form's Properties 51
    Extending the Code 53
    Fixing a Bug 53
Introducing Form Events 55
    The *Activate* Event 58
    The *Deactivate* Event 59
    The *DragDrop* Event 59
    The *Load* Event 60
    The *Resize* Event 61
    The *Unload* Event 62
Introducing Form Methods 63
Working with Multiple Document Interface (MDI) Forms 64
    Creating an MDI 65
    Improving an MDI 67
    Deciphering the Code 69
Using the Form Wizard 70
Summary of Skills Acquired 74

Skill 3.   **Selecting and Using Controls** **75**
Introducing Controls 75
Using Command Buttons 76
    Command Button Properties 77
    Command Button Events 79
    Command Button Methods 79
    Experimenting with a Control 80

Using Text Boxes 82
    Text Box Properties 82
    Text Box Events 84
    Text Box Methods 84
    Experimenting with Text Box Controls 85
Using Labels 88
    Label Properties 90
    Label Events 91
    Label Methods 92
    Experimenting with a Label Control 92
Using Option Buttons 93
    Option Button Properties 93
    Option Button Events 94
    Option Button Methods 96
Using Check Boxes 97
    Check Box Properties 98
    Check Box Events 99
    Check Box Methods 99
    Experimenting with Check Box Controls 100
Using Frame Controls 103
    Frame Properties 104
    Frame Events 104
    Frame Methods 105
Using List Boxes 106
    List Box Properties 106
    List Box Events 109
    List Box Methods 109
    Experimenting with List Box Controls 110
Using Combo Boxes 112
    Combo Box Properties 113
    Combo Box Events 114
    Combo Box Methods 115
    Experimenting with List and Combo Box Controls 116
Using Image Objects 118
    Image Properties 118
    Image Events 119
    Image Methods 119
    Experimenting with Image Controls 120
Using Picture Boxes 121
    Picture Box Properties 122
    Picture Box Events 123
    Picture Box Methods 124

Using Timers 125
    Timer Properties 125
    The Timer Event 126
    Timer Methods 126
    Experimenting with a Timer Control 126
Using Scroll Bars 128
    Scroll Bar Properties 129
    Scroll Bar Events 130
    Scroll Bar Methods 131
    Experimenting with Scroll Bar Controls 131
Using Drive Lists 133
    Drive List Box Properties 133
    Drive List Box Events 134
    Drive List Box Methods 135
Using Directory List Boxes 135
    Directory List Box Properties 135
    Directory List Box Events 136
    Directory List Box Methods 136
Using File List Boxes 136
    File List Box Properties 137
    File List Box Events 139
    File List Box Methods 140
    Experimenting with File List Box Controls 140
Adding Other Controls to the Toolbox 143
Summary of Skills Acquired 144

Skill 4.   **Working within Modules and Classes 145**
Introducing Code Modules 145
    Creating a Code Library 146
    Retrieving Code Modules 146
    Creating a Code Module 147
Using *Private* and *Public* Sub Procedures 149
Passing Parameters to Procedures 152
Creating and Using Functions 155
Adding Code Modules 160
Working with Class Modules 161
    Methods 163
    Properties 164
Summary of Skills Acquired 165

Skill 5.   **Creating and Using Menus and Toolbars** **167**

When to Use Menus and Toolbars 167

Understanding the Menu Object 168

     Menu Properties 169

     The Click Event 171

     Menu Methods 172

Creating a Menu with the Menu Editor 172

Considering a Menu's Design 176

Creating Toolbars 177

     Adding Buttons to Toolbars 178

     Adding Images to Toolbars 179

Summary of Skills Acquired 182

Skill 6.   **Using Variables, Arrays, and Constants** **183**

Introducing Variables 183

     What Is Memory? 183

Variable Types 184

     Using Byte-Sized Variables 185

     Working with a String: The Byte's Big Brother 187

     Using Integers 190

     Using Boolean Variables 192

     Variants — The Bane of a Programmer's Existence 193

     Determining the Scope of a Variable 194

     The Static Statement 198

Using Arrays 199

     Dynamic Arrays 201

Using Constants 202

Summary of Skills Acquired 204

Skill 7.   **Storing and Retrieving Data** **205**

Working with ASCII Files 205

     Understanding Sequential Mode 208

     Understanding Random Access Mode 211

     Understanding Binary Access Mode 214

Using Data Controls 224

     Adding the Data Control 225

     The Data Control Properties 227

The Anatomy of a Database 229

     Database Tables 229

     Database Queries 231

Creating Databases with Visual Data Manager 232

Creating a Database Table 234

    Defining a Table 236

    Adding Fields 237

    Entering Data 238

Creating a Query 240

    Primary Keys 243

    Counter Fields 244

    Number Fields 245

    Currency Fields 247

    Yes/No Fields 247

    Memo Fields 247

    Date/Time Fields 248

Modifying a Table 249

Summary of Skills Acquired 254

Skill 8.   **Printing** **255**

Making the Ultimate Use of Your Data 255

Understanding the *Print* Method 256

Viewing Values in the Immediate Window 257

    Viewing an Error in the Debug Window 258

    Fixing a Bug 259

Understanding the *PrintForm* Method 260

Using Crystal Reports Pro for Visual Basic 260

Using a Report in Your Application 262

Printing Your Source Code 263

    Using the Print Dialog Box 264

    Viewing the Results 267

    Deciphering the Code Listing 270

Summary of Skills Acquired 271

Skill 9.   **Using Dialog Boxes** **273**

Using Predefined Dialog Boxes 273

    Creating a Message Dialog Box 273

    Creating an Input Dialog Box 275

Creating Your Own Dialog Boxes 276

Doing Dialog Boxes with Class 278

Using the Dialogs Class 281

Summary of Skills Acquired 286

Skill 10.   **Working with the Mouse** **287**

Detecting Mouse Events 287

The *Click* Event 288
The *DblClick* Event 288
The *DragDrop* Event 288
The *DragOver* Event 289
The *MouseDown* Event 290
The *MouseMove* Event 291
The *MouseUp* Event 291

Using Drag-and-Drop Operations 292

Creating an Easter Egg 295

Summary of Skills Acquired 297

Skill 11.   **Creating and Using Help Files** **299**

Using Help Files in Your Application 299

Creating Your First Help File 301

Designing and Creating a Contents File 302
Writing a Topic File 305
Creating a Help Project File 313

Linking Your Application to Your Help File 318

Summary of Skills Acquired 322

Skill 12.   **Compiling and Distributing Your Application** **323**

Compiling Your Project 323

Using the Make Tab 324

Version Number 325
Application 326
Version Information 326
Command Line Arguments 328
Conditional Compilation 330

Compiler Settings 330

Compile to P-Code 331
Compile to Native Code 331

Using the Setup Wizard 334

Saving a Template 339

Scanning for Viruses 341

Distributing Your Program 342

Summary of Skills Acquired 343

Skill 13. **Learning and Using Object-Oriented Programming (OOP)** **345**

Defining OOP 345
    Why Should You Use OOP? 346
Characteristics of an Object 349
    The Properties of an Object 349
    The Methods of an Object 350
    The Inheritance Characteristic 351
    The Encapsulation Characteristic 352
    The Polymorphism Characteristic 353
Writing Reusable Code 354
    Creating a Human Resources Class 355
    Using the Human Resources Class 358
Summary of Skills Acquired 361

Skill 14. **Using ActiveX** **363**

Understanding the Active Platform 363
The Role of ActiveX 364
    ActiveX Requirements 365
    How Web Pages Work 366
Understanding the Role of ActiveX in Software Development 367
    Creating and Using ActiveX Documents 368
    Creating and Using ActiveX Controls 373
    Creating and Using ActiveX DLLs 380
Summary of Skills Acquired 383

Skill 15. **Using DLLs and the Windows API** **385**

Introducing Dynamic Link Libraries (DLLs) 385
DLL Calling Conventions 386
    Understanding DLL Calling Conventions 387
The API Viewer 389
Using the API in Your Applications 392
    Modifying the API Function 394
Adding an Application to the System Tray 395
    Creating the SysTray Control 395
    Using the SysTray Control 396
Looking to the Future 400
Summary of Skills Acquired 401

Index **403**

INTRODUCTION

Microsoft Visual Basic 5 is the newest version of the popular programming language. With its new features, Visual Basic is an even stronger contender in the application development arena than ever before.

The Visual Basic environment is great for creating almost any type of application you can think of. You can develop robust stand-alone applications, games, and utilities in less time than it takes in other languages. You can also use ActiveX technology to create Internet-enabled applications that are limited only by your imagination. When used in conjunction with the Windows API, you are armed with a serious programming tool for which you can do almost anything in your project development efforts.

The Complete Guide to Visual Basic 5 is designed to help you quickly become proficient in Visual Basic. This book will present you with the most important skills required to program a fully functional application—without requiring you to study every aspect in detail. You are not required to have prior experience with Visual Basic; the only requirements are a basic familiarity with the Windows environment and a desire to learn.

What Will You Learn from This Book?

This book aims to teach you everything you need to know about Visual Basic to use it effectively. The book is divided into skills that are designed to teach you a specific aspect of Visual Basic application development. Each skill demonstrates a particular feature or programming method, as well as offering you practical sample applications and routines. You do not need to read the book from cover to cover to learn a new skill. Simply jump to the skill you want to master and you are on your way!

In Skill 1, "Mastering the Integrated Development Environment (IDE)", you will discover the Visual Basic tools essential to working in Visual Basic, and you will create your very first application. In Skill 2, "Working with Forms", you'll understand and master the most basic element of application development. In Skill 3, "Selecting and Using Controls", you'll become familiar with many of the components that you will use in almost all of your applications. Skill 4, "Working within Modules and Classes", will help you to understand how and when to place procedures in code modules and class modules. You will learn how to create and link menus and toolbars, as well as learn the basics of interface design in Skill 5, "Creating and Using Menus and Toolbars".

In Skill 6, "Using Variables, Arrays, and Constants", you will take your programming knowledge a step further by learning how to manipulate memory objects, called *variables*, so your applications can perform useful tasks. Once you know how to work with variables, you can move on to Skill 7, "Storing and Retrieving Data". Here you will learn how to store data to disk and how to retrieve it. Skill 8, "Printing", teaches you how to perform basic printing services in your application and then introduces you to Crystal Reports Pro for Visual Basic.

In Skill 9, "Using Dialog Boxes", you will learn how to use the dialog boxes that are built-in to Visual Basic. Once you have mastered these, you will learn how to create your own reusable dialog boxes. Skill 10, "Working with the Mouse", teaches you how to program the mouse for your application. You will learn how to detect mouse-clicks, mouse movements, as well as create a drag-and-drop application. In Skill 11, "Creating and Using Help Files", you will learn how to use a utility that comes with Visual Basic— Help Compiler Workshop—to design and build your own help files, as well as link them to your Visual Basic application. This skill is a must for serious programmers. In Skill 12, "Compiling and Distributing Your Application", you will learn how to compile your program and distribute it to others. This skill also covers some special considerations that you, as a programmer, must consider when entering the marketplace with your application.

The last three skills deal with the more advanced features of Visual Basic. In Skill 13, "Using Object-Oriented Programming (OOP)", you will learn the basics of OOP and how to apply it in your application development efforts. It's easier than you think! In Skill 14, "Using ActiveX", you will learn about Microsoft's latest strategy for developing for the Internet: ActiveX. You will learn about its intent and specifications, as well as how to develop ActiveX components for your applications. Finally in, Skill 15, "Using DLLs and the Windows API", you will learn to do just that. You will use the Windows API to play a .WAV file as well as add an application to the System Tray. Using Visual Basic with the Windows API gives you almost endless possibilities for program development.

In addition to the skills within the book, you will find Notes, Tips, and Warnings that can help you become more productive within the Visual Basic environment.

I hope you will find this book to be a valuable resource that you will have by your side as you write your killer apps.

What This Book Assumes

This book assumes that you are familiar with the basics of the Windows environment:

- You know how to use Windows and navigate its interface enough to start an application.
- You know how to use the mouse and keyboard within Windows.

In addition, this book assumes that you have installed the sample applications on your Visual Basic CD. You will examine, as well as modify, some of these applications in this book.

Conventions Used in This Book

This book uses a number of conventions to convey more information accurately in a few pages:

- ➤ designates choosing a command from a menu. For example, "choose File ➤ Exit" means you should open the File menu and then choose Exit.
- \+ signs indicate key combinations. For example, "press Ctrl+Alt+Del" means that you should hold down the Ctrl and Alt keys, and press the Del key.
- **Boldface** indicates items that you want to type in exactly as it is printed.
- *Italics* are used to introduce new terms or information that may not be exactly the same from computer to computer, such as drive letters.
- An underscore character (_) in a code listing indicates that the line of code continues onto the next line. You should type these in as you see them in the book; Visual Basic recognises them as continuation of lines of code.

The Visual Basic 5 Virtual CD

This book has a companion Web site, from **http://www.computerstep.com**, that includes a number of helpful items for your Visual Basic needs, e.g:

Code Lists   Some chapters in this book include large-scale tutorials that require you to create new objects and enter code for the objects. If you're in a hurry or don't really feel like entering a lot of code, visit *The Complete Guide* section of the Web site for complete code listings organized by chapter.

Job Links   When you're ready to take your knowledge out in the field and pursue the high-paying, high-tech jobs, check out the job links.

SKILL
1

Mastering the Integrated Development Environment (IDE)

Featuring

- ❏ Introducing Visual Basic
- ❏ Learning the IDE features
- ❏ Working with multiple projects
- ❏ Customizing the IDE
- ❏ Creating an applet

Introducing Visual Basic

Visual Basic version 5 is the newest addition to the family of Visual Basic products. It allows you to quickly and easily create Windows applications for your PC without being an expert in C++ or other programming languages.

Visual Basic provides a graphical environment where you visually design the forms and controls that your applications use. Visual Basic supports many useful tools that will help you be more productive. These include, but are not limited to, projects, forms, object templates, custom controls, add-ins, and a database manager. You can use these tools together to create complete applications in months, weeks, or even days; this is compared to a much longer development time when you use other languages.

Version 5 of Visual Basic is specifically designed to utilize the Internet. It comes with several controls that allow you to create Web-based applications, called *ActiveX executables*. These will work just like stand-alone Visual Basic applications, but they are accessed through the Microsoft Internet Explorer Web browser. This allows you to revise your applications and distribute them through the Internet. We will discuss this feature in more detail later in the book (see Skill 14).

In addition, Visual Basic sports a new development environment, modelled after the Windows Explorer environment. This makes it easy for a computer user to jump right into creating applications with Visual Basic. Almost all of the objects and tools on the screen can be manipulated through a right mouse-click. You can set properties, add controls, and even view context-sensitive help with this single action.

When you start Visual Basic for the first time, the Project Wizard will open, and you will notice the New Project dialog box (see Figure 1.1).

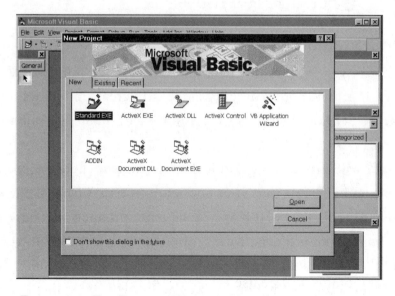

FIGURE 1.1: THE PROJECT WIZARD'S NEW PROJECT DIALOG BOX

From this window you can select from several types of *projects* that give you a head start on developing your applications. This window has three tabs: New, Existing, and Recent.

The New tab presents you with several project templates:

- Standard EXE
- ActiveX EXE
- ActiveX DLL
- ActiveX Control
- VB Application Wizard
- ADDIN
- ActiveX Document DLL
- ActiveX Document EXE

By selecting a project template from the New tab, you let Visual Basic create the foundation of your application. This can save you a lot of time designing an application, especially if you are new to Visual Basic. You may also notice the small check box at the bottom of the form: Don't Show This Dialog in the Future. If you prefer not to be bothered with selecting a project type, you can check this box and the window will not come up the next time you start Visual Basic.

Tip

Leave the Don't Show This Dialog in the Future check box empty. We will be using project templates throughout this book. When you are more experienced, you can check this option if you do not want to use templates in the future.

You will learn to use some of these templates later in the book. For most of the skills in this book, you will use the Standard EXE, but some of the ActiveX templates will be used in Skill 14, "ActiveX."

The Existing tab allows you to select an existing project. This could be a sample project included with Visual Basic, or it could be a project you have worked on in the past. As you work more with Visual Basic, you will choose this tab more frequently.

Finally, the Recent tab allows you to select from the most recently used (MRU) projects. The tab is similar to the Existing tab, but it presents you with a list of the existing projects you have worked on recently, instead of *all* of the existing projects.

You can use any of these tabs to help get you started on a project in Visual Basic. Now let's take a closer look at the Visual Basic integrated development environment (IDE).

Learning the IDE Features

Behind the Project Wizard window lies the integrated development environment, or IDE (see Figure 1.2). The IDE is an important part of Visual Basic; it's where you put together your applications and where you'll spend much of your time when you're creating applications.

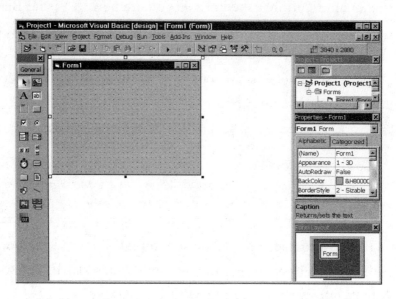

FIGURE 1.2: VISUAL BASIC'S INTEGRATED DEVELOPMENT ENVIRONMENT (IDE)

IDE is a term commonly used in the programming world to describe the interface and environment you use to create your applications. It is called *integrated* because you can access virtually all of the development tools you need from one screen, called an *interface*. The IDE is also commonly referred to as the *design environment*, the *program*, or just the *IDE*. We will use the latter term, so you can add your first programming buzzword to your vocabulary.

The IDE is made up of a number of components:

- Toolbar
- Project Explorer
- Properties window
- Form Layout window
- Toolbox
- Form Designer

The All-Important IDE

I cannot stress enough how important it is for you as a programmer to become familiar with your integrated development environment (IDE). If you jump right into coding without becoming comfortable with your IDE, you may spend a good deal of your development time learning the editor and tools, rather than writing code—which is what programming is all about.

Take some time to just play in the IDE. Tweak settings, move windows, and adjust toolbars. Just get comfortable. Not only will you be more productive, but your coworkers will sit in awe when you can be the first to show them all of the tricks you have learned.

After reading the next few sections and becoming familiar with Visual Basic's IDE, you'll be able to roll up your sleeves and get some bits and bytes under your fingernails!

The Toolbar

Immediately below the menu bar should be the Visual Basic toolbar (see Figure 1.3). If you can't see the toolbar, then click View ➤ Toolbars ➤ Standard. You can control the whole Visual Basic environment from the menu bar, but the toolbar gives you easy access to the menu-bar commands you'll use most frequently.

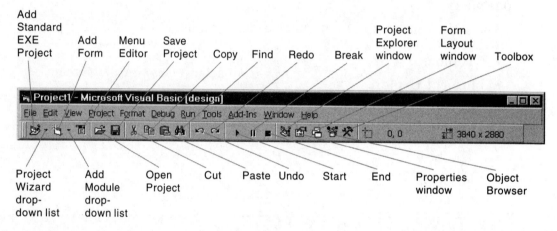

FIGURE 1.3: THE VISUAL BASIC TOOLBAR

The toolbar in version 5 of Visual Basic has inherited the characteristics of the toolbar in Microsoft Internet Explorer. You will notice when you move the mouse over the buttons they appear to raise themselves up from the toolbar. If you rest the mouse pointer over a button for a moment, you will also see the tool tip for that button.

Note

A tool tip is a little cream-coloured box that explains to you what the button's function is. You will most likely find yourself adding these helpful tips to your projects in the future.

One of the many enhancements in version 5 of Visual Basic is the provision of several toolbars. By selecting View ➤ Toolbars, you can also show or hide toolbars for the Edit, Debug, and Form Editor windows. If you are really finicky about your environment, you can even customize these toolbars to suit your preferences.

Moving a Toolbar Button

Let's say you want to move some buttons around on the Visual Basic toolbar to make them more accessible to you. You would follow these steps:

1. Right-click on the menu bar or toolbar at the top of the screen.
2. Select Customize... from the pop-up menu.
3. The Customize dialog box has three tabs: Toolbars, Commands, and Options. On the Toolbars tab, click the check box next to the toolbar you want to edit. (If the toolbar is already on the IDE like the standard toolbar, you can go straight to it. If it is not already available, checking the toolbar option will bring up the newly selected toolbar.)
4. Click the left mouse button on a toolbar button and hold the mouse button down. Now "drag" the button to a new position on the toolbar.
5. You will notice the I-bracket will move along the toolbar, under the button you are dragging. If the I-bracket is in the location where you want the button, let go of the mouse button and the toolbar button will "drop" into its new position.

Note

You can move toolbar buttons to the menu as well. Just drag the button to the menu title. When the menu drops down, drag the button to a position on the menu.

If you decide you don't want to keep the changes you have just made, click the Reset button to restore the buttons to their default positions. Otherwise, click Close to save your modifications.

Removing and Adding a Menu Item

If a toolbar does not contain the shortcuts you want, or you want to add another menu item, you can customize them even further to get what you want. Try the following:

1. Select the Commands tab from the Customize dialog box.
2. In the Categories list, scroll down to the bottom and select Built-in Menus.
3. Now go up to the Help menu on the Visual Basic menu bar and drag it to the Commands list. Once the menu item is over the list, drop it. The Help menu has been removed from your menu.
4. Select Help from the Commands list and drag it back to the menu and drop it back in its original position.
5. Click Close to save your modifications.

Now you have a good foundation for customizing the menu bar and toolbars. Experiment and get your environment set up the way you want it.

Note

The previous examples showed you a common Windows task called drag-and-drop. You will be using this frequently within the IDE, and you may even program this functionality in your own programs. See Skill 10 for more information on the drag-and-drop technique.

The Project Explorer

Docked to the right side of the screen, just under the toolbar, is the Project Explorer window (see Figure 1.4). The Project Explorer is your quick reference to the various elements—forms, classes, and modules—in your project.

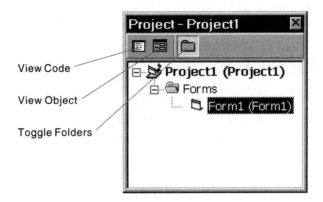

FIGURE 1.4: THE PROJECT EXPLORER WINDOW

The Project Explorer window is much like the Windows Explorer in that it allows you to expand and collapse the subfolders.

All of the objects that make up your application are packaged in a project. If you save it for later use, testing, debugging, or improvement, Visual Basic provides the default file extension .VBP (Visual Basic Project) to the project.

A simple project will typically contain one *form*, which is the window used by your application. In addition to forms, the Project Explorer window also lists code modules and classes. We will learn more about these later in Skill 4.

Note

Larger applications will often have a number of forms and modules. These too are listed in the Project Explorer window.

If you want to remove an object from your project, right-click on the name of the object in the Project Explorer window and select Remove... The name of the control will be listed after the Remove command. In this example you should see Remove Form1.

To view a form, select it in the Project Explorer and click the View Object button. (Any code associated with the form can be viewed in its own window by clicking the View Code button.)

If you right-click in the Project Explorer, you are presented with a pop-up menu that offers many options specific to that particular window. For instance, you can add, remove, and print forms and code modules from the pop-up menu.

Tip

Right-clicking on objects in Visual Basic will expose object-specific pop-up menus. These menus will allow you to quickly access tools that you can use to operate directly on the active object. I recommend getting used to doing this, because it will save time and wear and tear on your fingers.

The Properties Window

Docked right under the Project Explorer window is the Properties window. The Properties window exposes the various characteristics (or *properties*) of selected objects. To clarify this concept, consider that each and every form in an application is an *object*. Each and every *control* (a command button, for example) that appears on a form is also an object. Now, each object in Visual Basic has characteristics such as colour and size. Other characteristics affect not just the appearance of an object but the way it behaves, too. All these characteristics of an object are called its *properties*. Thus, a form

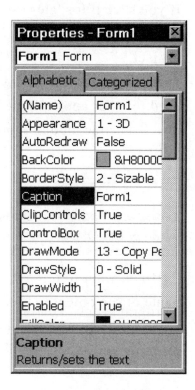

FIGURE 1.5: THE PROPERTIES WINDOW

has properties, and any controls placed on a form have properties, too. All of these properties are displayed in the Properties window (see Figure 1.5).

In the Properties window you will see a list of the properties belonging to an object. There are quite a few of them, and you may have to scroll to see them all. Fortunately, many of the properties are self-explanatory (Caption, Height, Width, and so on), while some of the others are rarely used. If you are not sure of what a specific property does, you can look at the brief description at the bottom of the Properties window. Besides scrolling to view properties, you can also view properties either alphabetically or by category. Whichever method you use is a matter of preference.

Tip

If you're not sure of a property's purpose, click on the property in the Properties window and press F1. This opens context-sensitive help on the highlighted property.

When a control (a command button, for example) is put on a form, the Properties window shows the properties for that control when it's selected. You can see the properties for different objects, including the underlying form, by clicking on each object in turn. Alternatively, use the drop-down list at the top of the Properties window to select the control and display its properties. Most properties are set at design time, though many can be changed at run time.

Most of the time, you will set properties directly from the Properties window when you are creating an application. When you're working in the IDE, it is referred to as working in "design time" because you are still designing your program. Sometimes you will need to change properties while a program runs. You may want to disable a command button, for example. You can do this by writing code that changes the property. This is done at "run time," when your program is actually running.

Note

When more than one control is selected on a form, you get to see only those properties shared by all the controls. Setting a property in those circumstances affects all the selected controls. Setting, say, the Top property of a number of controls simultaneously in this manner enables you to vertically align the controls. It's not possible to include the underlying form itself in a multiple selection.

The way to change a property setting depends on the range and type of values it can hold. Since the Visual Basic IDE is a visual environment, you will set most properties at design time. This saves you time by not requiring you to write the code to achieve the same results. Below are some examples of the most common types of properties and their uses.

To try these examples, start a new project by selecting File ➤ New Project from the menu. When the Project Wizard appears, select Standard EXE to create a standard executable project.

Boolean Value Properties

1. Open Form1 by double-clicking on it in the Project Explorer window. If the setting has a True or False value (called a *Boolean*), then you can change it by double-clicking the name of the property in the first column of the Properties window. Set the MaxButton property of Form1 to **False**.

2. Click Run ➤ Start. Your form will no longer have a Maximize button. This is handy if you don't want your application to cover the entire screen.

To stop the program, select Run ➤ End from the Visual Basic menu; this will bring you back into design mode.

Predefined Value Properties

If the setting has a number of predefined values (called an *enumerated list*), then double-click the property name cycles through all the permissible values. If there are a large number of options, then opening the drop-down list of values in the second column is probably quicker. To understand how an enumerated list works in the Properties window, you can experiment with the BorderStyle property of Form1.

1. Click on Form1 to make it the active control.
2. In the Properties window, click the drop-down arrow to the right of the BorderStyle property. You will see a list of possible values for this property:
    - Setting this value to 0-None removes all borders from the form. This is commonly seen on splash screens.
    - Setting 1-Fixed Single allows you to create a thin border that cannot be resized.
    - The default value of a form's BorderStyle property is 2-Sizable. Use this setting if you want your users to be able to stretch the window to a different size.
    - If you do not want your user to resize a dialog box for any reason, you can set the property to 3-Fixed Dialog. Warning messages that you receive in Windows use this style of border.
    - Finally, if you are creating a floating toolbar, also called a *tool window*, you can set the BorderStyle property to 4-Fixed Tool Window, or 5-Sizable Tool Window, depending on how you want the toolbar to behave.
3. Set the BorderStyle property to 3-Fixed Dialog. This will prevent the user from resizing your form.
4. Select Run ➤ Start from the menu to test your form. You will notice now the form has no Minimize or Maximize buttons. In addition, the form cannot be resized by stretching its borders.
5. When you are done examining the form, click its Close button.

String Value Properties

Some properties require text, called *strings* in programmer jargon. Two of the properties you will encounter the most—Name and Caption—require strings. When the setting requires you type an entry, then double-clicking the name is easier than clicking in the second column. The former highlights the entry (if any) in the second column so you can simply overtype instead of using the Delete or Backspace keys first. After you finish typing, it's safer to click back on the form or to press Enter—either of these removes the cursor from the settings box to prevent any accidental key presses from being added to the entry.

Let's change the name of the form and set a caption in the title bar of the form:

1. Click the form once to make it active.
2. In the Properties window, double-click on the Name property. It is at the top of the properties list. The value Form1 should be completely highlighted.
3. Type **frmMain** in this field. Notice the old name was automatically deleted as you started typing. Learning to overtype will save you time, not only in Visual Basic, but in other text applications as well. No longer do you have to continue hitting the Backspace key to edit text.
4. Hit the Enter key to set the Name property to **frmMain**.
5. Next, double-click on the Caption property to highlight the text Form 1.
6. Overtype the words **I can overtype text.** in the Caption field.

As you work with Visual Basic, you will notice that you use these two properties the most. The Name property identifies the form to the application, and the Caption property identifies the form to the user.

Hexadecimal Value Properties

Some of the entries look quite unfriendly, such as BackColor and the other colour settings. Fortunately, they're not as bad as they appear. A double-click on the property name in the first column opens a dialog box that contains two tabs. The Palette tab contains a Color Palette where you can choose a value by selecting its colour, rather than by typing a hexadecimal code. The System tab allows you to select colours based on the colour scheme defined in the Windows Control Panel. You can keep a Color Palette permanently visible by clicking View ➤ Color Palette. In this case a single click on the setting followed by a click in the palette is enough. BackColor is a good one to try out for frmMain—the ForeColor and FillColor will have no effect at this stage.

1. Double-click the BackColor property in the Properties window to bring up the Color dialog box.
2. Select the Palette tab to show the Color palette.
3. Click on the red colour to change the background of the form to red. This looks pretty ugly, so change the colour back to the default window colour:
4. Double-click the BackColor property again and select the System tab.
5. Select Button Face as the colour. If you select Window Background, the form will turn white. Because most controls in Windows are now 3-D controls, you can set the form's colour to the same as the command button's colour. This way it will be 3-D grey.

Note

While this is an easy way to set colours on your forms, you will almost always want to stick with the system colours defined on the System tab. This will allow your application to inherit the colours your users prefer. Keep them happy.

File Name Properties

A couple of properties have the setting (None). These are the ones that require a file reference. To pick a file, double-click the property name. For example, the Icon property for a form determines the icon that is displayed if you minimize the form at run time. Under Windows it also sets the icon that appears on the Taskbar and as the Control menu on the form. There are plenty of icons to evaluate in the \Graphics\Icons subdirectory of the Visual Basic directory. To reset one of these properties to (None), click once in the settings column and press Delete. To add an icon to the form:

1. Double-click the Icon property of frmMain. This will bring up the Load Icon dialog box.

2. Select Face02.ico from the \Graphics\Icons\Misc subdirectory. Click the Open button.

    The icon for your application is now a little yellow smiley face.

Size Properties

Four properties—Left, Top, Width, and Height—appear on the toolbar as well as in the Properties window. You can, if you want, type the values directly into the second column of the Properties window. However, there's another, easier way: If you drag the form in the Form Layout window and release the mouse button, the Left and Top property coordinates are updated on the toolbar—they're also updated in the Properties window. When you drag one of the form's borders and release the mouse button, then the Width and Height property coordinates are updated. You can move and resize controls on the form as well, only this time the coordinates are updated as you drag.

The Form Layout Window

The Form Layout window is a simple but useful tool (see Figure 1.6). Its purpose is to simply give you a thumbnail view of the current form, showing you what it looks like and how it is positioned on the screen at run-time.

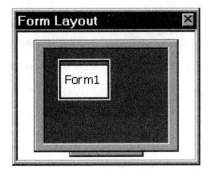

FIGURE 1.6: THE FORM LAYOUT WINDOW

The Form Layout window is useful for determining what screen real estate your form will use when your application is running. To use the Form Layout window, do the following:

1. Click on the form in the Form Layout window and move it to the centre of the monitor graphic in the middle of the window.
2. Run your program by selecting Run ➤ Start.

The Toolbox

As the name implies, the toolbox contains the bits and pieces you need to build your application interface. All the tools shown in Figure 1.7, with the exception of the pointer at the top left, correspond to the objects, or items, you might want to place on a form in your application. These tools or objects are referred to as *controls*. Most of them are an intrinsic part of Visual Basic and are called *built-in* or *standard* controls. Some examples include the command button control and the text box control. Skill 3 covers these controls in more detail. Depending on your Visual Basic setup, there may be a few more controls in the toolbox.

FIGURE 1.7: THE VISUAL BASIC TOOLBOX WITH THE CUSTOM CONTROLS

Organizing the toolbox

The toolbox in version 5 is similar to the toolbox in previous version of Visual Basic, but it has one major difference: It allows you to define tabs, which you can then use to organize your controls. You may want to organize your custom controls by category. For example, I like to keep all of my Internet custom controls on a separate tab.

To add a new Internet tab to your toolbox, follow these steps:

1. Right-click on a blank area of the toolbox.
2. Select Add Tab from the pop-up menu.
3. When Visual Basic prompts you to enter a new tab name, type **Internet**.
4. Click the OK button.
5. Now that you can create a new toolbox tab, you can drag whatever controls you'd like to the tab; for example, drag the image control to the Internet tab you just created. (You will not have any Internet-related controls on your toolbar at this time.)
6. To add custom controls—like those created by Microsoft and other third-party companies—right-click on the toolbox and select Components from the pop-up menu, or select Project ➤ Components.
7. Check the box next to the control you want to add from the list of available controls, in this case, Microsoft Internet Controls.
8. Click the OK button to add the controls to the toolbox.

The names of the tabs and the categories you define are strictly a matter of your personal preference. Create tabs you are comfortable with, and organize your controls the way you like them.

Removing a toolbox Control

To remove a control, simply turn off the appropriate check box in the Custom Controls dialog box. Be aware that you can't add or remove the built-in controls from the toolbox, so controls such as the command button will always be present. To remove the Internet controls:

1. Right-click on the toolbox.
2. Select Components from the pop-up menu.
3. Just as you added the components in the previous exercise, you remove them by removing the check from the box next to the control. Remove the check next to Microsoft Internet Controls.
4. Click the OK button.

The Form Designer

In the centre of the screen, between all of the toolboxes and other windows, you will see the Form Designer. This is the workspace where you actually design the visual layout of the form and the controls that lay on it.

In the Visual Basic IDE, you will see either one form at a time, or the Code window, in this space. (The Code window is discussed in the next section.)

Notice the form has little black dots in the centre of each side. These boxes are called anchors. You can drag an anchor with the mouse to resize the form.

Tip

If you want to make a form that is larger than the Form Designer window, you can stretch the border over the Project Explorer and Properties windows and Visual Basic will resize it accordingly. The form will then lie under the Project Explorer and Properties windows. You can use the scroll bars to uncover the hidden portions of the form.

Know Your Visual Basic Editor, and Know it Well

My Unix instructor's first words to the class were "Know your editor!" If any of you have ever had the dubious pleasure of working with the Unix's VI editor, you know exactly what he meant. These words have proven their meaning over and over to me during my years of programming.

In Visual Basic, the editor is called the *Code window* (see Figure 1.8). For all practical terms, it's just an editor. Regardless of what you want to call it, this is the window where you will do most of your work.

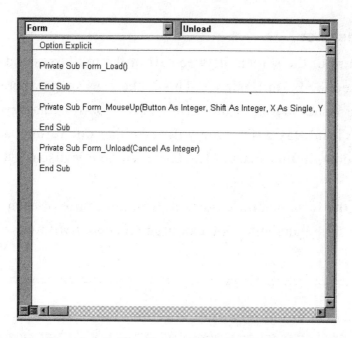

FIGURE 1.8: THE VISUAL BASIC CODE WINDOW

You can open the Code window by double-clicking on a form or control in the Form Layout window. If you double-click a form, you will be taken to a procedure for the form. If you double-click a control, you will be taken to a procedure for that control. Once the Code window is open, you can go to any procedure for any object on the selected form.

Like I said, you should get *really* familiar with your editor. Learn as much about its features as possible. Learn all of the shortcuts and keystrokes. Set your fonts and colours exactly the way you want them. Becoming as comfortable as possible now with the Visual Basic editor and the Code window will save you time later.

Depending on how you set your IDE options, you can have your Code window display multiple procedures at one time, as described in the next section. In addition, it can display object properties as you type, as well as give you visual cues as to the state of your code. We will cover these features in more detail later in this skill.

Working with Multiple Projects

Visual Basic allows you to work on multiple projects simultaneously. The Project Explorer window shows you the projects and their components in a tree view. If you are a beginner, you may not have an immediate need to open multiple projects at one time. However, when you start creating ActiveX objects (as you will do in Skill 14), you may want to open one project for the object and another to test the object.

If you have not already done so, you need to install the sample applications that come with Visual Basic. To install them follow these steps:

1. Start the Visual Basic 5 Setup program by selecting Add/Remove Programs from the Windows Control Panel.
2. Click the Add/Remove button to start the installation process.
3. When the Microsoft Visual Basic 5.0 Setup dialog box appears, press the Add/Remove button.
4. When the Microsoft Visual Basic 5.0 Maintenance dialog box appears, check the box next to "Online Help and Samples". If the check-box is greyed, press the Select All button.
5. Press Continue to finish the setup process.

Once you have installed the sample applications that come with Visual Basic, then you can try the following example to open multiple projects:

1. Select File ➤ Add Project.
2. In the Add Project dialog box, click the Existing tab.
3. Select FirstApp.vbp from the \Samples\PGuide\FirstApp subdirectory.
4. Click the Open button. This will add the FirstApp project to the IDE.
5. Select File ➤ Add Project to add another project.
6. Again, click the Existing tab in the Add Project dialog box.
7. Select Controls.vbp from the \Samples\PGuide\Controls subdirectory. This will add the Controls project to the IDE.

That's all there is to opening multiple projects. You can add more projects if you wish, but it will be very rare that you will need to do so. You will most likely start working with multiple projects when you start creating ActiveX servers and clients.

Note

Working with multiple projects is a skill you will perfect with experience. However, within this book we will only open one project at a time.

Customizing the IDE

While version 5 of Visual Basic has many enhancements to the IDE, you may still want to customize the IDE to suit your personal preferences. You can define the number of spaces of a tab, change the colour of your Code window, dock your toolbars, and much more. If you want to change any settings within the IDE, select Tools ➤ Options. The tabs of the Options dialog box categorize many IDE options you will become familiar with (see Figure 1.9).

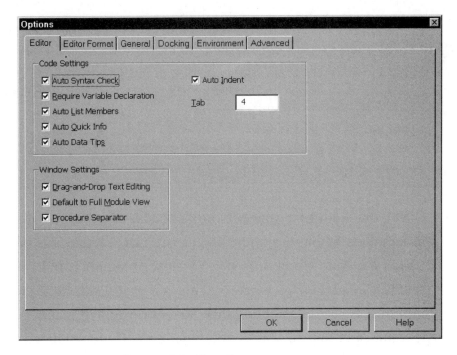

FIGURE 1.9: THE OPTIONS DIALOG BOX

The Editor Tab

The first tab of options I'll examine is the Editor tab. Within the Code Settings frame are the options that will affect your editor. After selecting Tools ➤ Options, experiment with these choices:

- Check the Auto Syntax Check box to force the editor to check your code for errors during design mode. Keep this setting enabled so you won't program errantly only to discover you have an error in your code.

- Check the Require Variable Declaration box to force you to declare all variables before using them in your code.

Note

Always use Require Variable Declaration in your code. This will place one line—Option Explicit—in the General Options portion of every form, module, and class. This will save you many hours of frustration when you start debugging larger applications in the future. As you gain programming experience, you will discover most of your errors will be the result of incorrect variable types and miscalculations. Setting variables to the appropriate type will minimize such errors. If you have not developed the habit of using this feature, take time to do so now.

- Check the Auto List Members box to cause the editor to display a list of members belonging to the object you just reference as you type.

- Check the Auto Quick Info box to show or suppress information about functions and their parameters. This is a useful setting if you are new to Visual Basic; by enabling this, Visual Basic will make recommendations to you as you type in the Code window.

- Check the Auto Data Tips box to toggle the display of the value of a variable under the cursor.

- Check the Auto Indent box to automatically indent your code a number of spaces. This is good for structured code. Neat code is easier to read, which is very helpful during the debugging process. As you read through the examples in the skills to follow, you will see what structured code looks like.

- Use the Tab box to set the number of spaces the editor will insert when you press the Tab button.

Within the Window Settings frame you can experiment with three options:

- Check the Drag-and-Drop Text Editing option if you want to drag text within the Code window.

- Check the Default to Full Module View if you want to see all of the procedures within an object in the editor. If you prefer viewing one procedure in the editor at a time, disable this option.

- Check the Procedure Separator option if you are in Full Module View mode and want a visual separator between your procedures.

The Editor Format Tab

Use this tab to set your colour and font preferences for your editor. Because this tab is self-explanatory, I will not cover it in detail.

The General Tab

The General tab allows you to fine-tune various aspects of the IDE, such as the gridlines on forms, error trapping, and compiling.

- You can set the grid-spacing units in the Form Grid Settings section. You use these lines to align controls on the form. Usually, the default settings will be sufficient.
- The Error Trapping section allows you to set the sensitivity of error trapping. You can have your application break on all errors, break in class modules, or break on all unhandled errors. Unhandled errors are errors that may be encountered that you have not written an error-trapping function for. Leave this option at its default.

The Compile section contains the following options:

- Set Compile on Demand to allow Visual Basic to compile your code as you write your code. This helps your program start sooner when you select Run ➤ Start. This setting is enabled by default.
- Enable Background Compile to allow yourself to continue working in Visual Basic while it compiles your application. This setting is enabled by default.
- Checking Show Tool Tips will allow Visual Basic to show you tool tips that describe the control under the mouse pointer. This is a helpful feature, especially if you are new to Visual Basic.

- Select Collapse Proj. Hides Windows to collapse the associated windows of a project when it is collapsed in the Project Explorer window.

The Docking Tab

By selecting the Docking tab, you can determine which windows within the IDE are dockable. These are self-explanatory.

Note
Docking allows windows to physically position themselves along borders of the screen or other objects. This is another feature that allows you to keep various windows out of the way.

The Environment Tab

The Environment tab is another place to change important settings within the IDE (see Figure 1.10).

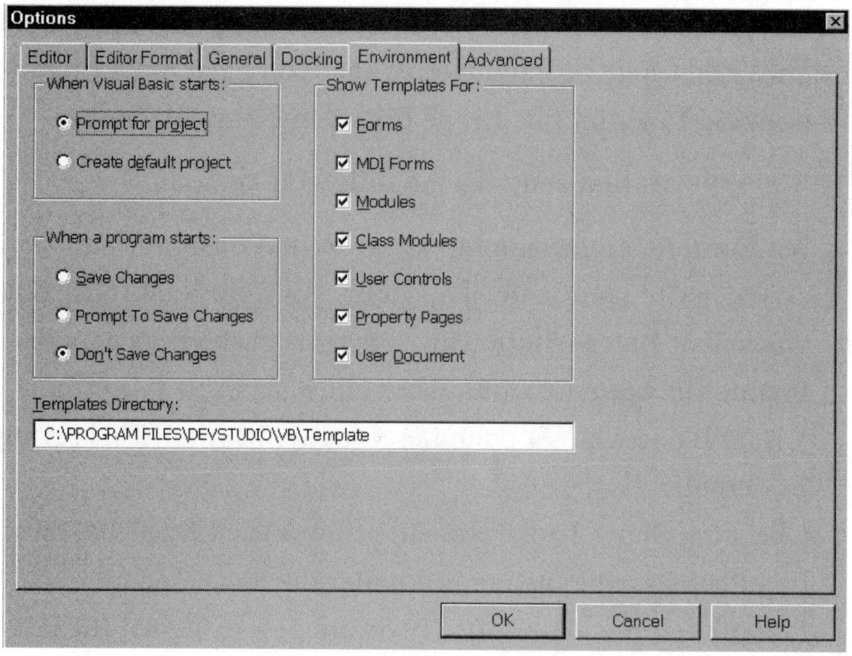

FIGURE 1.10: THE ENVIRONMENT TAB OF THE OPTIONS DIALOG BOX

If you decide you do not want the Project Wizard window disturbing you when you create a new project, you can deselect the Create Default Project option in the When Visual Basic Starts frame. However, leave this option checked for now. You will be using the Project Wizard window throughout this book.

In addition, if you do want the Project Wizard window but you want to remove some of the templates from the window, you can select and deselect them in the Show Templates For frame.

The most important settings, perhaps in the whole IDE, are the ones listed in the When a Program Starts frame. When you are involved in serious project development, you will want to save your work often. The best way to do this is to check the Prompt To Save Changes option. This will cause Visual Basic to ask you to save your project just before your application is run from the IDE.

If you take a look at Figure 1.10, you'll see the Don't Save Changes option checked. I use this when I am experimenting or demonstrating a series of programs that I do not want to keep.

The Advanced Tab

Finally, the Advanced tab has a few options that you will not need to worry about at this time, but I will briefly discuss them here.

- Select the Background Project Load option to force Visual Basic to load projects while you continue working. This is useful because it allows you to continue working while a project loads. This option is set by default.
- Leave the Notify When Changing Shared Project Items option checked. Some Visual Basic projects can use shared objects such as forms or modules. If you load multiple projects that use the same objects and change one of the shared objects, Visual Basic will notify

you that a shared object has been changed. Although you will not use shared objects within this book, you may do so as you become more proficient with Visual Basic.

• The SDI Development Environment option allows you to change your IDE from a multiple document interface (MDI) to a single document interface (SDI). All of the projects and examples used in this book were created in an MDI environment, so leave this option unchecked.

Note

Because we cannot possibly cover every aspect of the IDE in this skill, I recommend you take some time to snoop through each menu option and experiment with what it does. Most functions will be obvious, but for things that are not, you can always check the Visual Basic online help. As I mentioned earlier, get to know the Code window—as well as the whole IDE. With practice, using the IDE will become second nature to you, and your efforts will be spent on coding rather than fumbling through the IDE.

Creating Your First Applet

Now that you have had a chance to get familiar with the IDE and its new-and-improved tools, it's time to put all this knowledge to work by creating a simple application. You might not know it, but most programmers' first "real" application is the little Hello World program. Although it is simple to create, it will give you a feel for working with Visual Basic and using the IDE environment.

Hello World!

To create the Hello World application, follow these steps:

1. Click File ➤ New Project. You might be asked to save changes to the current project if you've been experimenting. If so, click the No button; if you want to keep your work, then click Yes.

2. If it is not already visible, open the Form Layout window by selecting View ➤ Form Layout Window.

3. Right-click on the form in the Form Layout window. Select Startup Position ➤ Center Screen from the pop-up menu.

Tip

You can move the form by dragging it around in the Form Layout window. The pop-up menu also offers other positioning options.

---

4. Resize the form by dragging its borders until it's about three inches wide and two inches high.

5. Double-click the command button control in the toolbox to create a command button of default size in the center of the form. Drag the button near the bottom center of the form.

6. Double-click the label control in the toolbox to create a label on the form. Drag the label so it sits just below the top of the form. Resize

the label so it is roughly the height of one line of text and wide enough to contain the text "Hello World." Your form should now look similar to the one shown here.

7. Now, click on the form once to select it. You can tell the form (as opposed to any of the controls) is selected because its properties are listed in the Properties window. If you can't see the Properties window, press F4.

8. Set the following two properties for the form by typing in the text under the Setting column in the appropriate property field:

Property	Setting
Caption	My First Application!
Name	frmHelloWorld

The Caption property setting appears in the title bar of the form. The Name property is a very important one and is used to refer to the form in program code. In Skill 3, I'll have a lot more to say about the Name property. For now, take it on faith that frmHelloWorld is a better name than the default one of Form1, which is the same as the default Caption property. The same applies to the Name property of the controls in this application. In each case the default Name property has been changed.

9. Next, click once on the label and set the next two properties:

Property	Setting
Name	lblHelloWorld
Text	Hello World.

10. Click once on the command button and set its properties as follows:

Property	Setting
Name	cmdOK
Caption	&OK

This time the Caption property shows as the text on the button. The ampersand character (&) before the first letter adds an underline to the letter "O"; this provides a quick keyboard alternative to a mouse-click to activate the button (here it's Alt+O). Happily, you can make many of your shortcut keys a mnemonic ("O" for "OK," in this example).

11. Now double-click the cmdOK button. Double-clicking a control (or a form) opens the Code window at the default event for the control. The default event for a command button is the Click event. You should be looking at a procedure template or *stub* for cmdOK_Click, as in Figure 1.11. You can afford to ignore the Private Sub prefix for now; the important point is the name of the procedure, cmdOK_Click. This means any code entered in the procedure will be executed when the user clicks the cmdOK button.

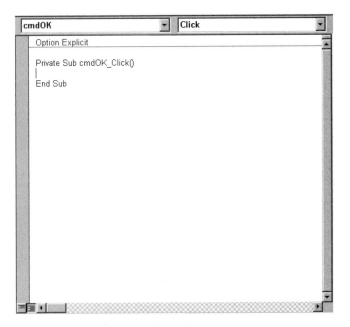

FIGURE 1.11: THE PROCEDURE IN THE CODE WINDOW

12. Type the following line of code between the Private Sub and End Sub lines:

```
Unload Me
Set frmHelloWorld = Nothing
```

When the user clicks the cmdHelloWorld button, the cmdOK_Click event occurs. This event tells the form to unload itself. Because this is the only form in the application, it also tells the application to end.

13. Click File ➤ Save Project. Enter **frmWorld.frm** as the name of the form and **World.vbp** as the name of the project. Before a project as a whole is saved, all the individual component files are saved. In this application there is one form and therefore one file corresponding to the form. The project file is basically a list of the component files.

Note

Notice that the form now has three descriptors—the Name property (frmHelloWorld), the Caption property (My First Application), and the file name (frmWorld.frm). It's vital that you understand the difference between these three descriptors. The Caption property appears in the title bar of the form, the Name property is used to reference the form in code, and the file name is used by the project file and your operating system to reference the form.

---

14. Click Run ➤ Start. If all goes well, you should see a form, similar to the one in Figure 1.12, that simply says, "Hello World."
15. Click the OK button to end. If things go wrong, check through the previous steps to find your mistake.

FIGURE 1.12: YOUR FIRST APPLICATION—THE HELLO WORLD APPLET

You've just created your first application! Congratulations—you're well on your way to being a master Visual Basic programmer.

Creating this simple applet was an example of
the Visual Basic IDE. Although the Hello World
allowed you to get a feel for working in Visual B:
will present you with more information about the
working with to build your killer app.

Summary of Skills Acquired

Now you can...

- ☑ use Visual Basic to create your own applications
- ☑ use the Project Wizard to help you get your application started
- ☑ right-click on objects to expose their properties
- ☑ effectively use the Code window
- ☑ work with multiple projects in the IDE
- ☑ customize the look and feel of the IDE to suit your preferences
- ☑ write a simple applet

SKILL 2

Working with Forms

Featuring

- ❏ Introducing forms
- ❏ Creating a form
- ❏ Changing a form's properties
- ❏ Becoming familiar with form events
- ❏ Understanding form methods
- ❏ Creating multiple document interface (MDI) forms
- ❏ Adding forms to your projects
- ❏ Using the Form Wizard

The Anatomy of a Form

The most basic object you will be working with in Visual Basic is the *form* object, which is the visual foundation of your application. It is basically a window that you can add different elements to in order to create a complete application. Every application you can see on the screen is based on some type of form. Before delving into the details of application development, let's take a look at the most basic form object that you will probably use the most often in your projects: the single form.

As you learn Visual Basic, most of your applications will only have one interface, which is the single form. When you become more experienced and start writing larger, editor-styled applications, you will want to use multiple forms, called *documents*. We will introduce these types of forms toward the end of this skill (see "Working with Multiple Document Interface (MDI) Forms"). To create a new form, select File ➤ New Project; you'll then see the various parts of a single form object, as shown in Figure 2.1. In the following sections, we will go through each of the parts that make up this object so you can become familiar with what forms are and how you will use them.

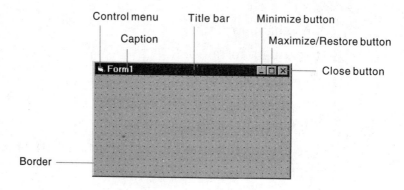

FIGURE 2.1: THE FORM OBJECT

The Border

The form's border is what gives the form its elasticity. Depending on the type of form you want to display, you can program the border to be fixed, sizable, or even nonexistent. These features can be set with the BorderStyle property.

The Caption

The form's caption is the text you see in the form's title bar. It can be used to identify the name of the application, the current function of the form, or as a status bar. What you put in the caption depends on what your program is trying to achieve.

If you set a form's BorderStyle property to None, then the caption (along with the whole title bar) is hidden. You can modify the caption by setting the form's Caption property in the Properties window to the text you want to display.

The Title Bar

The title bar is the coloured bar on the top of most forms. If your desktop colour scheme is set to the Windows default scheme, this bar will be blue. You can use the title bar to drag the window around the screen. In addition, double-clicking on it will alternately maximize and restore the form.

The Control Menu

The Control menu is a simple menu that allows you to restore, move, resize, minimize, maximize, and close a form. To enable this button on your form, set the form's ControlBox property to True in the form's Properties window.

The Minimize Button

The Minimize button is used to minimize the current form, that is, move it out of the way. To enable this button on your form, set the form's MinButton property to True in the form's Properties window.

The Maximize/Restore Button

The Maximize button has two purposes. If the form is in its normal state, that is, its normal size, you can click the Maximize button to stretch the current form to the size of the screen or container of the form. A form's *container* is also known as a multiple document interface (MDI) form, which is described in "Working with Multiple Document Interfaces (MDI) Forms" later in this skill. If the form is maximized, you can click this button again to restore the form to its original size. To enable this button on your form, set the form's MaxButton property to True in the Properties window.

The Close Button

The Close button's sole purpose is to close the current window. In Visual Basic, you can control whether the Close button is visible to the user with the ControlBox property. The Close button will not be visible if the Control box is not visible. If you decide not to enable the Close button or the Control box, then you must use a menu or a button to close the form. You will learn more about this in the next section.

Working with Form Properties

As you learned in Skill 1, properties describe the characteristics of an object. The following shows the properties for a form object.

ActiveControl	DrawWidth	HelpContextID	NegotiateMenus
ActiveForm	Enabled	hWnd	Picture
Appearance	FillColor	**Icon**	ScaleHeight
AutoRedraw	FillStyle	Image	ScaleLeft
BackColor	Font	KeyPreview	**ScaleMode**
BorderStyle	FontBold	**Left**	ScaleTop
Caption	FontItalic	LinkMode	ScaleWidth
ClipControls	FontName	LinkTopic	**ShowInTaskbar**
ControlBox	FontSize	**MaxButton**	Tag
Controls	FontStrikethru	MDIChild	Top
Count	FontTransparent	**MinButton**	Visible
CurrentX	FontUnderline	MouseIcon	WhatsThisButton
CurrentY	**ForeColor**	MousePointer	WhatsThisHelp
DrawMode	hDC	Moveable	**Width**
DrawStyle	**Height**	**Name**	**WindowState**

If you glance at the list of properties for a form in the Properties window, you'll see there are quite a lot of them. Fortunately, only a few of the properties are used frequently—these are boldface in the above list—the rest you'll probably only use occasionally.

Note

You won't see all these properties in the Properties window. If you can't see a certain property, it means it's a run-time–only property and can't be set at design time (see "Tweaking a Property" later in this chapter for more information).

Help is Just a Button Away

You can get help with a property at any time. Just highlight it in the Properties window and press the F1 function key. For example, highlight the Caption property in the Properties window, and you will see a screen similar to the one shown below.

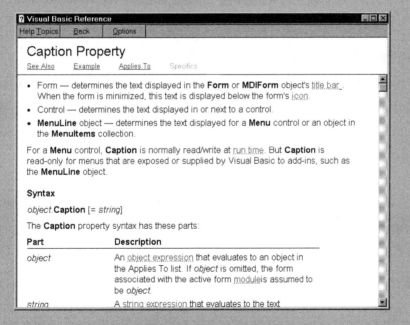

You can scroll through the information or click on links (text that is underlined) to find related information. The buttons at the top of the screen—Help Topics, Back, Options—offer you more options for finding help with Visual Basic topics.

Let's take a closer look at some of the properties that are used most often (the next sections are in alphabetically to act as a quick reference; the properties also appear in the Properties window in alphabetically).

The *BackColor* Property

The BackColor property sets the background colour of the form. You briefly met this property in Skill 1. You can set a form's background colour to any colour on the palette. When you double-click BackColor in the Properties window or click the drop-down arrow next to the colour selection, the Properties window will display a dialog box containing a colour palette and a system colour palette.

Usually you would not want to set a form's background colour because this prevents the user from utilizing their own colour scheme, which they may have defined in the Control Panel.

The *BorderStyle* Property

The BorderStyle property determines how the border of a form behaves. A form can have fixed borders that cannot be stretched and sizeable borders that can be stretched by dragging them with the mouse. Table 2.1 shows each option for the BorderStyle property.

Try out these options—you can use the form in the Hello World application that you created in Skill 1 to do this. Open the Hello World project from Skill 1 by selecting File ➤ Open Project. Select the project you saved in Skill 1.

1. In the Form Designer, click once on the form to make it the active control.
2. Because the Hello World form acts more as a dialog box than a useful form, set its BorderStyle property to **3 - Fixed Dialog**.
3. Run your modified Hello World program by selecting Run ➤ Start.

Notice that the form doesn't stretch: you have created a true dialog box.

Setting	Description
0 - None	Selecting this setting means the form can't be resized or moved. The Control menu, Close button, Maximize and Minimize buttons, and the form's title bar are all suppressed. Although you will not use this setting often, it is useful for making splash screens and screen savers.
1 - Fixed Single	This setting means the form can't be resized by dragging its borders. However, you can use the Maximize and Minimize buttons.
2 - Sizable	This is the default setting for Visual Basic forms and for most other Windows applications windows. The user can resize the form by dragging the form borders or by using the relevant buttons on the title bar.
3 - Fixed Dialog	As its name implies, this is usually the setting chosen for forms that act as dialog boxes. The user can't resize the form-the only options are to move or close it. If you want to force the user to interact with the form, you can set the ControlBox property to False. This prevents users from even closing the form. All they can do is to move the form by dragging its title bar. In that situation you would probably place one or more command buttons on the form-the Click events containing a line of code to close the form (for example, frmFormName.Hide).
4 - Fixed ToolWindow	This acts the same as the Fixed Dialog setting, but with the addition of a Close button (the caption in the title bar is also shown in a smaller font). The form will not appear on the Taskbar.
5 - Sizable ToolWindow	This is just the same as the Sizable style but does not include a Maximize or Minimize button. Under Windows 95 it shows the Close button but doesn't appear on the Taskbar.

TABLE 2.1: BORDERSTYLE SETTINGS

The *Caption* Property

A caption is the text that appears on the title bar of the form. If you set the BorderStyle property to None, then the caption (along with the entire title bar) is hidden. You can read more about changing the Caption property in "Tweaking a Property" later in this chapter.

The *ControlBox* Property

The True and False settings determine whether the Control menu is visible. Keep in mind the settings for BorderStyle, ControlBox, MaxButton, and MinButton are interdependent. For example, if you turn off the Maximize button and have the Control menu visible, the latter will not contain an option for maximizing the form. Or, to look at another example, if you set the BorderStyle to FixedToolWindow, then this turns off the ControlBox even if you explicitly turn it on.

Stop your Hello World application if you have not already done so. In design mode, do the following:

1. Make the form the active control by clicking on it.
2. In the Properties window, set the ControlBox property to False.
3. Run the program again (Run ➤ Start).

Notice this time there is not the Control menu on the left side of the title bar or a Close button on the right side. The only way to close this form is to click the OK button.

The *ForeColor* Property

This doesn't affect the colour of objects you place on a form, though it does affect the colour of text you print to a form. For example, if you wanted to print red text directly on the form, you would set the form's ForeColor property to red. Whenever you print text directly on the form using the Print method, it would be red. Don't worry too much about printing text directly on a form. It is very rarely used. Remember the colour of the form itself is set by the BackColor property.

Let's try adding a command button to a form and changing the colour of the text and the form itself:

1. Start a new project by Selecting File ➤ New Project.
2. Add a command button to Form1 by double-clicking the command button control in the Toolbox.
3. Once the button is on the form, double-click it to open the button's Click() event.
4. In the Click event procedure for the command button, enter the following line:

```
Print "Hello World"
```

Now experiment by changing the BackColor and ForeColor properties at design time using the Properties window. You can see how these properties work together. If you want to hide the text, you can set the BackColor and ForeColors to be equal. For example:

```
BackColor = ForeColor
```

The *Height* Property

Use this property to change the height of a form. You can also set the height by dragging the form's borders in design view. The default units for measuring the Height property (as well as for the Width, Left, and Top properties) are *twips*. Don't worry too much about the units of measurement right now. These are more important when you become more skilled in Visual Basic. If you require precise measurements for a form, or any other control for that matter, you can set its size in the Height and Width properties.

Using your form from the previous example:

1. In the Properties window, set the Width property to 3600.
2. Set the Height property to 3600.

Notice that even without running the program, the form has been resized in the Form Designer. This is not much use to you at this time, because you can visually size the form by dragging its borders in the Form Designer. You will find that the dimensions of a form will be set in code at run time. Try this example to see what I mean:

1. Double-click the form to open the Code window. The two boxes at the top of the Code window, called drop-down list boxes, should say Form and Load respectively. This means you are currently in the Form's Load event.

2. Scroll down the list on the right until it says Resize. This will take you to the form's Resize event.

3. In the Resize event, type the following line of code:

```
Width = Height
```

4. Select Run ➤ Start to run the project.

Resize the form by dragging the top or bottom border. Notice how the form automatically resizes itself to a perfect square? This is an example of setting properties at run time.

Try dragging the left or right border. The form does not resize, but it instead snaps back. This happens because the width will always equal the height, according to the code you entered. The width cannot change unless the height changes.

The *Icon* Property

Select an icon by double-clicking on this property. The Icon property determines the icon to display on the Taskbar when the form is minimized at run time. You have seen this property in action in Skill 1. This property has no effect if you can't minimize the form—you may have set its BorderStyle to Fixed Dialog.

If you installed all of the options for Visual Basic, then there are a large number of icons in the \Graphics\Icons folders—if they're not there, they'll always be found in the same directory on your Visual Basic CD-ROM. Helpfully, Windows lets you preview the icons before choosing one.

The *Left* Property

This property functions much like the Height and Width properties you learned about earlier. The difference is this property determines the distance of the form from the left of the screen. This property is commonly used in conjunction with the form's Top property, which sets the vertical spacing of the form. Try this example that centres the form on the screen:

1. Stop the program if you have not already done so.
2. Double-click the form to get back to the form's Resize event.
3. Add these two lines of code to the Resize event, below the Width = Height statement:

```
Left = (Screen.Width - Width) / 2
Top = (Screen.Height - Height) / 2
```

4. Run the program.

This time, the form will not only resize itself, but it will centre itself as well. If you want to see a cool elastic-style form, then change the last statement in the Resize event to:

```
Width = (Screen.Height - Height) / 2
```

The *MaxButton* Property

By setting this property to True, your form will show the standard Maximize button on the right side of the title bar. If you do not want your users to maximize the form, set this property to False.

The *MinButton* Property

By setting this property to True, your form will show the standard Minimize button on the right side of the title bar. If you do not want your users to minimize the form, set this property to False.

Tip

There may be instances when you do not want your users to resize the form. For example, you may have a graphic that must keep the same proportions on the form. Setting the MaxButton and MinButton properties to False will prevent this.

The *Name* Property

The Name property is the single most important property in Visual Basic. This is the name of a control that Visual Basic refers to when the program runs. In order to know exactly what your forms are, you should give them a descriptive name and prefix it with the letters frm. If you look back at your Hello World application in Skill 1, you will notice you named the form "frmHelloWorld." Although it is not so important to give a descriptive name in that particular application, imagine if you had 20 or 30 forms in your program! You wouldn't want to have to remember their names as Form17 or Form20; frmLogon and frmChangePassword are more descriptive. Descriptive names make it easier for you to identify forms and controls in your code.

As you read Skill 3, you will learn how to apply three-letter prefixes called *naming conventions* to your controls.

The *ScaleMode* Property

Although the Height, Width, Left, and Top properties of a form are in twips, you have a choice of scales for any controls you place on a form. If you wanted to set the size and position of a command button using the more familiar system of pixels, then set the ScaleMode property *for the form* to 3 - Pixel.

The *ShowInTaskbar* Property

This property is interesting, because it allows you to hide the form from the Taskbar. If you write an application that you want to reside in that little box in the right side of the Taskbar, called the *system tray*, or you just don't want your program noticed by the user, you will need to set this property to False. You can do this at run time in the form's Load event, as shown below:

```
Private Sub Form_Load()
  ShowInTaskBar = False
End Sub
```

The *Width* Property

This specifies the width of the form in twips. This is similar to and is commonly used in conjunction with the Height property.

The *WindowState* Property

The WindowState property is responsible for how the form starts up. There are three options; the following shows you what each option does.

You type...	Option	Effect
0	Normal	The form will open in its normal state.
1	Minimized	The form will open, but it will be minimized.
2	Maximized	The form will be maximized when it opens.

Tweaking a Form's Properties

Many properties can be set at run time as well as design time. A few can be set only at design time (for example, BorderStyle), and one or two can be set or read only at run time. Those that are only available at run time (for instance, a property called hWnd) do not appear in the Properties window at design time.

Note

To set properties at design time, you use the Properties window. To set them at run time, you set the properties through code.

One property you can easily change at run time is the Caption property. Here's a hands-on example to show you how to change "Hello" to "Bye." Afterward, you'll see how to extend the code slightly, and you'll learn to change the caption of an object on a form, too.

1. Start a new project (File ➤ New Project) and set the Name property of Form1 to **frmForm1** in the Properties window. Also set the Caption property to **Hello**.

2. Double-click the command button in the Toolbox to add a button to the form. Set its Name property to **cmdHello** and set its Caption property to **&Hello** in the Properties window.

3. Double-click the command button on the form to display the cmdHello_Click event procedure. Add the following lines to the procedure (as shown in Figure 2.2):

```
If frmForm1.Caption = "Hello" Then
  frmForm1.Caption = "Bye"
Else
  frmForm1.Caption = "Hello"
End If
```

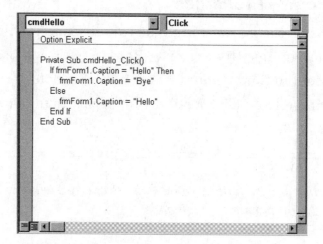

FIGURE 2.2: ADDING LINES TO A PROCEDURE

Note

If-Then-Else statements allow your program to make decisions. It operates much like it sounds: If condition1 is true, then do something, or else do something else. For more information about this kind of code, see Skill 13.

---

4. Run the application (Run ➤ Start) and click the command button.

All the code does is to check the current Caption property of the form. If it's "Hello," then it gets set to "Bye." If it's not "Hello" (that's the meaning of the Else statement), then set it gets set back to "Hello."

Extending the Code

The second example takes this a step further. Open the Code window for the command button's Click event. Amend the code to read:

```
If frmForm1.Caption = "Hello" Then
    frmForm1.Caption = "Bye"
    cmdHello.Caption = "&Hello"
Else
    frmForm1.Caption = "Hello"
    cmdHello.Caption = "&Bye"
End If
```

Note

When you set string properties in code, you must surround them in quotes. This lets the compiler know the properties are being set to actual values, rather than referencing the names of variables. When setting string valued properties in the Properties window, no quotes are necessary.

Fixing a Bug

As shown in Figure 2.3, the code now contains two additional lines that set the Caption property of the command button at run time:

```
cmdHello.Caption = "&Hello"
    .
    .
    .
cmdHello.Caption = "&Bye"
```

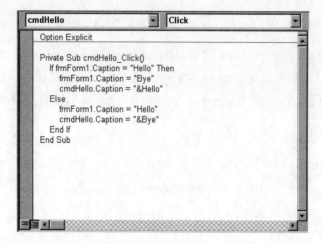

FIGURE 2.3: SETTING THE CAPTION PROPERTY

Watch how the entry in the Windows Taskbar is updated to reflect the current caption of the form. Also note there's something wrong with the application—when it first starts, the caption of the button is "Hello" when it should be "Bye." Of course, this is fixed by simply altering the Caption property of the button at design time, but there's also another way of doing it:

To fix the small bug in the code:

1. Double-click the form in the Form Designer to see the Form_Load event procedure.

2. Add the next line

    ```
    cmdHello.Caption = "&Bye"
    ```

    to that procedure (between the Private Sub and End Sub lines, as shown in Figure 2.4).

3. Now run the application (Run ➤ Start) and all is well.

What you did here was to use one of the events associated with a form. In the event procedure you changed one of the control properties at run time.

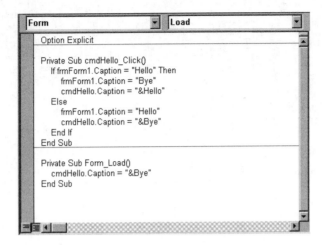

```
Form                    ▼   Load                    ▼
  Option Explicit

  Private Sub cmdHello_Click()
      If frmForm1.Caption = "Hello" Then
          frmForm1.Caption = "Bye"
          cmdHello.Caption = "&Hello"
      Else
          frmForm1.Caption = "Hello"
          cmdHello.Caption = "&Bye"
      End If
  End Sub

  Private Sub Form_Load()
      cmdHello.Caption = "&Bye"
  End Sub
```

FIGURE 2.4: ADDING ANOTHER LINE OF CODE

Now let's look at some of those events. Don't be concerned about the Private prefix to the Form_Load event procedure—the meaning of the prefix becomes clear in Skill 5.

Introducing Form Events

Before looking at the events for a form, let's learn what an event actually is. Windows is an *event-driven* operating system. This means it utilizes system events to react to the environment. Events are triggered by messages. Whenever you click on a button, move the mouse, resize a form, or anything else, Windows will generate a message that describes your action. This message then gets sent to the message queue. From here the message is sent to the appropriate control—for example, a form. When the control receives this message, it then generates an appropriate event. You can write your own code in an event to force a control to react precisely the way you want it to. You will learn more about events in this skill, and in the ones to follow. The more you program, the more familiar you will become with events. Now let's look at a form's events:

Activate	KeyDown	LostFocus	OLESetData
Click	KeyPress	MouseDown	OLEStartDrag
DblClick	KeyUp	MouseMove	Paint
Deactivate	LinkClose	MouseUp	QueryUnload
DragDrop	LinkError	OLECompleteDrag	Resize
DragOver	LinkExecute	OLEDragDrop	Terminate
GotFocus	LinkOpen	OLEDragOver	Unload
Initialize	Load	OLEGiveFeedback	

Just like properties, there are only a few of a form's events that are used a great deal of the time. Many of the events are rarely used, unless you're building a very complex application. The best way to view the events associated with a form is to double-click the form in design view to display the Code window. The form is already given in the Object drop-down box, so all you have to do is open the Proc drop-down list associated with it, shown in Figure 2.5.

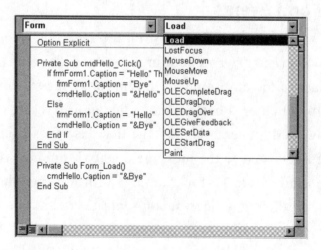

FIGURE 2.5: FORM EVENTS APPEARING IN A DROP-DOWN LIST

Getting On-line Help for Events

To find out what different events are, click once on a form in design mode to remove the focus from any other objects or windows. Then press F1 to show the Help window for the form object, as shown below.

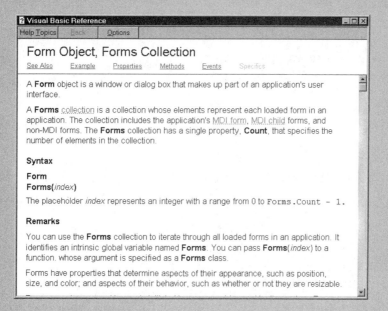

At the top of this window click the Events link—the link has a solid underline and is usually in green on a colour monitor. This jumps to a window that lists all the events for the form.

A further click on one of the events in the list leads to a full explanation of when the event occurs. Note that you can follow the same procedure to get help on the properties of a form and the methods applicable to a form—use the Properties and Methods link in the Form Object Help window.

The list of events is quite long, and some of them may appear to be fairly similar to their names—for example, the Activate event sounds similar to the Load event. You might think that a form can be displayed by activating it. However, the form must be loaded into memory before it can do anything. Once it is loaded, it can be activated and deactivated as needed. It all depends on the exact nature of the applications you want to create, but it's a fairly safe bet that, rather than using the less popular events, you'll want to use the ones described in the following sections.

The *Activate* Event

The Activate event sounds like it is similar to the Load event, which is discussed soon. There are also a couple of other events with which it may be confused—the Initialize and GotFocus events. You may think that activating a form and initializing a form are the same things, but they are not. A form is actually activated *after* it is initialized. The form then receives the focus after it has been activated.

These subtle differences appear between all of them. The most important difference is the order in which they occur in an application. The order is as follows:

Initialize   This event is triggered when a form is being configured before it is loaded.

Load   This event is called after the form has been initialised, and before the form is displayed on the screen. You can type code in a form's Load event to further tailor the appearance or behaviour of the form.

Activate   The Activate event is triggered when the form has been loaded into memory and when it becomes the active form.

GotFocus   If it occurs at all, this event is triggered when the form gets the focus, either when it is loaded or when a user accesses the form with a mouse-click.

Once a particular form is open, only the Activate and possibly the GotFocus events can occur from these four events—though the Initialize event can occur in certain special circumstances.

The Initialize event happens when Visual Basic first becomes aware of the form. At run time, this happens just as you click Run ➤ Start. This is followed by the Load event, as Visual Basic reads the form from disk to memory, or from a disk cache in memory. Once the form is loaded, then the Activate event occurs as the focus shifts to the form—in other words, as the form becomes active. This happens a millisecond or so before the GotFocus event. The GotFocus event, however, can only take place if there are no visible controls on the form. If there's a visible control, then it receives the focus rather than the form itself, and the form's GotFocus event is bypassed—though there will be a GotFocus event for the control.

In normal circumstances, then, there's always a Load event followed by an Activate event for the first form in the application when the application is started up. Of course, the application may have other windows. When the user or program switches back to the first window, then it receives another Activate event, so this time there's no Load event. However, there *is* a Load event if the form has been unloaded in the meantime.

To summarize, there's a Load event followed by an Activate event when the application starts. As the focus moves to other forms and back to the first form (provided it hasn't been unloaded), then the Activate event occurs without a preceding Load event.

The *Deactivate* Event

The Deactivate event is the converse of Activate. The Deactivate event occurs when the form ceases to be active. Depending on your Windows colour scheme, you might see the title bar of the form turning a different colour (or becoming fainter) as it stops being the active form.

The *DragDrop* Event

This event takes place when a dragged control is dropped onto a form. When you run the Hello World application, you'll find if you attempt to drag a command button, nothing appears to happen. To enable the DragDrop event, you must have something to drag and drop on the form in the first place. A fuller discussion of drag-and-drop comes later in Skill 10; but if you're impatient, follow these steps:

1. In the Properties window, set the DragMode property of the command button to **Automatic**.

2. Optionally, select an icon for the DragIcon property by double-clicking the DragIcon property in the Properties window.

3. Double-click the form to open the Code window.

4. Select the DragDrop event from the event drop-down list at the top of the Code window.

5. Finally, add the following statement to the DragDrop event procedure for the form:

```
Private Sub Form_DragDrop(Source As Control, _
 X As Single, Y As Single)
    Print "Dropped"
End Sub
```

Note

The DragDrop event can only happen if you have a "draggable" control to drag and drop. Some objects are not usually dragged around a form. For example, you would not drag a command button around. Other objects lend themselves to being dragged, such as picture boxes containing icons, or elements within list boxes. Examine other Windows applications when deciding what needs to be drag-and-drop enabled.

The *Load* Event

The Load event comes after the Initialize event, but it comes before the Activate event as a form is loaded into memory from disk or from a disk cache in memory. The Load event is a particularly important one and is the one most frequently used. It's extremely handy for specifying some of the contents of the form—for example, it's often used to centre a form on the screen.

When to Use Load/Unload or Activate/Deactivate

Before a form is visible on screen, it needs to be loaded into memory. When this happens, Windows sends a message to the form and a Load event is generated by the form. If you decided you wanted to perform checks for your program or wanted to change the position of your form, you would place the code to do so in this event.

For example, if you wanted to centre your form before it was displayed, you would write the following code:

```
Private Sub Form_Load()
    Move (Screen.Width - Width) / 2, (Screen.Height - Height) / 2
End Sub
```

Once the form is loaded, it gets activated because it becomes the active window. As a result, it generates an Activate event. In addition, this event is generated whenever an inactive form is acted upon. A good example of when to use the Activate event is in an e-mail program. You could write code in the Activate event that checks for new mail. As a result, every time you start working with the program, it will check for new mail for you.

The Deactivate event is generated when another form or application receives the focus. You could possibly use this event to minimize your application when you go to another program.

Finally, the Unload event is important, because this is your last chance to perform any "housekeeping" for your form. You will want to close any open databases or files in this event. This ensures memory is not wasted when the form is removed from memory.

The *Resize* Event

When the user or the program code alters the size of a form, the Resize event occurs. This has two main uses:

- You can resize the controls on the form (in the event procedure) with code.
- You can set the form back to its original size.

To do these you employ the Height and Width properties of objects. You can examine the code in the example dealing with the Height and Width properties.

Note

You can't resize a form that has been maximized or minimized. To prevent either of these from happening, the easiest solution is to set the MaxButton and MinButton properties to False.

The *Unload* Event

The Unload event is, logically, the opposite of Load. The most popular choice for an Unload event procedure is one that asks the user if they're sure they want to close the form (though another event procedure, QueryUnload, is a little more flexible in this respect). If you look at the Unload event in the Code window, you can see it's a little different from some of the others you've met. It has (Cancel As Integer) after the name of the procedure. You can use this argument to cancel the unloading of the form. You can see this in action with the following example:

1. Start a new project (File ➤ New Project), and select Standard EXE.
2. Double-click on Form1 in the Form Designer to open its Code window.
3. Select the Unload event from the events drop-down list box.
4. Add the following code:

```
Private Sub Form_Unload(Cancel As Integer)
 If MsgBox("Are you sure?", vbYesNo, _
"Quit?") = 6 Then
  Unload Me
```

```
    Set Form1 = Nothing
  Else
  Cancel = 1
  End If
End Sub
```

5. Close the Code window and run the program by selecting Run ➤ Start.

6. You should see a plain form on the screen. Click the Close button on the form. This will generate an Unload event.

Note

The MsgBox function is used to display a dialog box, called a message box, to the user. You can learn more about this function in Skill 9.

Because you added the code to the Unload event, Visual Basic executes this code, which asks you if you really want to exit. If you click the Yes button, the form will close. However, if you click No, the program sets the Cancel parameter to 1, which notifies Visual Basic not to unload the form.

Note

If you are creating an editor-style application—like a word processor or paint program—you should ask the user if they are sure about closing an application if they have not saved their edits and changes. You can place warning code, similar to the code is the previous example, in the form's Unload event.

Introducing Form Methods

Before we look at a form's methods, let me take a minute to explain what a method does. A method is a command you give to an object. You tell an object what to do through the use of a method. For example, you can tell a form to unload itself by calling the Unload method. The following are a form's methods:

Circle	Move	PSet	TextHeight
Cls	PaintPicture	Refresh	TextWidth
Hide	Point	Scale	**Unload**
Item	Print	SetFocus	ZOrder
Line	PrintForm	**Show**	

Show, Hide, and Unload are the three most popular methods to apply to a form. These are put into practice in the next section.

Working with Multiple Document Interface (MDI) Forms

Another breed of the form object is the multiple document interface (MDI) form. An MDI lets you open windows within a *parent container* window. If you look at a typical word processor—Word for Windows is a classic example—you can have many documents open simultaneously within the

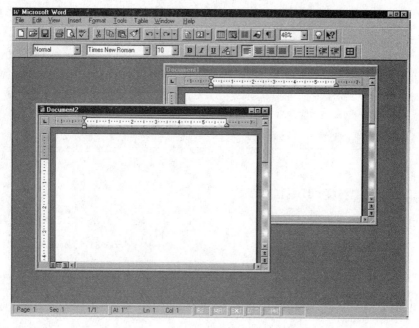

FIGURE 2.6: MULTIPLE DOCUMENTS OPEN SIMULTANEOUSLY WITHIN A PARENT CONTAINER WINDOW

main window (see Figure 2.6). This main window serves as the container—it contains multiple forms. The MDI application was originally developed back when previous versions of Windows were predominant. The multiple document nature allowed users to open more than one file at a time, without having to open several copies of the program itself. This not only saved time, but it also saved memory.

MDI interfaces are more commonly used for *document-centric* applications, like word processors and paint programs. A program is said to be document-centric when the main objects that you work on are documents. If you plan to allow your users to work on several similar forms at one time from within an application, you should use the MDI model. Visual Basic makes it very simple to create an MDI application.

Creating an MDI

To create an MDI application, you need at least two forms in the application. One is the parent, or containing form, and the second is the *child,* or *contained form.* To have more than one type of child form, you can add further forms to the project. But you only need one child form for the simplest of MDI projects. Here's how it's done:

1. Start a new project by selecting File ➤ New Project. Select Standard EXE as the project type if you have the Project Wizard enabled.
2. You will already have a form in the project. Set its Name property to **frmChild** and its Caption property to **MDI Child**.
3. To create the MDI parent form, right-click the Forms folder in the Project Explorer and select Add ➤ MDI Form. If the Form Wizard appears, select MDI Form.
4. Set the Name property to **frmMDI**, and the Caption property to **MDI Parent**.

5. Right-click Project1 in the Project Explorer, and select Project1 Properties from the pop-up menu. Set the Startup Object list to frmMDI. If you omit this, the application will start with the child form showing.

6. Select frmChild from the Project Explorer. Set the form's MDI Child property to True. This will cause this form, which is the child, to rest inside of the MDI Parent container.

7. Select frmMDI from the Project Explorer.

8. Start the Menu Designer by selecting Tools ➤ Menu Editor. You will see a window like the one in Figure 2.7. We are going to create a simple menu for this exercise. Don't worry about the details of creating a menu now. We will cover menus in detail in Skill 4, "Menus and Toolbars."

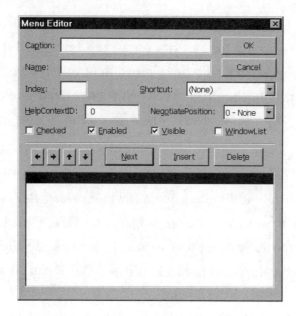

FIGURE 2.7: THE MENU EDITOR

9. Type **&File** in the Caption field.

10. In the Name field, type **mnuFile**.

11. Click the Next button.

12. Click the right arrow button. This will indent this menu item.

13. Enter **&New Form** in the Caption field.

14. Type **mnuFileNew** in the Name field.

15. Click the OK button to close the Menu Editor.

16. The frmMDI form should now have a File menu on it. Select File ➤ New from the MDI menu. This will open up the Code window.

17. In the Private Sub mnuFileNew_Click() event, type the following lines of code:

```
Dim frm As New frmChild
frm.Show
```

18. Save and run the project. You should now see the MDI shown here.

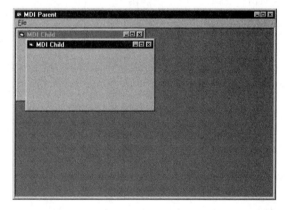

The code creates (or instantiates) new copies of frmChild and shows them. It does this each time you click File ➤ New. Try opening and closing a few child windows. You should have a functioning MDI application.

Improving an MDI

But there are a few additions to make before it really resembles a commercial Windows MDI application. For example, each child form has the same caption, so it's impossible to tell them apart. Let's fix that. It would also be nice to tile or cascade the children. Further, it's normal to have a menu option (called a *window list*), which lets you switch easily to children that get hidden behind other children.

1. Open the Menu Editor and add a **&Window** menu title to the MDI parent, frmMDI. Turn on the check box for WindowList in the Menu Editor as you do so.

2. Add a **Tile** and a **Cascade** item to this menu title. Name them **mnuWindowTile** and **mnuWindowCascade** respectively.

3. Click OK to close the Menu Editor.

4. Enter this code for the Click event of the mnuWindowTile object:

```
frmMDI.Arrange vbTileHorizontal
```

5. Enter this line for the mnuWindowCascade item:

```
frmMDI.Arrange vbCascade
```

The vbCascade and vbTileHorizontal terms are built-in Visual Basic constants.

6. Change the code for the mnuFileNew menu item so that it looks like this:

```
Private Sub mnuFileNew_Click()
 Static Counter As Integer
 Dim frm As New frmChild
 Counter = Counter + 1
 frm.Caption = "MDI Child" & Counter
 frm.Show
End Sub
```

7. Now save and run the application, and notice the difference in Figure 2.8.

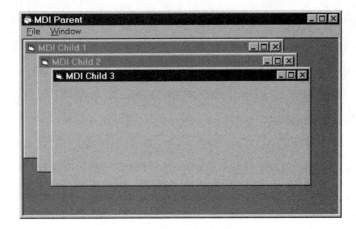

FIGURE 2.8: THE IMPROVED MDI APPLICATION

Deciphering the Code

The code you typed in the previous example may look Greek to you, but
don't worry. Many of the statements are explained in later skills in this book.
But let's take a quick look so you can get an idea of what's actually going
on when you type in code.

The first line (Static Counter As Integer) tells Visual Basic to create a
variable called Counter. The Static keyword tells Visual Basic to remember
the value of Counter every time this procedure is called. This allows Counter
to count the forms as they are created.

The second line (Dim frm As New frmChild) uses a Dim statement to
"dimension" a variable. In this case, it is dimensioning a variable called frm
and this variable will be based on, or derived, from the frmChild form. The
New keyword tells Visual Basic this will be a new form, not one of the
others created by this procedure.

Because Counter remembers its value, it can increment itself with the line:

```
Counter = Counter +1
```

In effect, if Counter was equal to the number 3, then it would say that Counter equals the value of Counter, three for example, plus one. The result would be that Counter equals three plus one, or four. Because Counter is a Static variable, it will remember this value, so it will be five the next time this procedure is called.

The next statement (frm.Caption = "MDI Child" & Counter) just changes the Caption property of the form to the text "MDI Child" and the number stored in Counter. For example, the second form would have the Caption "MDI Child 2."

The last statement brings the child to life, so to speak. It tells Visual Basic to show itself. Because you now understand how a form comes to be, you know the first event of a form is the Load event. Once the form is loaded, it is activated and then displayed on screen.

Using the Form Wizard

As you work with Visual Basic more often, you will find yourself adding forms to your projects. You have just done this in the multiple document interface (MDI) example. Because an single document interface (SDI) form cannot perform the functions of an MDI form very well, a special MDI form was created to handle the task. When you start writing your own applications, you may find that a single form is not enough to complete the task. At this point you will need to add a new form and customize it to do the task you need. With this version of Visual Basic, it is easier than ever to include a form; you can use the Form Wizard to select the style of form you would like to add to your project. Just right-click in the Project Explorer and select Add ➤ Form and the Form Wizard will display the Add Form dialog box (see Figure 2.9).

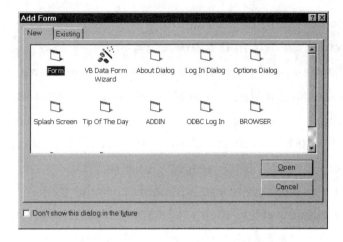

FIGURE 2.9: THE FORM WIZARD

As you can see, you have many form choices to choose from, including About Dialog, Splash Screen, Tip of the Day, and even a World Wide Web browser! When you select a form from the Wizard, Visual Basic will create a template complete with graphics and code and add it to your project. You will find that the Form Wizard can be a real time-saver, because it writes the code for a form automatically.

Tip

If you want to have standard-looking forms and do not want to code them yourself, you can use the Form Wizard to do the work for you.

Let's use the Form Wizard to add one last form to your project to spice it up a little.

1. To bring up the Form Wizard, right-click in the Project Explorer and select Add ➤ Form from the pop-up menu.

2. Add another form to your project by selecting About Dialog in the Add Form dialog box. The form will automatically name itself frmAbout.

3. Make the multiple document interface (MDI) form active by double-clicking frmMDI in the Project Explorer.

4. Go back to the Menu Editor, and add another menu by clicking the blank space directly under the &New Form caption. There should be no ellipses (the three dots) in this space. If there are, click the left arrow button to remove them. Now set its Caption property to **&Help**, and its Name property to **mnuHelp**.

5. Click the Next button to add another menu item.

6. Under the mnuHelp menu, add a menu item by clicking the right arrow once. Set the Caption Property to **&About**, and its Name property to **mnuHelpAbout**. Be sure to indent this menu item once by clicking the right arrow in the Menu Editor. This will ensure that this will be a menu item of the Help menu. Click OK to close the Menu Editor.

7. Right-click on Project1 in the Project Explorer and select Project1 Properties.

8. When the Project Properties dialog box comes up, click the Make tab.

9. Change the Title field to **A Sample MDI**.

10. In the Version Information frame, click on Company Name in the Type list, and type your name or your company name in the Value field.

11. Scroll down to the Product Name entry in the Type list, and enter **A Sample MDI**. Click OK when you are done.

12. Select Help ➤ About from the menu on your MDI form to open the Code window.

13. In the mnuHelpAbout_Click() sub, type the following line of code:

```
frmAbout.Show vbModal
```

Before you run this example, let's look at the keyword vbModal. As you will learn in Skill 5, "Modules and Classes," you will learn about passing parameters to procedures. In this case, the vbModal keyword is a parameter passed to the form's Show method. This tells Visual Basic to show the About dialog box in a modal state. A *modal* form gains the exclusive attention of the user. A user cannot access any other forms within an application until the modal dialog box has been addressed. This technique is used in many ways. You would most certainly want to make a login dialog box modal, because you do not want your users to gain access to a program without first being properly validate by the login process.

In addition to a simple modal form, you can also have *system modal* forms. These forms require the attention of the user and do not allow any other applications to be accessed until the dialog box has been addressed. A good example of a system modal dialog box is a screen saver. No applications can be accessed until the proper password is entered. This provides a small amount of security for your applications. (A full discussion of system modal dialog boxes is beyond the scope of this book.)

14. Run your application and check out the About dialog box (shown in Figure 2.10).

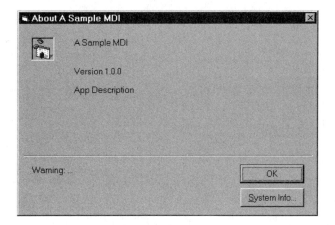

FIGURE 2.10: THE ABOUT DIALOG BOX CREATED BY THE FORM WIZARD

> ## Tip
> *If you find your Visual Basic design window becoming cluttered with lots of forms, close them. The quickest way to redisplay a form is to double-click its name in the Project Explorer.*

Summary of Skills Acquired

Now you can...

- ☑ create a new form
- ☑ work with forms in Visual Basic
- ☑ use the most important properties and methods to display your forms
- ☑ give your application some life by placing code in a form's events
- ☑ create a simple multiple document interface (MDI) with working menus
- ☑ use the Form Wizard to add specialized forms to your application

SKILL 3

Selecting and Using Controls

Featuring

- ❏ Introducing controls
- ❏ Learning about the Toolbox
- ❏ Using controls
- ❏ Grouping controls with frames
- ❏ Adding other controls to the Toolbox

Introducing Controls

Custom controls are the building blocks of a Visual Basic application. You can use them to add significant functionality to your programs. They are easy to use. You just double-click on the control you want to add to a form, or you can "draw" the control on a form by dragging the mouse around the area where you want the control to be.

After you add some controls, you can set most of their properties in the Properties window. You simply click on the control to make it the active control and change the appropriate properties in the Properties window.

The Toolbox is the containing window that holds the custom controls for your applications (see Figure 3.1). In this skill, we are going to take a look

at some of the basic controls you can use to
get your applications up and running.

There are also several advanced controls
that come with Visual Basic. Some controls
work with multimedia, and others utilize the
Internet. Best of all, you can now create your
own ActiveX custom controls and add them to
your Toolbox. You can also distribute your
custom controls to other developers through a
variety of methods. For more information
about creating and distributing these kinds of
controls, see Skill 14, "Using ActiveX."

FIGURE 3.1: THE
VISUAL BASIC TOOLBOX

Using Command Buttons

A command button control (shown here) is one of the most common
controls found in Windows applications. Visual Basic is no exception.
You can use a command button to elicit simple responses from the user or to
invoke special functions on forms. Surely you have encountered command
buttons before. Every time you click the OK button on a dialog box you
click a command button.

In the following sections we will look at some of the most important
properties, methods, and events of this simple but powerful control. In
"Command Button Methods" you will learn how a command button control
works; follow along with the exercise to get some hands-on experience.

Note

*Remember that properties describe the characteristics of an object. Methods are
actions that you can tell the object to perform, and events are triggered when a
control does something.*

Command Button Properties

Below is a list of the properties of a command button. The most commonly used properties appear in boldface. If you are interested in any properties not discussed below, you can select it in the Properties window and press the F1 key to get online help.

Appearance	**Enabled**	HelpContextID	**TabIndex**
BackColor	Font	hWnd	**TabStop**
Cancel	FontBold	Index	Tag
Caption	FontItalic	Left	ToolTipText
Container	FontName	MaskColor	Top
Default	FontSize	MouseIcon	UseMaskColor
DisabledPicture	FontStrikethru	**Name**	Value
DownPicture	FontUnderline	Parent	Visible
DragIcon	ForeColor	**Picture**	WhatsThisHelpID
DragMode	Height	**Style**	Width

The two most important properties of command buttons are Name and Caption. The Name property is used to give the control its own identity. This name is used by your code and Visual Basic to distinguish it from the rest of the controls. I will be discussing the Name property often throughout this book. The Caption property determines the text that appears on the command button. Placing an ampersand character (&) in the caption gives a keyboard access key alternative to a mouse-click. You access these controls by holding the Alt key down while you press the underlined letter of the control you wish to access. The user could also tab to the command button and press the spacebar to simulate a mouse-click on the button.

Two other useful properties are Cancel and Default. Setting the Default property to True means the user can simulate a click on the button by pressing Enter. Setting Cancel to True means the user can close a form by pressing Esc.

Note
When you add command buttons to a form, only one button can have its Default property set to True at a time. This button becomes the default button for the form. Likewise, only one command button can have its Cancel property set to True.

By setting the Style property, you can make the button contain text only, or you can add a picture to the button. If you want the button in its normal, unpressed state to have a picture, you can specify the picture's filename in the Picture property. You can also place other graphics on the button by setting them using the DisabledPicture and DownPicture properties.

Two properties can stop the user from accessing a command button—Enabled and Visible. If either is set to False, the command button will be unusable. Disabling a command button is a handy technique if you want to force the end user to complete certain actions (such as filling in text boxes) before clicking the next button in the process.

Note
When you want a button to be disabled, you should set the Enabled property to False rather than setting the Visible property to False. This lets the user know a control is available under certain conditions, rather than completely hiding the functionality of your program.

If the user moves around the form with the Tab key, you can determine the order in which they visit controls by specifying the TabIndex property. A control with a TabIndex of 0 (zero) is the first to receive the focus on a form, provided it's not disabled or invisible. If you alter the TabIndex of one control, the other controls' orders adjust to accommodate the new order. When you want to prevent a user from tabbing to a control, set its TabStop property to False, though this does not prevent a mouse-click on a control—to stop that, use the Enabled or Visible properties described previously.

Command Button Events

Without a doubt, the most frequently coded event procedure for a command button corresponds to the Click event; the other events for a command button are listed here:

Click	GotFocus	KeyUp	MouseMove
DragDrop	KeyDown	LostFocus	MouseUp
DragOver	KeyPress	**MouseDown**	

In your first programs, the Click event is probably the only event in which you'd be interested. It's the most commonly used event on a command button. You won't use many of the other events until you become more proficient in Visual Basic. However, you can also use the MouseUp event in place of the Click event. Many Windows applications use this event so it gives the user a chance to back out without causing a Click event.

Command Button Methods

Listed below are the methods for the command button. The most commonly used method is SetFocus.

Drag	Refresh	ZOrder
Move	**SetFocus**	

The SetFocus method is sometimes used to place the focus on a particular button. This comes in handy if you want the user to return to a default button after editing a text box on a form. If that were so, the code for the focus button looks like this:

```
cmdMyButton.SetFocus
```

and it might be placed in the Change event procedure for a text box.

Experimenting with a Control

Let's put the command button to use so you can see how to use it.

1. If you installed the sample applications from the Visual Basic CD, then open the project \Samples\Pguide\Controls\Controls.vbp.

Note

If you haven't already installed the sample applications, take a moment to refer back to the section "Working with Multiple Projects" in Skill 1. It covers how to install the sample applications. You will need to have these installed to do many of the exercises in this skill.

---

2. Click on Run ➤ Start from the Visual Basic menu to run the application. From the Control Examples dialog box, click Test Buttons. You will see a form like Figure 3.2.

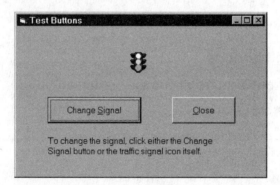

FIGURE 3.2: TESTING THE COMMAND BUTTON

3. Click the Change Signal button to watch the signal lights change. When you are done testing the buttons, click the Close button. With the command button control, you can enhance this form by placing the signal directly on the Change Signal button.

4. Stop the application by selecting Run ➤ End from the Visual Basic menu.

5. Make the Test Buttons form active by double-clicking frmButton in the Project Explorer.

6. Stretch the Change Signal button so it can fit an icon the size of the signal on it. In the Properties window, change the button's `Style` property to **1 - Graphical**.

7. Set the Visible property of the controls imgGreen, imgYellow, and imgRed to False.

8. Add the following code to the form's Load event:

```
Private Sub Form_Load()
  cmdChange.Picture = imgGreen.Picture
End Sub
```

9. Now change the ChangeSignal procedure to the following code:

```
Private Sub ChangeSignal()
  Static signal As Integer

  signal = signal + 1
  If signal > 3 Then signal = 1

  Select Case signal
    Case Is = 1
      cmdChange.Picture = imgYellow.Picture
    Case Is = 2
      cmdChange.Picture = imgRed.Picture
    Case Is = 3
      cmdChange.Picture = imgGreen.Picture
  End Select
End Sub
```

10. Run the program again (Run ➤ Start). Click Test Buttons again to get to the Test Buttons dialog box. When you click the Change Signal button, the signal icon on the command button will change in the same manner that the signal image did previously.

Although not sophisticated, this example shows you how the command button works. You can place other commands in the Click event so the button will perform any tasks you want it to. If you wanted the button to close your application, you could change the Click event procedure to:

```
Private Sub cmdChangeSignal_Click()
  End
End Sub
```

Tip

To add a graphic to your command buttons, set the Style property to 1 - Graphical. Then add the graphic by setting the Picture property to the filename of the graphic you want to use.

Using Text Boxes

Nearly every Visual Basic project involves at least one text box control (shown here). Text boxes are commonly used for accepting user input or for entering data. Their properties are, of course, specifically designed for these purposes. If you only want the simplest of user responses, you might consider using an InputBox instead. The InputBox displays a dialog box and prompts the user to enter something and returns this to the application. The Visual Basic InputBox and the converse MsgBox (message box) are discussed in Skill 9, "Using Dialog Boxes." A MsgBox is used for displaying simple messages to the user.

Text Box Properties

Here is the list of properties for the text box control. Again, the most important properties appear in boldface:

Alignment	FontItalic	LinkMode	SelStart
Appearance	FontName	LinkTimeout	SelText
BackColor	FontSize	LinkTopic	TabIndex
BorderStyle	FontStrikethru	Locked	TabStop
Container	FontUnderline	MaxLength	Tag
DataChanged	ForeColor	MouseIcon	Text
DataField	Height	MousePointer	ToolTipText
DataSource	HelpContextID	MultiLine	Top
DragIcon	HideSelection	Name	Visible
DragMode	hWnd	Parent	Width
Enabled	Index	PasswordChar	WhatsThisHelpID
Font	Left	ScrollBars	
FontBold	LinkItem	SelLength	

As always, the property you set first is the Name property. By convention this begins with the txt prefix. Notice that there is no Caption for a text box. Instead the text shown in the text box is determined by the Text property. You can provide a default entry in the text box by setting the Text property accordingly. It's possible you don't want any value in the text box—you want the user to enter something from scratch. In that case, delete the Text property setting and the text box appears blank. The MaxLength property is handy for limiting the user to a specified number of characters. This is often used in conjunction with the PasswordChar property. The latter is valuable for showing a default character (the asterisk character—*—is the best choice) when the user is entering a password. MaxLength and PasswordChar properties are often employed for a text box on a logon form.

The MultiLine property lets the user type more than one line of text into the text box. If MultiLine is used with the ScrollBars property, you can have a simple text editor with no coding—though you would need a couple of lines of code to save the user's typing.

The SelLength, SelStart, and SelText properties are useful for dealing with text appropriately. For example, the SelText property returns the text in the text box selected by the user or the application. From there it's easy to copy or cut the selected text to the Clipboard.

Note that the ReadOnly property from previous versions has been replaced by the Locked property. Setting the Locked property to True will cause the text box to display data, but permit no editing. You may have noticed this type of text box on licence agreement dialogs that appear during program installations. You can select and copy text, but you cannot type or delete text from the box.

To change the order in which the user tabs around the text boxes (and other controls) on a form, change the TabIndex setting. If you don't want the user to tab into a text box, set its TabStop property to False. To prevent a user from clicking in the text box with the mouse, set the Enabled property to False. There may be some situations where you would want to prevent the user from accessing a text box. For example, the user is not allowed to enter a message in an e-mail program until an address has been entered in the address text box. You will discover other examples of why you would want to use this feature as you become more proficient with Visual Basic.

Text Box Events

The textbox control supports a few events which are listed in the table here:

Change	GotFocus	LinkError	MouseMove
Click	KeyDown	LinkNotify	MouseMove
DblClick	KeyPress	LinkOpen	
DragDrop	KeyUp	LostFocus	
DragOver	LinkClose	MouseDown	

The Change event occurs every time the user inserts, replaces, or deletes a character in a text box. You can perform some elementary validation of user entry in the Change event. You can even use it to restrict entry to certain characters only. However, you may find that the Masked Edit control or one of the Key… events is more suitable for this purpose. The Microsoft Masked Edit control lets you specify entry templates or masks. It's a custom control that you need to add to the Toolbox if you want to use it. There's a full reference for all the custom controls bundled with Visual Basic in the *Books Online*, included on your Visual Basic CD.

Text Box Methods

Here is the list of methods supported by the text box control:

Drag	LinkRequest	SetFocus
LinkExecute	Move	ShowWhatsThis
LinkPoke	Refresh	ZOrder

Most of the methods here are not used very frequently, though the Link... methods are necessary if your text box is involved in a DDE (Dynamic Data Exchange) conversation. DDE allows one application to communicate with another. As the user interacts with one application, it sends data dynamically to the other application. Unfortunately, it is beyond the scope of this book to cover DDE in detail. If you are interested in pursuing it further check the online help.

The SetFocus method, though, is a boon in data entry applications. When the user clicks a command button (say, an Update one), the focus remains on that button. If the last statement in the Click event for the command button is a SetFocus method, you can force the focus back to the data entry text boxes. This saves the user from an extra mouse-click or excessive use of the Tab key just to get back into position. The syntax is:

```
txtMyTextBox.SetFocus
```

Experimenting with Text Box Controls

To see the SetFocus method in action, try the following example:

1. Open the project \Samples\Pguide\Controls\Controls.vbp if it is not already open.

2. Select Run ➤ Start to run the application. From the Control Examples dialog box, click Test Buttons. You will see a form similar to the one shown in Figure 3.3. The text box on the left of Figure 3.3 can be changed by selecting the options within the frame. The text box on the left has its MultiLine property set to True, and the text in the box indicates. Text editing applications often exploit the MultiLine and ScrollBars properties of a text box. Make the text box as large as the form and keep the form fixed in size (BorderStyle property). If you want the user to resize the form, or it's a multiple document interface (MDI) child form, you have to resize the text box dynamically as the

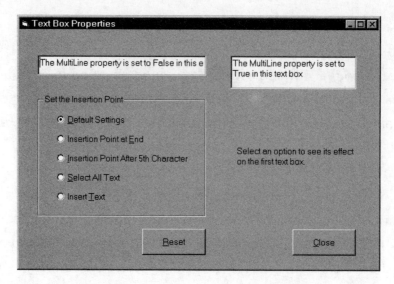

FIGURE 3.3: TESTING TEXT BOX CONTROLS

user alters the size of the form. One way of doing this is to add the following code to the form's Resize event procedure:

```
txtText1.Top = frmForm1.ScaleTop
txtText1.Left = frmForm1.ScaleLeft
txtText1.Width = frmForm1.ScaleWidth
txtText1.Height = frmForm1.ScaleHeight
```

The Scale… properties refer to the internal dimensions of a form. Thus a form's Height property is different from its ScaleHeight property. The latter makes allowances for title bars and borders.

3. Next, stop the application and make frmText active in the Form Designer.

4. Double-click the Insertion Point After 5th Character option to expose its procedure code, which looks like this:

```
Private Sub optInsert_Click()
    ' place the insertion point after 5th char
    txtDisplay.SelStart = 5
```

```
        ' set the focus to the text box so we can see
        ' the result of our settings
        txtDisplay.SetFocus
    End Sub
```

The SelStart property is used to select the starting position, in characters, of a selection within a text box. Here it is set to the 5th position. The SetFocus method sets the focus of the application back to txtDisplay.

5. Open the procedure for Click event of optSelect:

```
    Private Sub optSelect_Click()

     ' place the insertion point at the beginning
        txtDisplay.SelStart = 0
        ' find the length of the string and
        ' select that number of characters
        txtDisplay.SelLength = Len(txtDisplay.Text)

        ' set the focus to the text box so we can see
        ' the result of our settings
        txtDisplay.SetFocus
    End Sub
```

This code shows how you can select all of the text within a text box. So if you had a Select All menu option, you would call a procedure similar to this example. If you want to check the text that is highlighted, you can check the SelText property.

6. Replace the code in the cmdClose_Click event with the following:

```
    Private Sub cmdClose_Click()
        If txtDisplay.SelLength > 0 Then
            MsgBox "You selected " & txtDisplay.SelText
        End If

        End        ' Unload this form.
    End Sub
```

7. Run the application. In the Text Box Properties dialog box, select the word MultiLine and click the Close button. You will see something like Figure 3.4.

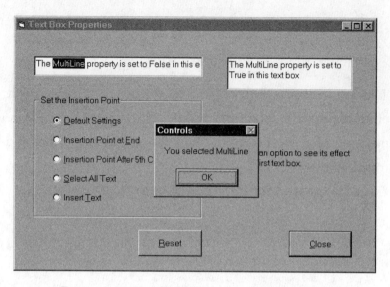

FIGURE 3.4: THE *SEL TEXT* PROPERTY CONTENTS

Using Labels

A label control (shown here) is similar to a text box control in that both display text. The main difference, however, is a label displays read-only text as far as the user is concerned, though you can alter the caption as a run-time property.

The property of interest in a label control is the Caption property, as opposed to a text box's Text property. Labels are often used for providing information to the user. This can be in the form of a message shown on the form itself or a prompt. The prompt is usually combined with a text box, list

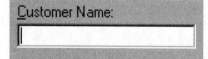

box, or other control. It gives the user an idea of the nature of the referenced control. For example, if you had a text box that allowed the user to enter the data for a customer's name, then you might place a label to the left or above the text box with its Caption property set to Customer Name.

Note – Setting Access Keys for a Label Control

Access keys are actually Alt+key combinations that allow the user to access a control by holding down the Alt key while pressing the underlined letter of text-type control. Access keys can only be set for controls that have a Caption property—for instance, command buttons and menu controls. Many controls text box controls for example, do not have a Caption property, so it's impossible for a keyboard user to jump straight to the control—unless they tab and the control just happens to be next in the tab order.

The workaround is to place a label control before the control in question. Make sure to set the TabIndex property of the label to one less than the TabIndex of the control the label is describing. Include an ampersand character (&) in the Caption property for the label to define the access key.

Let's try an example to give you an idea of what's required:

1. *If it's not already open, open the Controls.vbp project from the previous example.*
2. *Double-click on frmText in the Project Explorer to make it the active form.*
3. *Click on txtDisplay, the text box control on the upper-left side of the form, and examine its TabIndex property in the Properties window. It should be set to 0. This makes this control the first tab stop on the form.*
4. *Add a label control to the form and place it above txtDisplay. Set its Name property to lblDisplay in the Properties window. Set its Caption property to Dis&play. Be sure to place the ampersand before the letter P.*
5. *The TabIndex property of lblDisplay should be 11. Change it to 0.*
6. *Run the program by selecting Run ➤ Start.*
7. *From the Control Example form, click the Text Box button.*
8. *From the Text Box Properties form, click the Reset button to move the focus away from txtDisplay.*
9. *Now, hold down the Alt key and press the letter P.*

Now pressing Alt with the underlined letter moves the focus to the label. But if you look at the properties, events, and methods of a label (described shortly), you see that there's no TabStop property; no GotFocus or LostFocus events; and no SetFocus method. What this means is a label can never receive the focus—so moving the focus to a label with an access key actually moves the focus to the next control in the TabIndex property order.

Label Properties

You have already worked with some of the properties of a label control. Here is the complete list of properties for this control:

Alignment	DragMode	Index	Tag
Appearance	Enabled	Left	ToolTipText
AutoSize	**Font**	LinkItem	Top
BackColor	FontBold	LinkMode	**UseMnemonic**
BackStyle	FontItalic	LinkTimeout	Visible
BorderStyle	FontName	LinkTopic	WhatsThisHelpID
Caption	FontSize	MouseIcon	Width
Container	FontStrikethru	MousePointer	**WordWrap**
DataSource	FontUnderline	**Name**	
DataField	ForeColor	Parent	
DragIcon	Height	**TabIndex**	

As a reminder, the most important property at the outset is—once again—the Name property. For labels the prefix is normally lbl. The Caption property determines the text shown in the label. If you incorporate an ampersand (&) character in the caption, an access key is defined. This raises an interesting question. What happens if you want to show an actual ampersand in the caption? An ampersand does not display; instead, it remains hidden and causes the subsequent character to appear underlined.

Tip

If you do want an ampersand character to appear in a label, set the UseMnemonic property to False, because by default it's True. A mnemonic is an abbreviation or shorthand—in this context it means an access key.

You define the size of the label at design time. At run time you might wish to alter the Caption property, only to find it's too big to fit within the label control. You could calculate the length of the caption and adjust the label size accordingly, but this is messy and there's a danger of an enlarged label obscuring other controls. To simplify matters, use the AutoSize and WordWrap properties, either by themselves or in conjunction. That way the caption will fit and you can control whether the label expands vertically rather than horizontally.

One more interesting label control property is BorderStyle. This is not related to the form property of the same name—there are only two choices. But by setting BorderStyle to 1 - Fixed Single and the BackColor to white (or whatever), the label looks exactly like a text box, except that it's read-only. Labels are often used in this fashion to show data for browsing purposes only.

Label Events

The label control has many of the same events as any other controls:

Change	DragDrop	LinkError	MouseDown
Click	DragOver	LinkNotify	MouseMove
DblClick	LinkClose	LinkOpen	MouseUp

Most of the standard events are supported. But note the absence of any Key... events. This is consistent with a label not being able to receive the focus. The Mouse... events are there, because there's nothing to stop you from clicking on a label at run time. The ability to click on a control does not indicate it must necessarily receive the focus. The Link... events are not shared by many other controls (with the exception of text boxes and picture controls). These events are concerned with DDE (Dynamic Data Exchange) conversations. The Key... and Mouse... events are discussed later in Skill 10, "Working with the Mouse."

Label Methods

The label control also has methods, but you will probably not use them very often in your applications. The following shows the methods supported by the label control:

Drag	LinkPoke	Move	ShowWhatsThis
LinkExecute	**LinkRequest**	Refresh	ZOrder

The label methods are not particularly useful, although the LinkRequest method is sometimes used to update a non-automatic DDE link.

Experimenting with a Label Control

Although there is not much that can be done to show you how a label works, we will add a label to the main form in the Controls project that you have been working with in previous examples:

1. Make frmMain the active form in the Form Designer by double-clicking frmMain in the Project Explorer.
2. Add a label on the bottom of the form. Stretch it so it is almost the width of the form.
3. Set its Name property to **lblHelp** and set the Caption property to **Click a button to see how a control works**.
4. When you run the application, the main form should look like Figure 3.5.

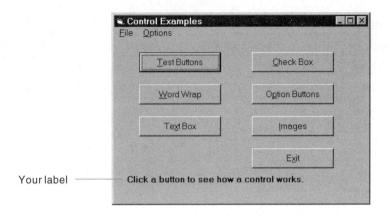

Your label ——————

FIGURE 3.5: YOUR LABEL ADDED TO THE FORM

Using Option Buttons

Option button controls (shown here) are used to allow the user to select one, and only one, option from a group of options. Usually option buttons are grouped together within a frame control (described later in this chapter), but they can also be grouped on a plain form, if there is to be only one group of option buttons. Thus, if you had a frame specifying a delivery method, you might have one button for Royal Mail and another for courier delivery. Products can only be shipped by *one* of these methods (not both—and not none). In contrast, option buttons representing, say, bold and italic settings for text would not make sense. Text can be both bold *and* italic, or neither (none).

Option Button Properties

The option button supports many properties, which are shown in the following table:

Alignment	FontSize	Picture
Appearance	FontStrikethru	Style
BackColor	FontUnderline	TabIndex
Caption	ForeColor	TabStop
Container	Height	Tag
DisabledPicture	HelpContextID	ToolTipText
DownPicture	hWnd	Top
DragIcon	Index	UseMaskColor
DragMode	Left	**Value**
Enabled	MaskColor	Visible
Font	MouseIcon	WhatsThisHelpID
FontBold	MousePointer	Width
FontItalic	**Name**	
FontName	Parent	

Once again the Name property is the one to set first; option buttons have an opt prefix by convention. The Caption property helps the user determine the purpose of an option button. The other popular property is Value. This is invaluable at both design time and run time. At run time you test the Value property to see if the user has turned on (or off) the option button. The property has two settings, True and False. At design time you can set the Value property to True for one of the buttons if you wish—the default setting is False. This means that the option button (and only that option button in a group) is pre-selected when the form opens. If you try to make Value for another button in the group True, then the previous one reverts to a False setting.

Option Button Events

The option button control has a few events, but only the Click event is really used:

Click	DragOver	KeyPress	MouseDown
DblClick	GotFocus	KeyUp	MouseMove
DragDrop	KeyDown	LostFocus	MouseUp

The typical way of dealing with option buttons is to test the Value property at run time to see if they're selected. Your code then initiates actions accordingly. It's common to test for the Value property in the Click event procedure for a command button that's clicked after the user has selected the option button of interest. This allows you to check for a condition before the next procedure is called. You test the Value property in an If ... End If or Select Case ... End Select construct. But there may be occasions when you want to initiate an action immediately after the user makes a choice. Then you may want to trap the option button's Click event. Try this example to see what I mean:

1. Run the Controls project by selecting Run ➤ Start.
2. Click the Option Buttons button on the Control Examples form.
3. Click on any of the option buttons and watch the label at the top of the form. The Click event of each option button is used to change the Caption property of the label.
4. When you are done watching the results, click the Close button to close the dialog box.
5. End the application by clicking the Exit button on the Control Examples form.

If you want to see the code that makes this example work, follow these steps:

1. Double-click on frmOptions in the Project Explorer to make it the active form.
2. Double-click on the option button next to 486 to open its Code window. You will see the following code:

```
Private Sub opt486_Click()
    ' assign a value to the first string variable
    strComputer = 486
     call the subroutine
    Call DisplayCaption
End Sub
```

Notice that the Click event sets the value of strComputer to 486. Then it calls another procedure to change the caption.

3. Select (General) from the left pull-down menu, called the *object pull-down*, at the top of the Code window. Then select (DisplayCaption) from the procedure pull-down on the upper right of the Code window. This will display the code for the DisplayCaption procedure:

```
Sub DisplayCaption()
    ' concatenate the caption with the two string
    ' variables.
    lblDisplay.Caption = "You selected a " & _
    strComputer & " running " & strSystem
End Sub
```

Notice how the Caption property of lblDisplay is set in this procedure, which is called in every Click event of every option button. That's all there is to it!

Option Button Methods

The methods for the option button are of little use in the Visual Basic environment:

Drag	Refresh	ShowWhatsThis
Move	SetFocus	ZOrder

Therefore, we will not deal with their explanations here.

Open and start the Control.vbp application in the \Samples\PGuide\Controls subdirectory of Visual Basic. Click the Option Buttons button to bring up the Options dialog box (see Figure 3.6).

The five option buttons are actually in two groups. The options labelled 486, Pentium, and Pentium Pro are in their own group directly on the form. The Windows 95 and Windows NT options are in a separate group on the Operating System frame. This frame then rests on the form and separates the

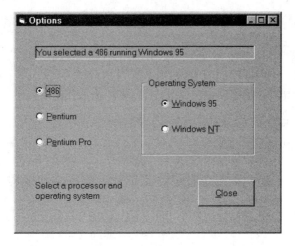

FIGURE 3.6: THE OPTIONS DIALOG BOX

two groups of option buttons. If you click on an option button, you will notice the other option buttons in the same group become deselected. Only one option can be selected in a group at a time.

Using Check Boxes

A check box control (shown here) is rather similar to an option button, which was described in the last section. Both often partake in groups, and the Value property is tested to see if a check box is on or off. But there are two fundamental differences between check boxes and option buttons: Check boxes are valid as single controls—a single option button is probably counter-intuitive. Check boxes (even when in a group) are not mutually exclusive. Finally, check boxes have three possible settings for the Value property.

An option button is either on or it's off. Therefore, Value can be either True or False. Check boxes can be in one of *three* states—on, off, or greyed. Greyed (dimmed) does *not* mean the same as disabled in this context—a greyed check box is neither on nor off, though the user can change its setting. If the check box were disabled, the user wouldn't be able to turn it on or off. A greyed check box is used to signify that some, but not all, options on another dialog box are selected. If you look at the dialog box in Figure 3.7, you will notice two of the check boxes are greyed. If you have installed Windows, then you understand what the greyed check box means. The Accessories check box is grey because I installed some, but not all, of the Windows accessories.

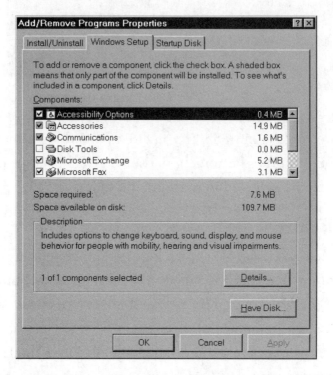

FIGURE 3.7: GREYED OR "DIMMED" CHECK BOXES

Check Box Properties

The following table lists the properties for the check box control. Again, as with option buttons, the three most popular properties are Name, Caption, and Value. When setting the Name property it's conventional to use a chk prefix.

Alignment	DragMode	Height	**TabIndex**
Appearance	**Enabled**	HelpContextID	**TabStop**
BackColor	**Font**	hWnd	Tag
Caption	FontBold	Index	ToolTipText
Container	FontItalic	Left	Top
DataChanged	FontName	MousePointer	UseMaskColor
DataField	FontSize	**Name**	**Value**
DisabledPicture	FontStrikethru	Parent	WhatsThisHelpID
DownPicture	FontUnderline	Picture	Width
DragIcon	ForeColor	Style	

Check Box Events

The following table shows you that the check box has similar events to the option button control:

Click	GotFocus	KeyUp	MouseMove
DragDrop	KeyDown	LostFocus	MouseUp
DragOver	KeyPress	MouseDown	

To carry out further processing as soon as the user has clicked the check box, use the Click event. Normally, though, if you do not put code directly within the Click event, you will have another procedure that will ascertain the value of a check box by retrieving its Value property.

Check Box Methods

Like the events of the check box control, its methods are similar to those for the option button control:

Drag	Refresh	ShowWhatsThis
Move	SetFocus	ZOrder

Like option buttons, the methods for the check box control are non-vital to the operation of the control.

If you want to test the functionality of the check box control, start the Controls application and click the Check Box button. The Check Box Example dialog box has two check boxes that manipulate the text box at the top (see Figure 3.8).

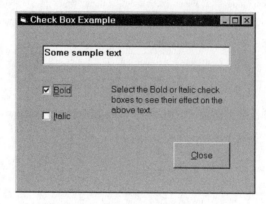

FIGURE 3.8: THE CHECK BOX EXAMPLE DIALOG BOX

Clicking the Bold check box turns the text bold, and the Italic option italicizes the text within the box. In the procedure below you can see how the FontBold property for the text box is modified in the Click event.

```
Private Sub chkBold_Click()
    ' The Click event occurs when the check box changes state.
    ' Value property indicates the new state of the check box.
    If chkBold.Value = 1 Then       ' If checked.
        txtDisplay.FontBold = True
    Else                            ' If not checked.
        txtDisplay.FontBold = False
    End If
End Sub
```

Experimenting with Check Box Controls

Try this example to see the check box work in all three of its states:

1. Start a new project by selecting File ➤ New Project.

2. In the Properties window, change the Name property of Form1 to
    frmMain.

3. Add a check box control to the form. Set its Name property to
    chkOptions, and its Caption property to **What do you want on your
    sandwich?**

4. Double-click on chkOptions to open the Code window. Select the
    (General)(Declarations) section from the object and procedure drop-
    down lists. Add the following code:

    ```
    Public PeanutButter As Boolean
    Public Jelly As Boolean
    ```

5. Add the following code to the MouseUp event of chkOptions:

    ```
    Private Sub chkOptions_MouseUp(Button As Integer, _
                    Shift As Integer, X As Single, Y As Single)
        frmOptions.Show vbModal

        If PeanutButter And Jelly Then
            chkOptions.Value = 1
            Exit Sub
        End If

        If PeanutButter Or Jelly Then
            chkOptions.Value = 2
            Exit Sub
        End If

        If Not PeanutButter And Not Jelly Then
            chkOptions.Value = 0
            Exit Sub
        End If
    End Sub
    ```

6. Right-click on the Project Explorer and select Add ➤ Form from the
    pop-up menu. Select Form from the Add Form dialog box.

7. In the Properties window, set the Name property of the new form to
    frmOptions. Set its Caption property to **Set Options**.

8. Add a check box control to frmOptions. Set its Name property to
    chkPeanutButter and its Caption to **Peanut Butter**.

9. Add another check box control. Set its Name property to **chkJelly** and its Caption to **Jelly**.

10. Double-click on frmOptions to open the Code window. Add the following code to the Load event of the form:

```
Private Sub Form_Load()
    If frmMain.PeanutButter Then
        chkPeanutButter.Value = 1
    Else
        chkPeanutButter.Value = 0
    End If

    If frmMain.Jelly Then
        chkJelly.Value = 1
    Else
        chkJelly.Value = 0
    End If
End Sub
```

11. Add the following code to the Click event of chkPeanutButter:

```
Private Sub chkPeanutButter_Click()
    If chkPeanutButter.Value = 1 Then
        frmMain.PeanutButter = True
    Else
            frmMain.PeanutButter = False
    End If
End Sub
```

12. Add the following code to the Click event of chkJelly:

```
Private Sub chkJelly_Click()
    If chkJelly.Value = 1 Then
        frmMain.Jelly = True
    Else
            frmMain.Jelly = False
    End If
End Sub
```

13. Select Run ➤ Start to start your application.

If you click on the check box on frmMain, you are presented with a dialog box offering you peanut butter and jelly. Some people like both, while others may like only one or the other. If you check both and close the dialog box, you will see the check box is solid. If you only select peanut butter or jelly, but not both, then the check box will be greyed. If you don't want either, the check box will be unchecked.

Using Frame Controls

When used by itself, the frame control (shown here) is not particularly useful. The controls normally placed in a frame are option buttons and check boxes. This has the effect of grouping them together so when the frame is moved, the other controls move too. For this to work you can't double-click a control (say, an option button) to add it to the form, and then drag it into position within the frame. Instead, you must single-click the control in the Toolbox and drag a location for it inside the frame. Then all the controls move together.

In addition, the option buttons function as a group—that is, if you select one at run time, the others become deselected. If you simply scatter option buttons randomly on a form, then they all function as one large group. To create separate groupings of option buttons, you place them in frames. The button items within each frame act as a self-contained group and have no effect on the option buttons in other frame groups.

Although a frame is often used as a container for check box groups too, each check box is completely independent. Thus the setting for one check box has no effect on the setting for the others in the same group. This is the behaviour you would expect of check boxes. Check boxes are not mutually exclusive. This contrasts with option buttons, where the buttons within a single group should be mutually exclusive. The reason then for placing check boxes in a frame is to enable you to move the group as a whole, when you reposition the frame at design time. The frame also serves as a visual grouping for the check boxes. For example, the check boxes relating to a particular feature can be in one frame and those pertinent to another feature in another frame.

A frame is usually given an fra prefix. You place the frame on the form before you place the controls it's going to contain.

Frame Properties

The frame control has several properties, listed below:

Appearance	Font	Height	Parent
BackColor	FontBold	HelpContextID	TabIndex
Caption	FontItalic	hWnd	Tag
Container	FontName	Index	ToolTipText
ClipControls	FontSize	Left	Top
DragIcon	FontStrikethru	MouseIcon	Visible
DragMode	FontUnderline	MousePointer	WhatsThisHelpID
Enabled	ForeColor	**Name**	Width

After the Name property, perhaps the single most important property is the Caption. You use this to give a meaningful title to the frame on the form. Then it's clear to the end user which feature the option buttons (or check boxes) in the frame refer to. To provide a clue as to how each option button affects the feature, you use the Caption property of the buttons. For example, in an order dispatch system you might have a frame with the caption Delivery. And within that frame you might have two option buttons, with the captions Normal and Express.

Frame Events

The frame control only supports a few events:

Click	MouseDown
DblClick	MouseMove
DragDrop	MouseUp
DragOver	

The frame control events are only rarely used. In an application that uses drag-and-drop, however, the DragDrop event is sometimes used to initiate actions when the user drops an object into a frame area. Drag-and-drop is covered in Skill 10.

Frame Methods

A frame object supports only a few methods. None are very helpful and they're hardly ever seen in Visual Basic projects:

Drag	Refresh	ZOrder
Move	ShowWhatsThis	

As you can see in Figure 3.9, a frame control serves as a container for other controls. You can group option buttons to separate them from other groups, or you can group other controls to provide visual organization to your form. Set the Caption property of the frame to the description of the functionality that the contained controls provide. In this example, the Caption is set to Set the Insertion Point.

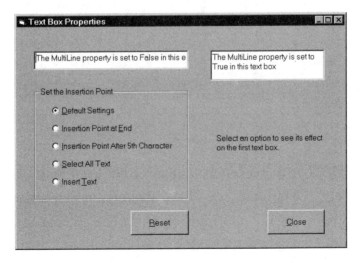

FIGURE 3.9: A FRAME CONTROL

Using List Boxes

If you're a regular user of Windows, then you're familiar with list box controls (shown here). A list box is an ideal way of presenting users with a list of data. Users can browse the data in the list box or select one or more items as the basis for further processing. The user can't edit the data in a list box directly—one way around that is to have a combo box instead; combo boxes are discussed next. When the list of data is too long for the list box then Visual Basic will add a vertical scrollbar. Let's examine most of the important list box control properties and methods.

List Box Properties

Many of the list box properties are shared by a combo box control, and some of them are essential for getting the best from the control:

Appearance	FontName	**ListCount**	TabIndex
BackColor	FontSize	**ListIndex**	TabStop
Columns	FontStrikethru	MouseIcon	Tag
Container	FontUnderline	MousePointer	Text
DataField	ForeColor	**MultiSelect**	ToolTip
DataSource	Height	**Name**	Top
DragIcon	HelpContextID	**NewIndex**	TopIndex
DragMode	hWnd	Parent	Visible
Enabled	Index	SelCount	WhatsThisHelpID
Font	ItemData	**Selected**	Width
FontBold	Left	**Sorted**	
FontItalic	**List**	**Style**	

The Columns property lets you create a multi-column list box. Unfortunately, the columns are of the snaking, or newspaper, type. There's no direct support for the multiple columns of an Access-style list box where different data items are displayed in separate columns. Instead Visual Basic wraps the same type of data items from column to column.

Tip

You can't have a true multiple-column list box in Visual Basic. One workaround is to concatenate (join) the different data items into one string and add that string to a single-column Visual Basic list box. To line up the columns, you can embed spaces or tab characters (Chr(9)) in the concatenated string. Alternatively, use fixed-length strings to hold the items to be concatenated. However, this does not work when you're using a proportional font.

The List property sets or returns the value of an item in the list. You use the index of the item with the List property. The index positions of items in a list box start at 0 (zero) and run to 1 less than the total number of items in a list. Thus, if you had 10 items in the list box, the index positions run from 0 to 9.

Note

Don't confuse the index position in a list box with the Index property of a list box. The latter is displayed in the Properties window—the index position is not shown anywhere. The Index property is used when you create a control array of list boxes.

You use the List property to get the value of any item in the list. For example, to return the value of the third item in the list, use the following:

```
lstList1.List(2)
```

To get the value of the currently selected item in the list, simply use the Text property of the list box. The ListIndex property sets or returns the index position of the currently selected item—if no item is selected, the ListIndex property is -1.

Note

"lstList1.List(lstList1.ListIndex)" and "lstList1.Text" are the same.

You can pick up the index position of the last item added to a list (see the AddItem method shortly) with the NewIndex property. The ListCount property returns the number of items in a list box. Confusingly, this is always 1 greater than the value returned by the NewIndex property—this is because the index positions count from 0 (zero) while the ListCount property starts counting from 1 for the first item. ListCount returns 0 if the list box is empty.

The MultiSelect property determines whether the user can select one item or whether they can select more than one. List boxes support both a simple and an extended multiple selection. A simple multiple selection allows the user to select contiguous items—usually accomplished with the mouse and the Shift key. An extended multiple selection lets the user select contiguous and non-contiguous items—usually done by mouse clicks in conjunction with the Ctrl key.

The Selected property is a Boolean property and is a run-time property only. A Boolean property is one that can take only a True or False setting. The following line preselects the third item in a list box:

```
lstList1.Selected(2) = True
```

Note the use of index position (2) to reference the *third* item in the list.

The final property that we're going to consider is the Sorted property. This is one of those properties that you can set only at design time. You can read it, or return it, at run time (that is, see if it's True or False) but you can't set it (that is, change an unsorted list into a sorted one or vice versa). When you set the Sorted property to True at design time, then any items you add to a list box (typically, with the AddItem method) are sorted in alphabetical order. The sort can only be in ascending order and it's not case-sensitive.

List Box Events

The list box control supports a few events, shown here:

Click	KeyDown	MouseMove
DblClick	KeyPress	MouseUp
DragDrop	KeyUp	Scroll
DragOver	LostFocus	
GotFocus	MouseDown	

Perhaps the most commonly used event for a list box is DblClick. This coincides with the normal operation of list boxes in Windows applications. The first thing to do with a list box is usually to fill it with items for the list. The AddItem method can be used to do this (see "List Box Methods"). You can then, if you want, preselect one of the items in the list by setting the Selected property to True. The user either accepts the default selection or chooses another item with a single-click. Then a clicking on an OK command button carries out a process using the Text property, which returns the value of the selected item. However, a popular shortcut is to double-click the item in the list—that way, the user can both select an item and initiate a process based on that item in a single action. Many Windows applications adopt this technique to copy one item from a list box into another list box.

List Box Methods

The list box has many of its own methods, as well as some common to the other controls discussed so far:

AddItem	Move	SetFocus
Clear	Refresh	ShowWhatsThis
Drag	**RemoveItem**	ZOrder

There are three methods here worthy of note—AddItem, Clear, and RemoveItem. AddItem, as already indicated, is for adding items to a list box control. The RemoveItem method, as you might expect, removes items from a list box. To remove all the items in one fell swoop, use the Clear method.

An example of the simplest syntax for the AddItem method is:

```
lstList1.AddItem "Hello"
```

This adds the word "Hello" to the list box. Often you employ a number of AddItem methods, one after the other, to populate (fill in) a list box. Many developers place the AddItem methods in a Form_Load event procedure so the list box is filling as the form loads. You can specify the position that an item will take in a list by specifying the index position:

```
lstList1.AddItem "Hello" 3
```

This places the text "Hello" at the *fourth* position in the list. If you omit the index position, the item is added to the end of the list—or if the Sorted property is True, the item is placed in the correct order.

Caution

Be careful when using the AddItem method with a specified index position in a sorted list box. The Sorted property automatically calculates the index position of added items. If the position you specify does not match the one generated by the Sorted property, then Visual Basic gets confused and the results are unpredictable.

Experimenting with List Box Controls

Now that you have read about what makes a list box work, try this example to see it in action:

1. Start a new project by selecting File ➤ New Project. Select Standard EXE from the Project Wizard.

2. Add two list box controls to Form1.

3. Place one list box on the upper half of the form, and the other on the lower half of the form. Size both list boxes until they are almost as wide as the form.

4. Double-click on the form to open the Code window. Add the following code to the Load event:

```
Private Sub Form_Load()
    List1.AddItem "Nuts"
    List1.AddItem "Bolts"
    List1.AddItem "Nails"
    List1.AddItem "L-Brackets"
    List1.AddItem "Hammers"
    List1.AddItem "Saw"
    List1.AddItem "Drill"
    List1.AddItem "File"
    List1.AddItem "Sandpaper"
    List1.AddItem "Planer"
End Sub
```

5. Add the following code to the DblClick event of List1:

```
Private Sub List1_DblClick()
    'Add the item to the other list
    List2.AddItem List1.Text

    'Remove the item from this list
    List1.RemoveItem List1.ListIndex
End Sub
```

6. Add the following code to the DblClick event of List2:

```
Private Sub List2_DblClick()
    'Add the item to the other list
    List1.AddItem List2.Text

    'Remove the item from this list
    List2.RemoveItem List2.ListIndex
End Sub
```

7. Finally, run the program by selecting Run ➤ Start.

You can double-click on any product to move it to the opposite list box. If you look at the code in steps 5 and 6, you will notice the item is added to the other list box before it is removed from the current one. The AddItem must be called *before* the RemoveItem method because the AddItem needs to know what to add to the other list. If you call RemoveItem first, then the wrong list item will be added to the opposite list. You will learn more about lists in the next section.

Using Combo Boxes

The name combo box comes from "combination box"; the control is shown here. The idea is that a combo box combines the features of both a text box and a list box. A potential problem with list boxes—in some situations anyway—is that you're stuck with the entries displayed. You can't directly edit an item in the list or select an entry that's not already there. Of course, if you *want* to restrict the user, then a list box is fine in this respect. A combo box control (at least in two of its styles available in Visual Basic) allows you to select a predefined item from a list *or* to enter a new item not in the list. A combo box can also incorporate a drop-down section—that means it takes less room on a form than a normal list box. In all, there are three types of combo boxes to choose from at design time: a drop-down combo, a simple combo, and a drop-down list. You can specify the type by setting the Style property.

Apart from the Style property, the properties, events, and methods of combo boxes are very similar to those of list boxes, described shortly. However, the Text property is different. With a list box, the Text property returns the text of the currently selected item at run time. With a combo box, on the other hand, you can assign a value to the Text property at run time—in effect, you can set the text, even if the item is not already in the list. The results of choosing a different Style property are covered in the next section.

Note that the combo box discussed here is the built-in combo box control. There's also another combo box (DBCombo, or the data-bound combo box). This has a few more features that let you work with data from databases.

Combo Box Properties

These are the properties for the combo box control:

Appearance	FontName	**List**	**Style**
BackColor	FontSize	**ListCount**	TabIndex
Container	FontStrikethru	**ListIndex**	TabStop
DataField	FontUnderline	MouseIcon	Tag
DataSource	ForeColor	MousePointer	Text
DragIcon	Height	**Name**	Top
DragMode	HelpContextID	**NewIndex**	Visible
Enabled	hWnd	Parent	Width
Font	Index	**SelCount**	
FontBold	ItemData	**Selected**	
FontItalic	Left	Sorted	

The List, ListCount, ListIndex, NewIndex, and Sorted properties are identical to those for a list box. The property that's different, and that consists of one of the fundamentals of designing combo boxes, is the Style property. There are three settings for Style, and the behaviour and appearance of the combo box are determined by the setting you choose. The styles are numbered from 0 to 2 and represent, in order, a drop-down combo, a simple combo, and a drop-down list:

- The drop-down combo looks like a standard text box with a drop-down arrow to the right. Clicking the arrow opens a list beneath the text box. The user has the choice of selecting an item from the list, which places it in the text box, or of entering their own text in the text box. In other words, this is the true combo box.

- The simple combo is a variation on this theme—the only difference being that the list is permanently displayed. This one's an option if your form is not too crowded.

- The final style, the drop-down list, is really a type of list box rather than a combo box. It looks identical to a drop-down combo but, as the name suggests, the user is confined to selecting a predefined item from the list. The advantage of this latter style is that it takes up less space then a conventional list box.

Combo Box Events

Here are the events for the combo box:

Change	DragOver	KeyPress	MouseUp
Click	**DropDown**	KeyUp	Scroll
DblClick	GotFocus	LostFocus	
DragDrop	KeyDown	MouseDown	

Most of the events for a combo box control are the standard ones. However, the DropDown event is specific to combo boxes—though not supported by the simple combo box, which is already "dropped-down."

The Change event is not supported by the drop-down list (style 2), because the user can't change the entry in the text box section. To see if that type of combo box has been accessed by the user, try the Click or the DropDown event procedures.

The DblClick event is only relevant to the simple combo box, for it's the only one where the user can see the full list by default. Usually, the DblClick event procedure calls the Click event for a command button. This means the user can simply double-click an item in the list, rather than using a single-click to select followed by a click on a command button to carry out some processing based on the user selection.

Combo Box Methods

The methods you can apply to a combo box control are the same as those for a list box:

AddItem	Move	SetFocus
Clear	Refresh	ShowWhatsThis
Drag	RemoveItem	ZOrder

Again, the important methods are AddItem, Clear, and RemoveItem. And, just as with a list box control, it's common practice to populate a combo box with a series of AddItem methods in the Load event of a form.

Incidentally, especially if you've worked with the database application Microsoft Access, you may be wondering about the flexibility of list and combo boxes. What do you do if the predetermined items in the list continually change? Do you continually have to recode the AddItem methods? How can you do this anyway in a stand-alone .EXE you generate from your .VBP project? Another concern of yours could be regarding the actual tedium of typing long series of AddItem methods.

All of these questions are easily resolved if you exploit the RowSource and ListField properties of a data-bound list or data-bound combo box. Even more flexibility is provided by these data-bound versions of those two controls (DBList and DBCombo). For more information on these and other data-bound controls, consult the Visual Basic online help.

Note

Often you want the user first to select an item from a list box and then to click a command button. The button initiates an action using the selected item. An accepted practice is for the user to simply double-click the item in the list. This both selects the item and carries out the action. To do this, you can call the button's Click event procedure from the list box's DblClick event procedure.

The code listed below populates the list and combo boxes in Figure 3.10. The following example will show you the difference between a list and a combo box by simulating a grocery list. In the list I added some fruits. The combo box lists different types of bread. Because I obviously haven't covered all of the different types of bread, you can type another type of bread in the combo box to add it to your list.

```
Private Sub Form_Load()
    'Add items to list box
    lstItems.AddItem "Apples"
    lstItems.AddItem "Oranges"
    lstItems.AddItem "Grapes"
    lstItems.AddItem "Tangerines"
    lstItems.AddItem "Lemons"
    lstItems.AddItem "Bananas"

    'add items to combo box
    cboCombination.AddItem "Wheat"
    cboCombination.AddItem "White"
    cboCombination.AddItem "Rye"
    cboCombination.AddItem "Sourdough"
    cboCombination.AddItem "French"
    cboCombination.AddItem "Pita"
End Sub
```

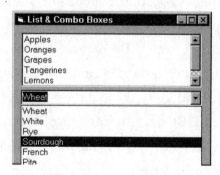

FIGURE 3.10: THE LIST AND COMBO BOX

Experimenting with List and Combo Box Controls

Let's modify this form to function like a grocery list. You code the form to allow you to select items from the combo box and add them to your grocery list box.

1. Start a new project and add one list box to a form and set its Name to **lstGroceries**.

2. Add a combo box below the list box and set its Name to **cboProducts**, and its Caption to **Wheat**.

3. Add two labels to a form. Place the first label above the list box and set its Caption property to **Grocery List**.

4. Place the second label between the list box and the combo box. Set its Caption to **Store Items**.

5. Add a command button to the bottom centre of the form. Set its Name property to **cmdAdd**, and its Caption to **&Add**.

6. Modify the Form_Load event as follows:

```
Private Sub Form_Load()
    'Clear the list box
    lstGroceries.Clear

    'add items to combo box
    cboProducts.AddItem "Wheat"
    cboProducts.AddItem "Cereal"
    cboProducts.AddItem "Steak"
    cboProducts.AddItem "Pasta"
    cboProducts.AddItem "Candy"
    cboProducts.AddItem "Soda"
End Sub
```

7. Add the following code to the cmdAdd_Click event:

```
Private Sub cmdAdd_Click()
    lstGroceries.AddItem cboProducts.Text
End Sub
```

8. Run the program. You can select a product from the combo box. If you want to add it to the grocery list, click the Add button.

9. Notice that this store doesn't carry any ice cream. You can type this in the combo box and click the Add button. The store will have to special order it for you.

Note

To call the event procedure for another control, you type the name of the procedure, as in cmdListAdd_Click. But to initiate command buttons' Click events there's an alternative method. You set the Value property of the button to True, as in cmdListAdd.Value = True.

Using Image Objects

The image control (its prefix is often img) is a lightweight equivalent of the picture box control, which is described in a later section. But unlike the picture control, the image control can't act as a container for other objects. In some of its other properties it's not as versatile, but it's a good choice if you simply want to display a picture on a form. Image controls consume far less memory than picture controls.

The image control that comes with Visual Basic can now display bitmap (.BMP), icon (.ICO), metafile (.WMF), JPEG (.JPG) and GIF (.GIF) files. This makes it easier to display graphics from the World Wide Web, as well as graphics from other popular graphics program.

Image Properties

The image control utilizes several properties, but less than the picture box, discussed later.

Appearance	Enabled	**Name**	Tag
BorderStyle	Height	OLEDragMode	Top
DataField	Index	OLEDropMode	Visible
DataSource	Left	Parent	Width
DragIcon	MouseIcon	**Picture**	
DragMode	MousePointer	**Stretch**	

As with most other graphical controls, you add the graphic by setting the Picture property. Perhaps the most interesting property here is Stretch. This is a Boolean property—meaning it takes only the values True or False. When Stretch is set to False (the default), the control resizes to the size of the picture placed inside it. If you later resize the control, then the loaded picture either is cropped or has empty space showing around it, or both, depending on the relative directions of horizontal and vertical resizing. But if you set Stretch to True, the picture resizes with the control. Thus you can make the enclosed picture larger or smaller, or fatter or thinner, by resizing the control after the picture is loaded. A picture control has no Stretch property. Its nearest equivalent is the AutoSize property. When AutoSize is set to True for a picture box, then the control adapts to the size of the loaded picture. However, unlike an image control with Stretch turned on, if the picture box is resized the enclosed picture remains the same—the picture does not "stretch" with the picture box control.

Image Events

The image control doesn't use many events, and of those, you may only use a few if any.

Click	DragDrop	MouseDown	MouseUp
DblClick	DragOver	MouseMove	

Image controls are sometimes handy as drag-and-drop destinations. This is because you can have a picture inside that gives an indication of the results of dropping onto the control. Drag-and-drop is discussed later in Skill 10, "Working with the Mouse."

Image Methods

The following are properties of an image control:

Drag	Move	Refresh	ZOrder

You will most likely not use any of these methods in your applications.

Note

There's a catalogue of bundled icons included with your Visual Basic documentation. They can be found in the \Graphics\Icons subdirectory of Visual Basic as well as on the CD.

Experimenting with Image Controls

Let's take a look at some image controls in action.

1. Open the Controls.vbp project from earlier in the \Samples\PGuide\Controls\ subdirectory.

2. Run the program and click the Images button.

As you can see in Figure 3.11, you can click on one of the four card icons and the program will notify you that it is selected. The code listed below is fairly straightforward.

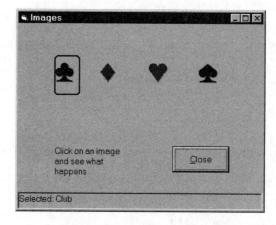

FIGURE 3.11: THE IMAGE CONTROL

```
Private Sub imgClub_Click()
    shpCard.Left = imgClub.Left
    picStatus.Cls
    picStatus.Print "Selected: Club"
End Sub
Private Sub imgDiamond_Click()
    shpCard.Left = imgDiamond.Left
```

```
        picStatus.Cls
        picStatus.Print "Selected: Diamond"
End Sub
Private Sub imgHeart_Click()
        shpCard.Left = imgHeart.Left
        picStatus.Cls
        picStatus.Print "Selected: Heart"
End Sub
Private Sub imgSpade_Click()
        shpCard.Left = imgSpade.Left
        picStatus.Cls
        picStatus.Print "Selected: Spade"
End Sub
```

The card outline is actually a shape control that is actually moved off the left side of the form. This is done in the Form's Load event by setting the shape's Left property to -500. This achieves the same results as hiding a control by setting its Visible property to False.

As you can see in any of the procedures, the shape is moved to the same coordinates as the image that was clicked. This creates the effect of outlining the image. So the result is a small card with an image in it.

Using Picture Boxes

 As you might expect, picture boxes (shown here) often display graphics (for example, bitmaps, icons, JPEGs, and GIFs). In this role, picture boxes are similar to image controls. However, picture boxes and images have slightly different properties and therefore behave differently. If you just want to show a picture, then an image control is usually a better choice than a picture box. Images take up less memory and are a lightweight version of picture boxes. However, if you want to move the graphic around the form, a picture box produces a smoother display. In addition, you can create text and use graphics methods in a picture box at run time. The graphics methods enable you to draw lines, circles, and rectangles at run time. But, most importantly for this application, picture boxes can act as containers for other controls. Thus, you can place a command button within a picture box. In this respect, picture boxes function as "forms within forms."

Picture Box Properties

The table below lists the properties for the picture box control. Notice that there are many more properties for this control than there are for the image control.

Align	FillStyle	LinkTopic
Appearance	Font	MouseIcon
AutoRedraw	FontBold	MousePointer
AutoSize	FontItalic	**Name**
BackColor	FontName	Parent
BorderStyle	FontSize	**Picture**
ClipControls	FontStrikethru	ScaleHeight
Container	FontTransparent	ScaleLeft
CurrentX	FontUnderline	ScaleMode
CurrentY	ForeColor	ScaleTop
DataChanged	hDC	ScaleWidth
DataField	Height	TabIndex
DataSource	HelpContextID	TabStop
DragIcon	hWnd	Tag
DragMode	**Image**	ToolTipText
DrawMode	Index	Top
DrawStyle	Left	Visible
DrawWidth	LinkItem	WhatsThisHelpID
Enabled	LinkMode	Width
FillColor	LinkTimeout	

Quite a lot of properties this time! When you put a picture into a picture box, it appears at its normal size. If it's too big for the picture box, the graphic is clipped. Setting the AutoSize property to True causes the picture box to resize to match the size of the graphic. The graphic displayed in the picture box is determined by the Picture property—you can change this property at both design time and run time. There's a similar-sounding property—the Image property. This one's only available at run time, and it's for making a copy from one picture box to another. The syntax for doing this is:

```
Picture2.Picture = Picture1.Image
```

You can place this line of code in any event where it is relevant. For example, maybe you want to change the picture in a picture box when the user selects a different record in a database.

The line above places a copy (image) of the picture in the first picture box into the second picture box (using its Picture property). You can even change the picture directly at run time. The syntax is:

```
Picture1.Picture = LoadPicture _ ("filename")
```

To empty a picture box, use the Visual Basic LoadPicture function with no parameter:

```
Picture1.Picture = LoadPicture()
```

Picture Box Events

The picture box events are listed in the following table:

Change	GotFocus	LinkError	MouseMove
Click	KeyDown	LinkNotify	MouseUp
DblClick	KeyPress	LinkOpen	Paint
DragDrop	KeyUp	LostFocus	Resize
DragOver	LinkClose	MouseDown	

Two of the popular events for picture boxes are the Click and DragDrop events. The Click event is, with any luck, self-explanatory by now. The DragDrop event is discussed in detail in Skill 10, "Working with the Mouse," later in the book.

Picture Box Methods

The picture box control supports more methods than its counterpart, the image box. The most important once are listed in boldface in the following table:

Circle	LinkPoke	Point	SetFocus
Cls	LinkRequest	**Print**	ShowWhatsThis
Drag	LinkSend	**PSet**	TextHeight
Line	Move	Refresh	TextWidth
LinkExecute	**PaintPicture**	Scale	**ZOrder**

The Circle, Cls, Line, PaintPicture, Print, and PSet methods are all concerned with drawing graphics or text in the picture box at run time—Cls (like the old DOS command for "clear screen") is actually used to erase entries. The ZOrder method is the run-time equivalent of Format ➤ Order ➤ Bring to Front or Format ➤ Order ➤ Send to Back. You can use ZOrder to determine which controls overlap other controls. However, you should be aware that there are three layers on a form—ZOrder only works within the layer that contains the control. All the nongraphical controls except labels (for example, command buttons) belong to the top layer. Picture boxes and other graphical controls (as well as labels) belong to the middle layer. The bottom layer contains the results of the graphics methods—for instance, a circle drawn with the Circle method is on the bottom layer. This contrasts with a circle drawn with the Shape control, which is in the middle layer. What all this means is that you can't position a picture box over a command button with ZOrder—the picture box is permanently relegated to the layer behind. The ZOrder method is for rearranging objects *within* one layer.

Note

Z-order determines the relative positions of objects within the same layer or level of a form. In design view, use Format ➤ Order ➤ Bring to Front, or Format ➤ Order ➤ Send to Back to change relative positions. At run time you can use the ZOrder method.

Using Timers

The timer control (shown here) is one of the few controls always hidden at run time. This means you don't have to find room for it on a form—it can go anywhere, even on top of existing controls. The timer basically does just one thing: It checks the system clock and acts accordingly.

Timer Properties

The timer control does not have many properties as you can see in this table:

Enabled	Left	Tag
Index	**Name**	Top
Interval	Parent	

Apart from the Name property (a tmr prefix is recommended), there's only one important property for the timer control—the Interval property. Indeed, you have to set this property to get the timer to do anything at all (assuming the Enabled property is at its default, True). The Left and Top properties are virtually superfluous—it makes little difference where you put a timer on a form.

The Interval property is measured in milliseconds. This means if you want to count seconds, you have to multiply the number of seconds by 1,000. Once an interval has elapsed (provided the timer is enabled), the timer generates its own Timer event. It does this by checking the system clock at frequent intervals.

Tip

The Interval property is measured in milliseconds. If you want to count the number of seconds elapsed, you have to set the Interval property to the number of seconds multiplied by 1,000.

The Timer Event

The timer control has only one event called, appropriately, a Timer event. As already stated, this event takes place every time an interval elapses. The interval is determined by the Interval property. To stop the Timer event from occurring, you can set the timer's Enabled property to False at run time.

Timer Methods

The timer control does not support any methods at all.

Experimenting with a Timer Control

To give you an idea of how the timer works, let's create a Caption Bar clock:

1. Start a new project by selecting File ➤ New project. Select Standard EXE as the project type.
2. Set the Name property of Form1 to **frmMain**. Set its Caption property to **Application Time**.
3. Add a timer to the frmMain. Set its Name property to tmrTime.
4. Set the timer's Interval property to **500**. We want to have the clock check itself every half-second. We do this because the timer control is

not as precise as other timer-type controls, but it will perform well for this example.

5. Add the following code to the (General)(Declarations) procedure for frmMain:

```
Private OldCaption As String
Option Explicit
```

6. Add the following code to the Form_Load event:

```
Private Sub Form_Load()
    OldCaption = Me.Caption
End Sub
```

7. Now add the following code to the Timer event of the timer.

```
Private Sub tmrTimer_Timer()
    Dim msg As String

    msg = OldCaption & ": " & Time$
    Caption = msg
End Sub
```

8. Save and run the application by selecting Run ➤ Start. Your Caption Bar clock should now look like Figure 3.12.

FIGURE 3.12: THE CAPTION BAR CLOCK

You may notice that the caption flickers a bit. You can minimize this by changing the code in the Timer event to minimize the number of refreshes to the Caption:

```
Private Sub tmrTimer_Timer()
    Dim msg As String

    msg = OldCaption & ": " & Time$
    If msg <> Caption Then
        Caption = msg
    End If
End Sub
```

The If...Then statement checks to see if the time, returned through Time$, has changed. If the msg string is different than Caption, the you update the Caption property to reflect the time change. Otherwise you do nothing to cause a refresh on the Caption. The flicker will go away.

Tip

You can use the Format function to change the format of the display. Format accepts many named parameters as well as ones you define yourself. You can use the function to format the display of numbers and strings—it's not just confined to date and time. To see some of the possibilities, search help for the Format function. Once you reach the topic entitled Format Function, click the See Also pop-up text at the top of the window.

Using Scroll Bars

A scroll bar control (shown here) on a form is not to be confused with a scroll bar on a large text box or list box. The scroll bar controls are completely independent objects that exist without reference to any other control (this is not the case with large text boxes or list boxes). The horizontal scroll bar and the vertical scroll bar are identical (except for their orientation). Both controls share the same properties, events, and methods. When the term "scroll bar" is used in this section it means both the horizontal scroll bar and the vertical scroll bar.

A scroll bar control is typically employed to increase or decrease a value. For example, you may want to change a colour setting, a number, or the volume of a media device. The scroll bar acts as a sliding scale with a starting point and an ending point, including all the values in between. If you simply want to increment or decrement a number, then you should also take a look at the spin button custom control.

One problem with a scroll bar is that once it is used it retains the focus and may flicker on screen. To circumvent this, change the focus to another control.

Tip

To avoid scroll bar flicker, add a SetFocus method on another control as the last statement in the scroll bar control's Change event procedure.

Scroll Bar Properties

The scroll bar control has a few properties worth noting:

Appearance	hWnd	MousePointer	Top
Container	Index	**Name**	**Value**
DragIcon	**LargeChange**	Parent	Visible
DragMode	Left	**SmallChange**	WhatsThisHelpID
Enabled	**Max**	TabIndex	Width
Height	**Min**	TabStop	
HelpContextID	MouseIcon	Tag	

The properties most commonly set for scroll bars are the Max, Min, LargeChange, and SmallChange properties. The Min and Max properties determine the limits for the Value property of the scroll bar. You can set the Min property to the lowest value allowed, for example 0. You can set Max to the maximum allowed. For example, the following code could be used to define the lowest and highest volume allowed by your application:

```
Private Sub Form_Load()
  hscVolume.Min = 0        'The lowest volume
  hscVolume.Max = 255      'The maximum volume
End Sub
```

The LargeChange property determines how much the Value property changes when the user clicks in the scroll bar. The SmallChange property sets the amount the Value property changes when the user clicks one of the scroll arrows. You don't have to worry about the direction of the change, only the amount; Visual Basic figures out whether it's an increase or decrease, depending on where you click. There is no property setting to correspond to the user dragging the scroll box (also called *thumb* or *elevator*) within the scroll bar. This is because there's no way of predicting how far the scroll box will be dragged. However, it automatically updates the Value property. You ascertain the new Value in the Change event procedure for the scroll bar. The Value property can also be set at design time to place the scroll box at a certain point within the scroll bar.

The Value, LargeChange, and SmallChange property settings must lie within the range dictated by the Min and Max properties. Value is usually set equal to Min or Max so the scroll box is at one end of the scroll bar. LargeChange is ordinarily some integral multiple of SmallChange. Max can be less than Min, which is often counter-intuitive. Max and Min, or both, can also be negative.

Scroll Bar Events

This is the list of events supported by the horizontal and vertical scroll bars:

Change	GotFocus	KeyUp
DragDrop	KeyDown	LostFocus
DragOver	KeyPress	**Scroll**

There are two vital events here—Change and Scroll. The Change event occurs whenever the Value property of the scroll bar is altered at run time. The Value property, in turn, is changed whenever the user clicks on a scroll arrow (SmallChange), clicks in the scroll bar to one side of the scroll box

(LargeChange), or stops dragging the scroll box along the scroll bar. The latter induces a Value change depending on the length of the drag—though the Value change can never be greater than the difference between the Min and Max properties.

Although the Change event is generated when the user stops dragging the scroll box, it does not occur during the drag. If you want to generate the Change event *as the user drags,* then you must call it from the Scroll event. The Scroll event is continually generated as the user drags the scroll box. By calling the Change event from the Scroll event, you can continually generate a Change event. If you don't, you have to wait until the user stops dragging to ascertain the results of the action. On the other hand, any kind of click on the scroll bar produces an immediate Change event.

Scroll Bar Methods

The following scroll bar methods are not terribly important and are beneficial only rarely.

Drag	Refresh	ShowWhatsThis
Move	SetFocus	ZOrder

Experimenting with Scroll Bar Controls

To see how a scroll bar works by adding a horizontal scroll bar to a project, follow these steps:

1. Start a new project by selecting File ➤ New Project.2. Add a horizontal scroll bar to Form1 and set its Name property to **hscVolume** in the Properties window.

2. Set the Min property of hscVolume to **0**. Set its Max property to **100**. Set its Value property to **50**.

3. Set the SmallChange property to **1**, and the LargeChange property to **10**.

4. Add a label control to the top of the form and set its Name property to **lblVolume**. Set its Caption to **50**.

5. Click on Font in the Properties window to set the Font Size property of the label to **24**.

6. Set the AutoSize property of the label to **True**. Centre the control on the form above the scroll bar.

Your form should now look similar to Figure 3.13.

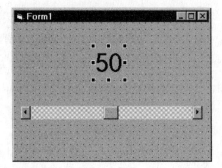

FIGURE 3.13: THE SCROLL BAR DEMO

7. Double-click on the scroll bar to open the Code window.

8. Add the following code to the Change event of the scroll bar:

```
Private Sub hscVolume_Change()
    lblVolume.Caption = Trim$(Str$(hscVolume.Value))
End Sub
```

9. Finally, select Run ➤ Start .

The program is very simple. It just displays the volume setting, which you control by moving the slider within the scroll bar. You can move it by clicking either of the direction arrows, by dragging the slider, or by clicking between the slider and an arrow.

Perhaps the parts of the program that deserve the most attention are the Trim$ and Str$ functions. First, the Str$ function is used to convert a numeric value to a string. You need to make this conversion because the

Caption of lblVolume expects either a string or a variant. However, the Value property of the scroll bar is an integer. So, the value returned by the function:

```
Str$(hscVolume)
```

will be suitable for the Caption property. The Trim$ function trims the leading and trailing spaces from a string. When you convert a number to a string, the string result will contain leading spaces. So to keep the formatting neat, you can use the combination:

```
Trim$(Str$(hscVolume))
```

Using Drive Lists

The drive list box control (or just *drive*), which is shown here, is normally used in conjunction with the directory list and the file list controls. At its most fundamental these three controls allow the user to select a file in a particular directory on a particular drive. The user changes to another drive via the drive control. They switch directories with the directories control, and they select the file from the file control. You can also use the drive and directory controls to let the user choose a destination for a file they wish to save. Although a common dialog control is better suited for retrieving filenames, we will look at these three controls in the following sections. You will be able to find other uses for them as you develop your skills.

Drive List Box Properties

The following table lists the many properties for the drive list box control:

Appearance	FontName	Left	TabIndex
BackColor	FontSize	List	TabStop
DragIcon	FontStrikethru	ListCount	Tag
DragMode	FontUnderline	ListIndex	ToolTipText
Drive	ForeColor	MouseIcon	Top
Enabled	Height	MousePointer	Visible
Font	HelpContextID	**Name**	WhatsThisHelpID
FontBold	hWnd	OLEDropMode	Width
FontItalic	Index	Parent	

For the Name property a drv prefix is normally adopted. Apart from the Name, the single most important property is Drive. This is a run-time property only. It's used to return the drive the user has selected in the drive control. Your code should then deal appropriately with the user's choice. The Drive property is invariably accessed in the Change event procedure for the drive control (see the next section).

Drive List Box Events

The drive list box has a few events, but few are useful to the beginning programmer.

Change	GotFocus	KeyUp
DragDrop	KeyDown	LostFocus
DragOver	KeyPress	Scroll

The Change event is the most popular one to trap. This occurs whenever the user makes a selection of a drive in the drive control. The Drive property of the control is used to update the display of directories in the directory list control. Thus, the directories shown are always those on the currently selected drive. A fuller discussion of how to do this appears under the section on the file control, which follows shortly.

Drive List Box Methods

Below is the list of methods for this control.

Drag	Refresh	ShowWhatsThis
Move	SetFocus	Zorder

These methods are rarely used.

Using Directory List Boxes

As already stated, the directory list box (or simply *directory*) control, which is shown here, is used in conjunction with the drive control, described earlier, and file control. The user can select a directory on the current drive from the directory list. However, it's important to update the directories displayed when the user changes drives in the drive control. Further, it's also important to update the files shown in a file control, too. To do these, the directory's Path property and Change event are used.

Directory List Box Properties

The following are the directory list box properties:

Appearance	FontStrikethru	ListIndex	Tag
BackColor	FontUnderline	MouseIcon	ToolTipText
DragIcon	ForeColor	MousePointer	Top
DragMode	Height	**Name**	TopIndex
Enabled	HelpContextID	OLEDragMode	Visible
Font	hWnd	OLEDropMode	WhatsThisHelpID
FontBold	Index	Parent	Width
FontItalic	Left	**Path**	
FontName	List	TabIndex	
FontSize	ListCount	TabStop	

A directory control is often given a Name property with a dir prefix. The Path property is a run-time property that sets or returns the path to the directory in the directory list. It's usually seen in the Change event for the *drive* control—where it updates the list of directories to match the drive selected by the user. The Path property is also used in the *directory* control's Change event procedure to update the list of files in a file control when the user changes directories or drives.

Directory List Box Events

The table below shows the events used by the directory list box.

Change	GotFocus	LostFocus	Scroll
Click	KeyDown	MouseDown	
DragDrop	KeyPress	MouseMove	
DragOver	KeyUp	MouseUp	

Although you may use the Click event in your code, the Change event procedure is where you will place code to update the files in a file list control.

Directory List Box Methods

You probably won't be working with the following directory list box methods too often:

Drag	Refresh	ShowWhatsThis
Move	SetFocus	ZOrder

Using File List Boxes

The file list box control (shown here) comes at the end of the drive-directory-file chain. It is used to list the actual filenames that are in the directory specified by the Path property, as shown in Figure 3.14.

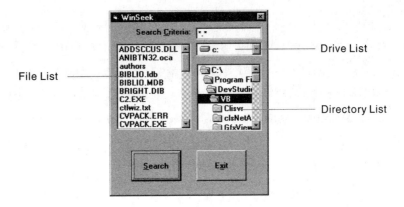

File List

Drive List

Directory List

FIGURE 3.14: THE DRIVE, DIRECTORY, AND FILE LIST CONTROLS

To reiterate, the file control is updated in the directory Change event. The directory control, itself, is updated when the user selects a directory in the directory control—it's also updated when the user selects a new drive in the drive control. For these links to work you must code *two* Change event procedures correctly (this is explained in the example coming up in the next section).

File List Box Properties

File list boxes have a lot of properties—and many of them quite valuable:

Appearance	FontSize	ListIndex	ReadOnly
Archive	FontStrikethru	Locked	**Selected**
BackColor	FontUnderline	MouseIcon	**System**
Container	ForeColor	MousePointer	TabIndex
DragIcon	Height	MultiSelect	TabStop
DragMode	HelpContextID	**Name**	Tag
Enabled	**Hidden**	**Normal**	ToolTipText
FileName	hWnd	OLEDragMode	Top
Font	Index	OLEDropMode	TopIndex
FontBold	Left	Parent	Visible
FontItalic	List	**Path**	Width
FontName	ListCount	**Pattern**	

Let's concentrate on just a few. The Path property is vitally important. It's a run-time property and is often both set and returned. When the Path property is returned, Visual Basic is aware of the path to the currently selected file in the file control. To ascertain the path and the filename together (sometimes called a *fully qualified path*), you have to concatenate the Path property with the FileName property. The fully qualified path can then be used as a basis for opening files.

Saving files is not quite so straightforward—you'll also need to provide a text box for the user to enter a new filename rather than writing over the selected file. An alternative approach is to generate the filename for a saved file automatically and use the controls to determine only the drive and directory for the file. In that case, you might want to disable the file control or make it invisible.

The Path is set in response to users changing the drive (in a drive control) or the directory (in a directory control). You must code the series of possible events correctly for this to work. Let's experiment with using the default control names for now:

1. In the Drive1_Change event you add a line like this:

   ```
   Dir1.Path = Drive1.Drive
   ```

   This line updates the directory list to reflect the selected drive. The fact that the directory Path property changes in code generates a Change event for the directory control as well. And the same event is generated if the user manually changes directories in the directory control.

2. You now code the Change event for the directory as follows:

   ```
   File1.Path = Dir1.Path
   ```

This ensures that the files displayed (governed by the file control's Path property) reflect both the currently selected drive and the directory. Changing a drive automatically selects a new directory.

The Pattern property can be set at design time—it can also be changed at run time. By default the Pattern property is *.*, which shows all files in the file control. You can narrow down the list of files by providing a suitable template, for example, *.txt to display just your text files.

The Archive, Hidden, Normal, ReadOnly, and System properties can all be used to further narrow or expand the list of files. Hidden and System are False by default—ideally, you wouldn't want the end user even to be aware that hidden and system files exist.

Tip

If you're designing a project for a system administrator or a network manager, you may want the hidden and system files to be visible. To do this, set the Hidden and System properties to True.

By using the above code, you will also synchronize the controls when the application begins.

File List Box Events

This is the list of events supported by the file list box control.

Click	GotFocus	LostFocus	**PathChange**
DblClick	KeyDown	MouseDown	**PatternChange**
DragDrop	KeyPress	MouseMove	Scroll
DragOver	KeyUp	MouseUp	

In a sense, the events for a file list control are similar to those of an ordinary list box. The standard approach is to have a command button's Click event procedure carry out some processing based on the Path and

FileName properties of the file control. However, it's often helpful to give the user a double-click alternative. The way to do this, if you recall from an earlier discussion on list boxes, is to code the file control's DblClick event procedure to call the command button's Click event.

Two events that are specific to a file control are PathChange and PatternChange. The PathChange event occurs when the file's Path property alters. Similarly, the PatternChange event occurs when the Pattern property is changed in code. It's common practice to let the user enter a pattern in a text box and translate this into the Pattern property at run time. You can then use the PatternChange event procedure to reset the Pattern if the user has entered a pattern that might be dangerous, for example, *.ini.

File List Box Methods

This control only supports a few methods, listed in the table below. None of them are particularly useful for the operation of the control.

Drag	Refresh	ShowWhatsThis
Move	SetFocus	ZOrder

Experimenting with File List Box Controls

To get a look at the drive, directory, and file list boxes in action let's experiment with the WinSeek.vbp sample project. This program will simply search the current drive and directory for files matching a file specification, such as an AVI extension (see Figure 3.15).

1. Load and run the WinSeek project by double-clicking on WinSeek.vbp in the \Samples\Misc\FileCtls\ subdirectoy.

2. Set the drive list control to C: if it has not defaulted to it already.

3. Set the directory list box to the root directory of the drive. You should be in the C:\ directory.

FIGURE 3.15: THE WINSEEK APPLICATION

4. In the Search Criteria field, type a file specification (filespec) of a file type you want to search for, such as ***.AVI**. By entering an asterisk, the program will find any filename that ends with the .AVI extension.

5. Click the Search button and watch WinSeek find matching files. You will see search results similar to those in Figure 3.16.

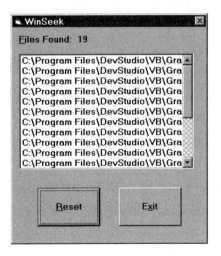

FIGURE 3.16: THE WINSEEK RESULTS

When you are done experimenting with the WinSeek application, stop it by selecting Run ➤ End from the Visual Basic menu. Double-click on frmWinSeek to open the Code window. The procedures you want to examine are the Change events for drvList and dirList. Let's start by looking at the drvList_Change event:

```
Private Sub DrvList_Change()
    On Error GoTo DriveHandler
    dirList.Path = drvList.Drive
    Exit Sub

DriveHandler:
    drvList.Drive = dirList.Path
    Exit Sub
End Sub
```

The first thing you will notice is the On Error statement. The procedure calls an error-trapping routine because the drive list box is the most likely of the three controls to cause an error. The reason is the user could select a floppy drive that has no disk in it, which would cause an error. By trapping this error the program can resume gracefully.

Also notice that this event triggers a Change event in the directory list by setting the Path property. This, in turn, triggers a Change event in the file list box. It is sort of like the domino theory. You trigger one event and it will trigger the next object and so on down the line. As you can see below, the directory list Change event modifies the path of the file list box.

```
Private Sub DirList_Change()
    ' Update the file list box to synchronize with the directory list box.
    filList.Path = dirList.Path
End Sub
```

The drive, directory, and file list boxes are almost always used together. However, there may be some instances where you will only need the functionality of one of the controls. If you do use them all together you will place the relevant synchronization code in the Change event of each control.

Adding Other Controls to the Toolbox

Before we move on to the next skill, you should learn how to add controls to your Toolbox. There are many more controls included with Visual Basic than those described in this skill. As you move through this book, you will continually learn more about these controls as well as the others not covered here.

You can add other controls by following a few simple steps:

• Add a tab to the Toolbox to keep it neat
• Select the controls to add
• Move them to the appropriate tab if necessary

To teach you how to add controls to the Toolbox, let's add some Internet controls.

1. Right-click on the Toolbox to display its pop-up menu.
2. Select Add Tab... from the pop-up menu.
3. When prompted for the tab name, type in **Internet** and click the OK button.
4. Now that the Internet tab has been added to the Toolbox, click on it to make it the active tab.
5. Right-click on the Toolbox and select Components from the pop-up menu.
6. From the Controls tab on the Components dialog box, click the check boxes next to Microsoft Internet Controls and Microsoft Internet Transfer Control 5.0.
7. Click the OK button to add the controls to the tab.

If the controls don't "land" on the appropriate tab, you can move them by dragging them to the appropriate tab on the Toolbox.

That's all there is to adding controls to the Toolbox. It is a good idea to create tabs that you can categorize your controls by. This will help make it easier for you to locate the control you need. Use the tabs to avoid Toolbox clutter.

There are obviously too many controls to cover in this skill. To cover all of the controls would almost require its own book. Fortunately, we cover some of the other controls throughout this book and provide sample code, so you can learn how to use each one. If you have read this entire skill, then you are more than ready to start using the controls covered here, as well as those that have not been covered yet. The nice thing about custom controls is that once you are familiar with one, it is easy to become familiar with others.

Summary of Skills Acquired

Now you can...

- ☑ understand when to use a control
- ☑ use the controls in the Toolbox
- ☑ group controls with frames
- ☑ coordinate the drive, directory, and file list box controls
- ☑ add controls to the Toolbox

SKILL 4

Working within Modules and Classes

Featuring

- ❏ Introducing code modules
- ❏ Using Private and Public sub procedures
- ❏ Passing parameters to procedures
- ❏ Creating and using functions
- ❏ Adding code modules
- ❏ Working with class modules

Introducing Code Modules

You have already worked with two of the three major building blocks of Visual Basic in earlier skills: forms and controls. Now we're going to take a look at the third fundamental building block—the *code module*. You have actually already used code modules in working with forms, although you probably didn't know it. In fact, every time you open the Code window to add code to your forms, you are actually working with a kind of code module.

Note

A code module is actually an ASCII text file that contains procedures of code. They are useful for combining related procedures that are available to your programs.

Because code modules are in their own file, you can include them in more than one project. This is one way of writing reusable code. For example, I have several code modules with related procedures in them. One has many dialog box functions for use in my shareware programs. Another module has functions that make accessing multimedia devices much easier. By combining similar functions into one code module, you can create a *code library*. If you place these modules within one directory, or a logical set of subdirectories, you can reuse them in other projects. This saves you time by not requiring you to write the same code more than once. In addition, if the procedures in the modules are debugged, then you can use them reliably within other projects.

Creating a Code Library

Create a separate directory on your hard disk to store your code libraries. Then you can include the required modules in your project so you don't have to constantly rewrite the same code.

To create your own code library, follow these steps:

1. Open Windows Explorer.
2. Create a directory, also called a *folder*, named Library. The location of this folder must be in a location that is easy to find and to back up. You don't want to accidentally delete this directory if you re-install software.
3. Close Windows Explorer.

Retrieving Code Modules

Now when you write code modules that are generic in nature, you can save them in the Library directory. When you need to use this code module in another project, just follow these steps:

1. Right-click in the Project Explorer.

2. Select Add > Add File from the pop-up menu.

3. Select the appropriate code module from the Library directory.

Creating a Code Module

Now that you have set up a code library directory, you can create your first reusable code module. I have included three simple but useful procedures you can use when you include this code module in your projects. Follow these steps to create the code module:

1. From Visual Basic, select File ➤ New Project to create a new project.

2. Right-click in the Project Explorer and select Add ➤ Module.

3. Select Module from the Add Module dialog box. Click the Open button.

4. In the Properties window set the Name property to **MyLibrary**.

5. Go to the Code window and add the following function:

```
Public Function IsFile(Filename As String) As Boolean
  If Len(Dir(Filename)) > 0 Then
    'Filename exists
    IsFile = True
  Else
    'Filename does not exist
    IsFile = False
  End If
End Function
```

6. Add the following code to the module:

```
Public Sub ShowHourglass()
  Screen.MousePointer = 11
End Sub
```

7. Add the following code to the module:

```
Public Sub ShowMousePointer()
  Screen.MousePointer = 0
End Sub
```

8. Select File ➤ Save MyLibrary from the Visual Basic menu.

9. In the Save File As dialog box, save the file as **MyLibrary.bas** in the Library folder.

Now that you have your first reusable code module, you can include it in your projects to perform simple tasks. The IsFile function is used to detect if a file exists on the hard disk. You will want to do this before you attempt to open files in your programs. All you have to do is tell it what file to look for using the following syntax:

```
If IsFile("C:\CONFIG.SYS") Then
  …Your code goes here…
End If
```

The ShowHourglass and ShowMousePointer procedures are useful when you want the user to wait because a task is running. To use them, just call ShowHourglass before the task, and call ShowMousePointer when the task is done. For example:

```
ShowHourglass
    IndexLargeDatabase
ShowMousePointer
```

You can add to this code module in the future when you start writing your own useful procedures and functions.

The code modules that make up forms consist of procedures that support the form and the controls on that form. While examining event procedures of forms in previous examples you may have noticed these procedures have the word Private in front of the Sub keyword. These procedures are declared Private because they are private to the form—they cannot be called from outside that form.

There are ways to make that code accessible to other forms and procedures in code modules, however:

- By declaring the procedure Public, you make the procedure available to other components within your application.

- The other method is to create a separate code module that contains procedures and variables that can be utilized by any object within the scope of the application. You accomplished this in the previous example.

Using *Private* and *Public* Sub Procedures

All the programming in this book so far is fairly straightforward. The code you have worked with in previous skills has been entirely contained in the event procedures for forms. Now, to extend the capabilities of Visual Basic, it's necessary to move on from this rather limited approach. In particular, you'll learn how to create your own procedures and your own modules. You have already created a simple code module in the previous section, but you will soon want to add to it. This will allow you to extend your code library so you can spend more time designing rather than coding.

If you open the controls sample application in the \Samples\Pguide\Controls directory, then a glance at the Project window shows a total of seven forms (see Figure 4.1). Each form file contains the design of the form and the controls on the form.

FIGURE 4.1: SEVEN FORMS IN THE PROJECT WINDOW

Each form file also includes all the event procedures coded for the form, which is called *code behind forms* (CBF). This code behind the form is called a *form module*. A module is a self-contained collection of procedures. These procedures can be called by events on the form or from other procedures in the same module.

Each of the event procedures is preceded by the keyword Private. This indicates that the procedure can't be called from outside its own form module: Its scope is module-level, and it's not visible outside the form, meaning it's private or local. All form event procedures are Private by default. But you can add your own procedures to a form and make them application-level (public or global) by using the Public prefix. Such procedures can be called from any other form (or standard module) in the project. If you leave out the Private or the Public prefix, the procedure is application-level by default.

You can add your own procedures by clicking Tools ➤ Add Procedure and selecting options in the Add Procedure dialog box (see Figure 4.2). This option is only available when the Code window is open.

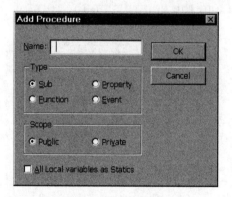

FIGURE 4.2: THE ADD PROCEDURE DIALOG BOX

A Quicker Way to Add Procedures

Instead of selecting Tools ➤ Add Procedure, a quick way to add a procedure is to follow these steps:

1. *Type Public Sub ProcedureName on a blank line anywhere in the Code window.*

   You could also type Private Sub ProcedureName to make a private procedure, or you could type just Sub ProcedureName, which will automatically default to a public procedure.

2. *Press Enter, and Visual Basic will create a procedure stub or template for you.*

   For this example, Visual Basic's Code window will look like the one shown here.

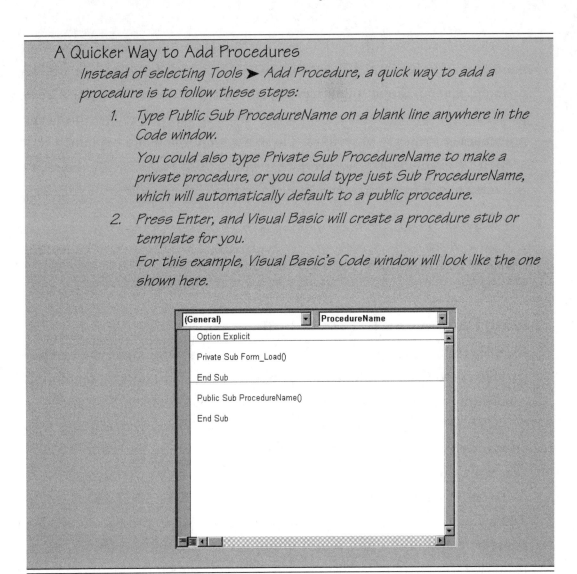

You can run a form's public procedure (or a private procedure) by typing the name of the procedure in another procedure behind the form. For example, if you have a procedure named *test* you would enter the following line to run it:

```
test
```

Strictly speaking, this is only true for Sub procedures. There is another main type of procedure, a Function procedure, which is called in a slightly different manner. Function procedures are discussed shortly in the "Creating and Using Functions" section. You will also see references to a third type of procedure, a Property procedure. These are mentioned and explained in the section "Working with Class Modules" later in this skill.

Tip

To call a public procedure in a form module (from outside the form) you must prefix the call with the name of the form. For example, to call a public Sub procedure with the name test in frmForm1, you type: frmForm1.test

Passing Parameters to Procedures

If you want to tailor your procedures to accept varying input you can pass parameters to them. With parameter passing, you can allow a function or procedure to perform the same tasks on different variables. This allows you to write only one procedure that can be used over and over, which is the first step to writing re-usable code. The parameters that are passed to the procedure are sometimes called arguments.

To better understand how parameter passing works, think about a blender. The blender's sole purpose is to chop things up. What you put in the blender could be considered a parameter. If you put a carrot in the blender, the result will be carrot juice. If you put in celery, you get celery juice. So if you wrote a function called Blender, you could put something in it, the parameter, and it would work on it and return a type of juice, called the result.

The procedures, whether they are subs or functions, should be narrowed down to perform one discrete task. This task may consist of many sub-tasks, but they should all work neatly together to perform one desired result. For example, add the following code for a Sub procedure to change the Caption property of your form:

```
Private Sub AlterCaption(X As String)
  frmMyForm.Caption = X
End Sub
```

Your Code window will look similar to the one shown here.

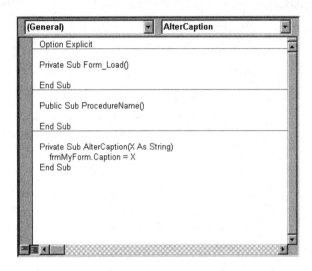

When you're finished, your application will look like Figure 4.3.

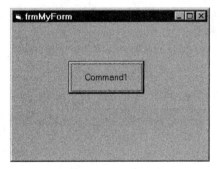

FIGURE 4.3: RUNNING THE SAMPLE APPLICATION

This procedure has one argument, X. The name you give to the argument isn't important. However, in this case, the procedure will only work if you pass a string (text) value. You could create a string variable called

MyTitleText and set it to **New Caption**. Then you could pass MyTitleText as the parameter to the procedure. Thus, you pass a string variable or the raw text enclosed in quotation marks, called a literal, to the procedure. To call this Sub procedure (say, in a command button's Click event procedure), try entering something like the following code (show in the Code window below):

```
AlterCaption "New Caption"
```

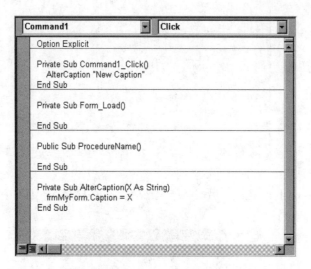

The text after the procedure name is a string literal—note the use of quotes around a string literal. This text is the parameter that meets the argument X. To pass a string variable, try the following code (shown in the Code window below).

```
Dim Y As String
Y = "New Caption"
AlterCaption Y
```

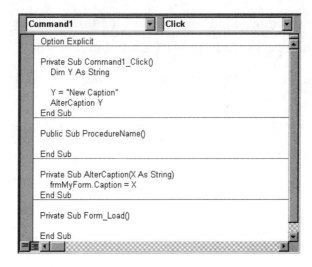

Note the lack of quotes this time. Also note the lack of parentheses around the parameter—though the argument it's passed to is in parentheses. Your form should look like the shown here in Figure 4.4.

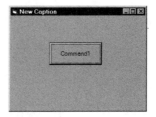

FIGURE 4.4: CHANGING THE CAPTION PROPERTY THROUGH CODE

Creating and Using Functions

You've now met two types of Sub procedures. The first type (Private by default) is the *event* Sub procedure behind forms and controls. These event procedures are already defined for you. The second type, the ones you add yourself, are called *general* Sub procedures. There are also Function procedures. These you must create yourself, and they can be Private or Public. Function procedures return a value to the procedures that call them.

The best way to understand Function procedures is to try one out. Here's one that calculates the cube root of a number.

1. Open a form's Code window by double-clicking it in the Form Designer.

2. Create the template by typing the following on a blank line in a form's Code window and pressing Enter:

```
Public Function CubeRoot
```

This creates the following code:

```
Public Function CubeRoot()
End Function
```

3. Now alter the template as follows (see Figure 4.5):

```
Public Function CubeRoot(x As Double) As Double
  If x = 0 Then
    CubeRoot = 0
    Exit Function
  End If
  CubeRoot = 10 ^ ((Log(Abs(x)) / Log(10)) / 3)
  If x < 0 Then
    CubeRoot = - CubeRoot
  End If
End Function
```

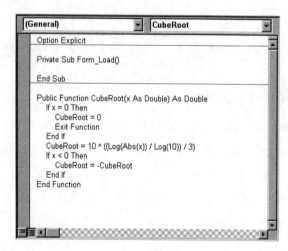

FIGURE 4.5: THE CODE WINDOW TO CALCULATE A CUBE ROOT

The maths involved here isn't important. But a few other things are:

- The Function ends with an End Function rather than an End Sub.
- You can jump out of a Function with Exit Function.
- The Function must return a value—the line CubeRoot = 0 is one of three possible lines that do that.
- You can specify the type of value returned—here it's a Double (a numeric variable that can handle very large and small values as well as decimals) by adding the statement As followed by the data type of the returned value.

4. To call this function, you must assign its return value to another variable. Try the following code in a Click event for a form (see Figure 4.6):

```
Dim Y As Double
 Y = CubeRoot(27)
Print Y
```

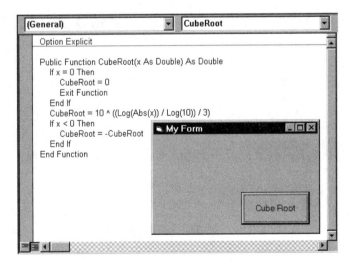

FIGURE 4.6: THE CODE WINDOW AND DESIGN FORM

5. Now run the application and click the command button. You should see a form similar to the one shown in Figure 4.7.

This code prints the return value straight onto the form (see Figure 4.7).

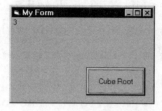

FIGURE 4.7: THE FUNCTION RETURNS THE CUBED ROOT 3.

Normally, you may want to assign the return value to a control on the form, such as a text box control (see Figure 4.8) as in:

```
txtText1.Text = Y
```

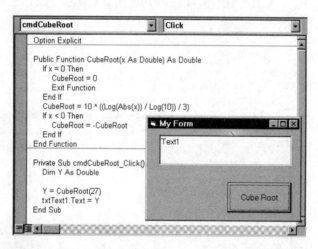

FIGURE 4.8: THE MODIFIED CODE WINDOW AND DESIGN FORM

The result is shown is Figure 4.9.

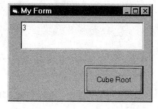

FIGURE 4.9: THE MODIFIED APPLICATION

Alternatively, you can have just the line (see Figure 4.10):

```
txtText1.Text = CubeRoot(27)
```

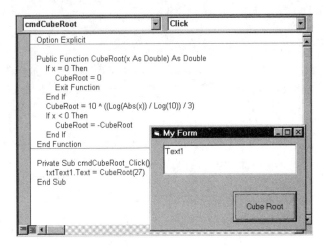

FIGURE 4.10: THE ADJUSTED CLICK EVENT

Here the return value is being assigned directly to a control.

Note

When you call a Function procedure, you must enclose the parameter(s) in parentheses. This contrasts with calling a Sub procedure.

Testing from the Immediate Window

You can test both Sub and Function procedures from the Immediate window.

First, run your project. Then click Run ➤ Break. This usually brings the Immediate window to the front (shown below).

If you lose it, click View > Immediate Window. You're now in Break or Debug mode. To run a Sub procedure from the Debug window, type the name of the procedure and press Enter. If the procedure accepts parameters, then add those too. For example:

```
AlterCaption "New Caption"
```

To run a Function procedure, you need to see its return value. You can do this by printing the return value to the Immediate window. For example:

```
Print CubeRoot(27)
```

or just:

```
? CubeRoot(27)
```

Adding Code Modules

In addition to creating your own procedures, you can also create your own modules. You can then add your procedures to these modules. To make a new form (.FRM) module, simply click Insert ➤ Form. To create a new standard (.BAS) or general module, click Insert ➤ Module (see Figure 4.11).

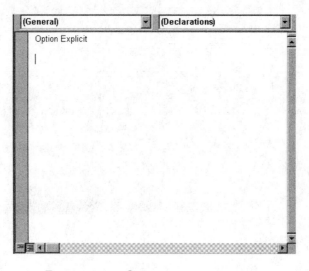

FIGURE 4.11: CREATING A NEW MODULE

Such standard modules typically contain libraries of routines you use from many places in a project. Unlike form modules, they don't have any predefined event procedures. Rather, they hold Sub and Function procedures that you create yourself. These can be public or private. If they're public, they can be called from anywhere. If they're private, they can only be called from other procedures within the same module.

Tip

To call a public Sub procedure in a standard module, just type its name. This contrasts with a public Sub procedure in a form module. There you must preface the procedure with the Name property of the form, if you're calling it from outside the form.

If you examine some of the sample applications that ship with Visual Basic you will see references to other types of modules called *classes*. These too can appear in a Project window.

Working with Class Modules

Another type of code module that deserves some discussion is the *class module*, or simply the *class*. Classes are the fundamental building blocks to a type of programming called *object-oriented programming* (OOP). OOP is a programming style that allows you to think of your program in terms of objects. You use these same objects throughout the entire project development process. You can learn more about OOP in Skill 13.

A class allows you to compartmentalise the functionality of a program into a single object. This helps make the program easier to design and develop. When you optimise your class objects, you minimize the risk of one piece of code interfering with another piece of code. These objects basically mimic real-world situations.

In Visual Basic, you can insert classes into your projects, or you can compile them to make ActiveX controls, such as dynamic link libraries (DLLs) and custom controls, formerly referred to as OCXs. When you make an ActiveX control, you can link it to your program or you can link or embed it into World Wide Wed documents. The sample application in Skill 9 shows you how to create a custom dialogs class and compile it to an ActiveX DLL. Skill 14 presents you with more of the specific details of ActiveX. For now, we will discuss the class module and how it pertains to your project.

A class contains properties and methods that all work together to perform a set of related operations. The class is a self sufficient piece of code. This means you can move the class from one project to another and it will work properly without any modification whatsoever. Objects are created from the class framework. For example, a command button object is actually created from a class object. The command button works by itself in any application you add it to, without modification. The classes you design should do the same thing.

Much like a standard code module, a class is just a formless file, but it comes with two procedures, Class_Initialize() and Class_Terminate():

- You use the Class_Initialize() procedure to set any properties to their defaults or configure anything the class requires before it is executed. For example, you can create a class that displays a dialog box before it is run for the first time, or you can have it check the registry to check a setting before it runs.

- You can place code in the Class_Terminate() procedure that cleans up anything that needs it. Maybe your class creates temporary files on the hard disk. You would want to clean these up when you are done working on them, so the Class_Terminate() procedure could be a place to do it.

Methods

Adding a method to a class is just like adding a procedure to a code module. You can prefix the method name with Private or Public, depending on the scope of the method. Public methods serve as the interface to the programmer. Your program can access these without any problems. Private methods are used by the class to perform operations that cannot be called from outside the class.

A good example of a method that should be private is one that retrieves personnel information from a personnel database. You would not want to allow anyone access to this data, so it should be retrieved in a private method. Then you could write a public method that calls the private method. This shields you from the information and the data retrieval process altogether. Here is another example that shows how an ATM class could work:

```
Private Function GetBalance(AccountNo as String) as Double
    GetBalance = 10000
    'Don't we all wish we could have that much!
End Function
Public Function DisplayAccountInfo(AccountNo as String, PIN as _
String) as Double
    If AccountNo = "123456" And PIN = "5551289" Then
        DisplayAccountInfo = GetBalance(AccountNo)
    End If
End Sub
```

The GetBalance function is declared private because we don't want just anybody looking at people's account balances. Imagine how many new relatives you would get if someone knew you had 10 million dollars in your account! To prevent this, we require the user to go through the DisplayAccountInfo procedure. Their account number and personal identification number (PIN) are verified before the account balance is retrieved.

Properties

Methods are used to manipulate the data within the class. Properties are used to retrieve and return data from these methods. Like methods, properties can be public and private as well. Public properties can be accessed by the program, whereas private properties are used by the class only.

Class properties are accessed through the Property Get and Property Let statements. Property Get serves as the public interface to retrieve the values of variables inside the class that the program does not have access to. Property Let does just the opposite. It allows you to set the values of variables within the class. You can also create properties by declaring them as public within the class. Then they can be shared between your code and the class. The Property Get and Property Let statements create a sort of security model for the class properties.

Going back to our ATM example, two good properties would be AccountNo and PIN. You could rework the class so you set the properties and then call the methods without passing any parameters. For example:

```
Public AccountNo as String
Public PIN as String
Private Function GetBalance() as Double
    GetBalance = 10000
    'Don't we all wish we could have that much!
End Function
Public Function DisplayAccountInfo() as Double
    If AccountNo = "123456" And PIN = "5551289" Then
        DisplayAccountInfo = GetBalance()
    End If
End Sub
```

Here is the same code using the Property Let and Property Get statements:

```
Private AcctNo As String
Private PINNo As String
Public Property Let AccountNo(x As String)
    AcctNo = x
End Property
```

```
Public Property Let PIN(x As String)
    PINNo = x
End Property
Private Function GetBalance() As Double
    GetBalance = 10000
    'Don't we all wish we could have that much!
End Function
Public Function DisplayAccountInfo() As Double
    If AcctNo = "123456" And PINNo = "5551289" Then
        DisplayAccountInfo = GetBalance()
    End If
End Function
```

Tip

Use the Private keyword to encapsulate properties and methods within your classes. This helps protect the internals of your class from tampering by the calling program. Use the Public keyword to expose only the properties and methods that absolutely need to be accessed by the calling program.

These are the basics of class development. Forms, code modules, and controls are the building blocks of a Visual Basic application. Now that you understand the fundamentals, let's dig a little deeper to understand how to use these building blocks to create something useful.

We will discuss class objects and OOP in more detail in Skill 13.

Summary of Skills Acquired

Now you can...

- ☑ use code modules to write code behind your forms and controls
- ☑ create your own Sub procedures and functions
- ☑ pass parameters to sub procedures and functions
- ☑ design a simple class object
- ☑ expose properties and methods using the Public keyword
- ☑ encapsulate properties and methods using the Private keyword

SKILL 5

Creating and Using Menus and Toolbars

Featuring

- ❏ When to use menus and toolbars
- ❏ Creating and using menus
- ❏ Using the Menu Editor
- ❏ Considering a menu's design
- ❏ Creating toolbars
- ❏ Using toolbar custom controls
- ❏ Linking images with an image list

When to Use Menus and Toolbars

By now you may have noticed most applications written for Windows have a somewhat standard interface. Most of them have title bars, sizable borders, and Control menu buttons. In addition, many have menus and toolbars to help you access special functions within the program. Visual Basic itself offers menus and toolbars to help make your job easier (see Figure 5.1).

FIGURE 5.1: THE VISUAL BASIC MENU AND TOOLBAR

Menus expose many of the underlying functions built into an application that are not necessarily obvious at first glance. Menu options can be enabled, disabled, checked, and even popped-up on an object. In addition, you can create a window list, which is a menu that has an option for each MDI child form within the form. As you have noticed in Visual Basic, menus can be docked to another control, be context sensitive, and pop-up directly on an object. You will create a menu later in this skill (see "Creating a Menu with the Menu Editor").

Toolbars, on the other hand, are used to provide quick access to the functions that are also available in menus. For instance, you have probably seen the Cut, Copy, and Paste buttons on menus and toolbars before. It is much easier and quicker for a user to press a button on a toolbar than it is to select Edit ➤ Copy from the menu. Toolbars are even more helpful if they expose functions that are buried under a menu of options or hidden deep in nested submenus. You will create a toolbar later in this skill (see "Creating Toolbars").

When you decide to create a large application, be sure to use menus and toolbars effectively. Make sure they conform to the Windows Graphical User Interface (GUI) standards (described in "Considering a Menu's Design" later in this chapter). Not only will this help reduce the learning curve of your application, it will make your application user-friendly and will be more likely to welcome new users.

Understanding the Menu Object

As stated in the previous section, a menu exposes functions to the user in a clean and, usually, user-friendly manner. To create a menu in Visual Basic, you will use the menu control. The menu control is just like any other control you add to a form except the menu control does not appear in the Toolbox. Instead, you can start the Menu Editor from the Visual Basic menu or toolbar and create your menu from there.

A menu control has several properties and one event, but no methods. To place a menu control on a form, you set that particular form as the active control. With the desired form selected, click Tools ➤ Menu Editor, or use the toolbar alternative to open the Menu Editor (see Figure 5.2).

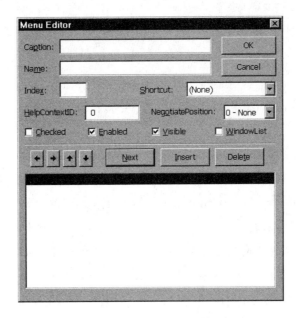

FIGURE 5.2: THE MENU EDITOR

The Menu Editor is where you design your menu. A menu consists of one or more menu titles (for example, File) across the menu. Each menu title on the menu bar contains one or more menu items (for example, Exit). You can even include a separator to group related items together within one menu. You end up with a series of menu controls rather than a single control. Every menu title and menu item (including separators) is a distinct control with its own properties and Click event.

Menu Properties

The design-time properties, which are listed below, are exposed in the Menu Editor rather than in the Properties window.

Appearance	HelpContextID	Parent	**Visible**
Caption	Index	**ShortCut**	WindowList
Checked	**Name**	Tag	
Enabled	NegotiatePosition		

The following explains some of the more important properties to remember:

- The Caption property determines the text you see in the menu—using an ampersand (&) character gives an access key alternative to the mouse.

- The Checked property places (or removes) a check mark next to the menu item. This is handy for toggle items, and you can turn the check mark off and on at run time by setting the Checked property appropriately.

- The Enabled property is sometimes set to False when the menu item is not relevant. For example, you may want to disable a Save item until the user has entered some data. Once again, you can reset the Enabled property at run time.

- A variation of the previous item is to use the Visible property and hide the item when it's not required—though it's less confusing for the user if you disable rather than hide items.

- The Name property is, as always, the first one to define—by convention, menu controls begin with the mnu prefix.

- The Shortcut property determines the keyboard alternative to the menu item. This is not quite the same as an access key (which is determined with the ampersand character).

Note

A shortcut key immediately generates the Click event for the menu control. With access keys, there are two actions to carry out first—one, you press the Alt+key combination to open the menu, and then you press the key corresponding to the underlined letter in the menu caption. For example, you might press Alt+H to open a Help menu and then press C to see the contents page of the help file. With a shortcut key, all you have to do is press, say, F1 to see the same page.

You can open the menus created in the Menu Editor from the form when it is in design view. To see the code for the Click event procedure, you click the menu item in design view. Alternatively, choose the menu control's name from the Object drop-down list in the Code window. You can easily see the properties for a menu item by reopening the Menu Editor and selecting the menu item from the list at the bottom of the editor. You can also view menu control properties by selecting their names from the drop-down list at the top of the Properties window.

Tip

The properties are not displayed when you click the menu control in design view—this contrasts with all other controls. Usually, you set, review, and alter properties in the Menu Editor—but you may prefer to use the Properties window to make further changes.

The Click Event

This is the only event for a menu control; this event is also generated when either access or shortcut keys are used. You place the code for the actions relevant to the menu item being selected in the Click event procedure.

Each menu title has a Click event, too. Usually, this event is ignored, as you don't want anything to happen if the user has merely opened the menu by clicking the menu title. However, advanced Visual Basic developers often use the Index property in conjunction with this event to dynamically add or remove items from the menu that is about to open. Dynamic menus are actually menu control arrays. Each menu item is similar, and resides in the same block of memory. Then rather than referring to the menu item by name, you refer to it by its index in the array. For more information on arrays, please refer to Skill 6.

Menu Methods

There are no methods for menu controls, at least not for the type of menus being discussed here.

Creating a Menu with the Menu Editor

The Menu Editor is where you will do most of the work designing menus for your applications. To define your first menu, open the Menu Editor by clicking Tools ➤ Menu Editor (as shown previously in Figure 5.2). Notice the following items in the Menu Editor:

- As you might expect, you enter the Caption property and the Name property in the first two text boxes in the Menu Editor.
- You can also choose a shortcut key for the current menu control.
- Typically, leave the Checked, Enabled, and Visible property check boxes at their default settings.
- The left and right arrow buttons are for indenting and outdenting menu controls. A menu title must be flush with the left margin of the menu list box at the bottom. A menu item is usually indented once. You would indent a second time to create a submenu item (cascading menu) from the previous menu item.
- The up and down arrow buttons are for changing the order in which menu titles and menu items appear.

To create a menu title or menu item, the minimum requirements are the Caption and Name properties. You create a title first, and then you add the items that are to appear under that title's menu. Each menu item must be indented once from the left. Then you add the next title and its items, and so on. To add each entry, click the Next button. If you leave out an entry, then either add it at the bottom and use the up arrow button, or select the one after the insertion point and click the Insert button. To remove entries, click the Delete button. If you want to have a separator bar in a menu, set its Caption property to a hyphen character (-). But you *must* give a separator a Name property. A separator must be at the same level of indentation as the items it's separating.

The accepted prefix for menu titles and menu items is mnu. For instance, a File menu title might have the name mnuFile. Any item under that title usually incorporates the title's name. For example, an Exit menu item in the File menu would have a Name property like mnuFileExit. A single separator in the File menu may have a name like mnuFileSep1. A Name property such as mnuExit is probably not sufficient for an Exit item. When you're reading code or debugging, it's not immediately apparent which menu this item belongs to.

Let's create a simple menu so you can get some practice working with a menu object:

1. Start a new project using File ➤ New Project.
2. Select Standard EXE as the project type.
3. Click on Form1 to make it active.
4. Open the Menu Editor by selecting Tools ➤ Menu Editor or selecting Ctrl+E.
5. Create the File menu by typing **&File** in the Caption field, and **mnuFile** in the Name field.
6. Click the Next button to start the next menu item.
7. You want to make this a menu item of the File menu, so click the right arrow button to indent this menu item.

8. Set the Caption property of the next item to **&Exit**. Set its Name property to **mnuFileExit**.

9. Now that you have created your first menu, finish making the Edit and Help menus by setting the properties below and clicking the Next button after you set each Name property:

Edit Menu	
Caption:	**&Edit**
Name:	**mnuEdit**
Edit Menu Items	
Caption:	**Cu&t**
Name:	**mnuEditCut**
Caption:	**&Copy**
Name:	**mnuEditCopy**
Caption:	**&Paste**
Name:	**mnuEditPaste**
Help Menu	
Caption:	**&Help**
Name:	**mnuHelp**
Help Menu Items	
Caption:	**&About...**
Name:	**mnuHelpAbout**

When you are done creating these menu objects, the Menu Editor should look like Figure 5.3. You can make any changes you may need to by clicking on the appropriate menu item and changing its properties. When the menu is designed like Figure 5.3, click the OK button.

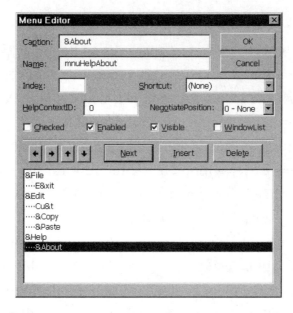

FIGURE 5.3: CREATING A MENU WITH THE MENU EDITOR

Now you can see what your menu will look and behave like. If you click on the Edit menu, it will expose the Edit menu items (see Figure 5.4). If you click on Paste, it will take you directly to the mnuEditPaste_Click() procedure in the Code window. You place your code to paste in the Code window.

FIGURE 5.4: YOUR MENU IN ACTION

Click on File ➤ Exit on your newly designed menu so you can place code in the mnuFileExit_Click() procedure. Place the End statement in the procedure and run your application. All of the menus should expand and collapse properly. Clicking the Exit menu item should end your application.

Considering a Menu's Design

Windows is an operating system that uses a Graphical User Interface, or GUI. The reason that it is called this is because you work more with graphics, forms, and icons, for example, than typing text. The GUI is what makes the environment and its programs user-friendly. Rather than trying to remember cryptic commands and their parameters, called *switches*, you can remember things easier with pictures. In order for the GUI to be effective, it must be standardized. All similar controls and forms should look alike and operate in pretty much the same fashion.

Before looking at toolbars, let's examine an often overlooked aspect of Windows application design: standards. When you design your menus, you should strive to make them as standard as possible. While it is beyond the scope of this book to go into too much detail regarding GUI standards, it makes sense to get you started on the right track.

When you lay out your menus, try to make them as close to standard Windows applications as possible. While many applications have different menus and no two applications are exactly alike, you can duplicate the layouts of other menus to make yours standardized.

You may notice how the File menu is always the left-most menu, and the Help menu is always right-most. Make your applications the same way. The Edit menu is almost always to the right of the File menu, and the Window menu is to the left of the Help menu. If you incorporate Edit and Window menus, be sure to keep them in this order. Proficient Windows users get accustomed to moving the mouse in particular fashions to access menus. Don't throw them off by rearranging your menus.

As menu layout is standardized, your shortcut keys should be standardized as well. Notice the letter "t" is underlined in the Cut menu option. Your first instinct might be to place the ampersand in front of the "C," but when a user decides to copy something from the clipboard, they may be in for a shock when half of their document disappears! Many menu shortcuts are standardized. If you are in question as to what shortcuts to use, you can launch any of your other Windows applications and examine how they are designed.

Creating Toolbars

Toolbars are an extremely useful enhancement to menus. They provide mouse-driven shortcuts to menu options.

When designing toolbars, it is important to consider design standardization as well. You may want to use standard-sized buttons or standardized icons so your users know exactly what a button does without having to depend on a manual or on-line help to navigate your application. You can duplicate toolbar designs from other applications in much the same way as you can with menus.

Let's create a toolbar to enhance the menu you just created in the section "Creating a Menu with the Menu Editor." Before you can work on the toolbar, you need to make sure it is added to your Toolbox. If you need to add it, right-click on the Toolbox and click on the Components menu item. When the Components dialog box appears, check the boxes next to Microsoft Windows Common Controls 5.0 and Microsoft Windows Common Controls 5.0-2.

Now, to create a toolbar, follow these steps:

1. Add a toolbar control to your form. Set its Name property to **tbrToolbar** and set its Align property to **1 - vbAlignTop**.
2. From the Properties window, select Custom.
3. When the Property Pages dialog box appears, select the Buttons tab.
4. Notice how most toolbars are indented a bit from the left of the screen. To duplicate this, add a separator before you add your first button. Click Insert Button to place the first button on the toolbar.

5. Click on the Style drop-down box and select 3 - tbrSeparator (see Figure 5.5).

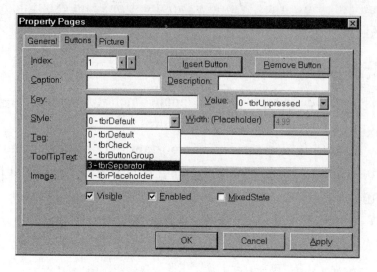

FIGURE 5.5: SETTING THE STYLE PROPERTY

Adding Buttons to Toolbars

Now you can add some buttons to your toolbar:

1. Click Insert Button to add a new button. Set Key to **New** and Style to **0 - tbrDefault**.

2. Click Insert Button again to add another button. Set the Key property to **Open** and set the Style property to **0 - tbrDefault**.

3. Click Insert Button to add the last button. Set the Key property to **Save** and set the Style property to **0 - tbrDefault**.

4. Click the OK button to see what the toolbar looks like.

If you had no problems, your toolbar should now look like Figure 5.6. Again, notice the separator on the left of the toolbar that gives it the indent.

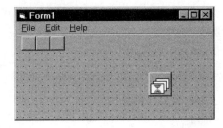

FIGURE 5.6: A FORM WITH YOUR TOOLBAR

Adding Images to Toolbars

Now you need to add some images to the toolbar. Unfortunately, you cannot do it directly by setting a Picture property. Instead, you need to link the toolbar with an image list. Here's how to do it:

1. Add an image list to your form and set its Name property to **imlToolbar**. This control was added to your Toolbox when you added the Microsoft Common Controls 5.0.2.
2. Open up the Property Pages by selecting Custom from the Properties window.
3. When the Property Pages dialog appears, click on the Images tab so you can add some images.
4. The first image you want to add is the standard blank page which is used to represent a New file. Click Insert Picture.
5. Select New.bmp from the Graphics\Bitmaps\Tlbr_w95 directory.
6. After the blank page appears, click it so the next image will be placed after it in the list.
7. Click Insert Picture. Select Open.bmp. When it is added, click the yellow folder.
8. Click Insert Picture one last time and select Save.bmp. Your Image List should look like Figure 5.7. Click the OK button to close the Property Pages dialog box.

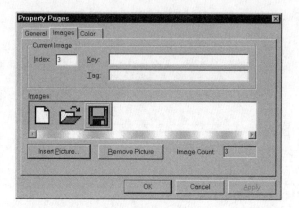

FIGURE 5.7: INSERTING BITMAPS IN AN IMAGE LIST

9. Select tbrToolbar and open its property pages again by selecting the Custom property from the Properties window.

10. On the General tab, set the ImageList property to imlToolbar, as in Figure 5.8.

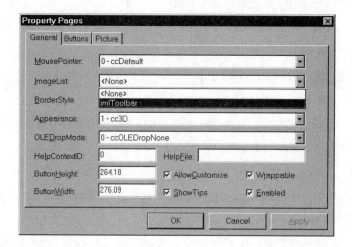

FIGURE 5.8: LINKING THE TOOLBAR TO THE IMAGE LIST

11. Click the Buttons tab.

12. Set the Index property to **2**, and set the Image property to **1**. This will place the image in index position 1, the blank document, on the button in position 2. Remember that button 1 is actually a separator.

13. Set Index to **3** and Image to **2**. This places the folder icon on the Open button on the toolbar.

14. Set Index to **4** and Image to **3**. This puts the disk icon on the Save button on the toolbar.

15. When you are done, click the OK button. Your toolbar will look like Figure 5.9.

FIGURE 5.9: THE TOOLBAR WITH ICONS

That's all there is to designing the layout of a toolbar and adding graphics to it, but the toolbar is not finished yet. You need to add code to the toolbar so it will know what button the user is pressing. Double-click on the toolbar to open the tbrToolbar_ButtonClick() event. Notice that the Button parameter is passed to this event. This is actually the index value of the button that was clicked. You will use this index to help identify the appropriate button. Add the following code to the event:

```
Private Sub tbrToolbar_ButtonClick(ByVal Button As ComctlLib.Button)
  Select Case Button.Key
    Case Is = "New"
      MsgBox "You clicked the New button."
    Case Is = "Open"
      MsgBox "You clicked the Open button."
    Case Is = "Save"
      MsgBox "You clicked the Save button."
  End Select
End Sub
```

Notice that you used a Select Case statement to determine which button was pressed. This is like a supercharged If...Then statement. It allows us greater flexibility when dealing with multiple conditions. As you can see from the code above, you used three Case Is statements rather than three separate If...Then code blocks. When using a toolbar, be sure to set the Key property appropriately. You will need to reference this value to determine which button was clicked.

And that's all there is to creating menus and toolbars! Remember, menus and toolbars offer simple and convenient ways to provide added functionality to your applications. By making your menus look and feel like other Windows-based applications, you give your applications an advantage over poorly designed ones: your app will be more useable than nonstandard applications, and users will thank you for it.

Summary of Skills Acquired

Now you can...

- ☑ determine when to use menus and toolbars
- ☑ create a menu using the Menu Editor
- ☑ design your menus to resemble those in other Windows apps
- ☑ create a toolbar using the toolbar control
- ☑ add images to the toolbar using an image list
- ☑ write code to make your toolbar function

SKILL 6

Using Variables, Arrays, and Constants

Featuring

- ❑ Understanding variable types
- ❑ Using variables
- ❑ Using arrays
- ❑ Using constants

Introducing Variables

The most important aspect of programming you must learn in any language is how to use variables, arrays, and constants. These elements are crucial to making your application run. So what is a variable? A *variable* is an area in memory that stores values. As its name indicates, a variable can change its value; in other words, it can vary.

What Is Memory?

In order to better understand how variables work, you must understand a little bit about memory first. To get a visual picture of memory, consider a piece of graph paper. Each square is .0625 square inches in size, or ¼ inch wide by ¼ inch high. If the piece of graph paper was a computer's memory, then a square would equal one byte of memory. One kilobyte of memory, which is equal to 1,024 bytes, would cover a piece of graph paper eight inches by eight inches. That may not seem like much, but imagine how large a megabyte would be. One megabyte equals 1,024 kilobytes, so one megabyte would cover a sheet of graph paper 21.33 feet by 21.33 feet in size, or 5,461.33 square feet. Now that's one large piece of graph paper! Assuming your computer has 16 megabytes of memory, the sheet of graph paper would be 87,381.33 square feet, or approximately 85.33 feet wide and 85.33 feet high. That's almost one third the area of an American football field!

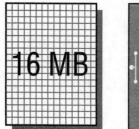 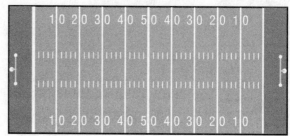

Imagine how big it would be if you actually broke down each byte into bits. Because a byte is made up of eight bits, the graph paper would almost be the size of three football fields. Fortunately, you don't need to use bits at this beginning level. Now that you have a general idea of what memory looks like, you can start to understand how the different variable types work.

Variable Types

When you start presenting, retrieving, and storing data in your applications, you will invariably start using variables, arrays, and constants. These are fundamental coding tools designed to hold temporary values in memory. Not only will you use these tools in Visual Basic, you will probably use them in other languages as well. Let's look at variables in a little more detail.

A variable is a name that references an area of memory that holds a temporary value that can change while an application is running. Variables are used in an unimaginable variety of tasks, most of which you will learn through experience. There are several types of variables, called *data types*, in Visual Basic. Each data type has its own characteristics, which you can see in Table 6.1.

Data Type	Purpose
Integer	A numeric variable, holds values in the range -32,768 to 32,767
Long	A numeric variable—holds a wider range of integers than Integer
Single	A numeric variable—holds numbers with decimal places
Double	A numeric variable with a wider range than Single
Currency	For holding monetary values
String	For holding text or string values
Byte	A numeric variable—range 0 to 255, even less than Integer
Boolean	For holding True or False values
Date	For holding date values
Object	For holding references to objects in Visual Basic and other applications
Variant	A general-purpose variable that can hold most other types of variable values

TABLE 6.1: DATA TYPES FOR VARIABLES AND CONSTANTS

As you can see from Table 6.1, there are lots of different variable types. For the scope of this book, you will only need to learn about some of the most common variable types: bytes, strings, integers, booleans, and variants.

The object type can be further subdivided into types such as form, control, printer, and so on. The variant type is quite clever in that it can hold all the other types but can cause headaches when debugging larger applications.

Using Byte-Sized Variables

No pun intended, but the most basic type of variable is a byte. A byte can only hold one value at a time. Without getting too involved in the complexities of binary maths, take my word that a byte's value must always be between 0 and 255. If you look at Figure 6.1, you can see how a byte fits into the larger memory scheme.

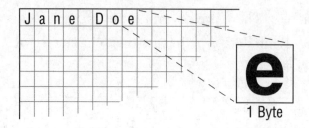

FIGURE 6.1: THE BYTE DATA TYPE

A byte is useful for dealing with smaller-sized numbers. Bytes are particularly useful when working with the ASCII character set and binary data. Try the following example to learn how the byte works:

1. Start a new project by selecting File ➤ New Project.
2. From the Project Wizard, select Standard EXE.
3. After Visual Basic creates the project, remove Form1 from the project by right-clicking on Form1 in the Project Explorer. Select **Remove Form1** from the pop-up menu.
4. If Visual Basic asks you to save Form1, click the No button.
5. Right-click in the Project Explorer and select Add ➤ Module from the pop-up menu.
6. Select Module from the Add Module dialog box. This will add a blank code module to your project.
7. If it is not already open, double-click on Module1 in the Project Explorer to open its Code window.
8. Add the following code to the module:

```
Option Explicit

Private Sub Main()
 Dim b As Byte
 Dim text As String

 Debug.Print "ASCII Table Example"
 For b = 0 To 63
   text = Str$(b) & "   " & Chr$(b)
```

```
        text = text & Chr$(9) & Chr$(9)
        text = text & Str$(b + 64) & "   " & Chr$(b + 64)
        text = text & Chr$(9) & Chr$(9)
        text = text & Str$(b + 128) & "  " & Chr$(b + 128)
        text = text & Chr$(9) & Chr$(9)
        text = text & Str$(b + 192) & "  " & Chr$(b + 192)

        Debug.Print text
    Next

    End
End Sub
```

9. Select Run ➤ Start to run the program.

After a brief moment you will see a list of numbers and characters scroll by in the Immediate window. This list is known to programmers as an *ASCII table*. It consists of a list of values between 0 and 255, which fit neatly into a byte data type. Next to each number is the corresponding ASCII character for the number. You can use these numbers to add unprintable and other special characters to your code. For example, the code contains several references to Chr$(9). The value of nine represents the ASCII tab character. Because you cannot print this character directly in your text, you must use Chr$(9). The Debug.Print command allows you to print directly to the Immediate window. You can learn more about this in Skill 8, "Printing."

Tip

If you want to add a character to your text that cannot be accessed from the keyboard, look up the character in an ASCII table and use the function Chr$() with the ASCII value of the character between the parentheses.

Working with a String: The Byte's Big Brother

Now that you understand how a byte works, let's look at a more useful method of using them. A string-type variable, called a *string*, is made of up several consecutive bytes in memory that can contain letters and numbers. When used together, these bytes can form mnemonics, words, and even sentences. Figure 6.2 shows you a simple string in memory. Notice that it is actually 13 bytes long, with each byte consisting of one ASCII character.

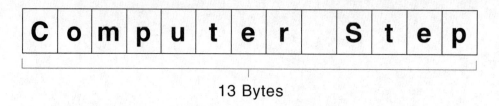

13 Bytes

FIGURE 6.2: THE STRING DATA TYPE

A couple of the properties you have already worked with are actually string variables. The Name and Caption properties require alphanumeric values. To use a string variable, you must do a couple of things:

- Pick a name for the variable
- Dimension the variable as a string data type
- Give the variable a value

Let's create a simple string variable called strName. The str naming convention is used to denote that the variable is a string type. This is useful when you are debugging and are not sure what data type a variable is.

The next step is to dimension the variable as a string. This is done using the Dim keyword:

```
Dim strName as String
```

Once the variable is declared, and area in memory is set aside for it. Visual Basic will allocate enough memory for the proper type of data to fit in it.

Finally, you can set the string to a value, as shown below:

```
strName = "Jane"
```

When you assign values to a string, you must enclose the value in quotes. If you don't, then strName would assume that its value can be found in the variable named Jane.

Once you assign a value to the variable, you can use the value assigned to the variable as a basis for further processing. For example, you can pass the value as a parameter to a procedure or assign the value to a control on a form:

```
Form1.Caption = strName
```

To give you a better idea of how this works, try the following example:

1. Start a new project using File ➤ New Project.
2. Double-click on Form1 in the Form Designer to open the Code window.
3. Select the form's Click event from the Events drop-down list in the Code window.
4. Add the following code to the Click event:

```
Private Sub Form_Click()
  Dim msg As String

  msg = "Ooh. That tickles!"
  Caption = msg
End Sub
```

5. Run the project by selecting Run ➤ Start.
6. Click on the form once and watch the caption change.

This is a very simple example of how you can use string variables in your applications. As you continue to work through this book you will see many more examples that demonstrate how strings work.

It can sometimes get quite difficult to remember to dimension your variables, so you can force explicit declaration by typing **Option Explicit** in the (General) (Declarations) section of your form's Code window. You can put this in the same section for every form and in the same section for any standard .BAS modules you create.

Tip

To force explicit declaration of variables in all modules, click Tools ➤ Options. Select the check box for Require Variable Declaration in the Editor tab of the Options dialog box (see Figure 6.3). Once you've done this, Visual Basic will add an Option Explicit line in the (General) (Declarations) section of every module.

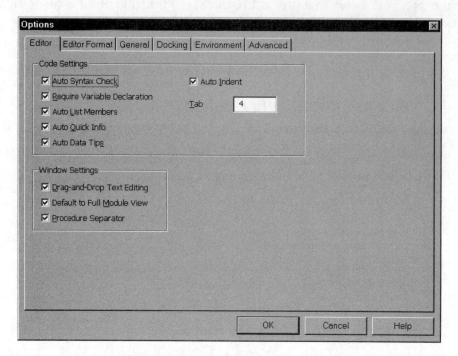

FIGURE 6.3: THE OPTIONS DIALOG BOX

Using Integers

Another fundamental data type is the integer. An integer is a numeric data type much like a byte data type except that it can be *signed* (be positive or negative) and can hold a minimum value of -32768 and a maximum value of 32767. Integers are useful for simple mathematics where you know that values are not going to exceed the integer's range. Integers are also useful for counters.

To see an integer data type in action, try this example:

1. Start a new project.
2. Add a command button to the form.

3. Double-click on the command button to open the Code window.

4. Add the following code to the command button's Click event:

```
Dim A As Integer
Dim B As Integer
A = 2
B = A + 1
Print B
```

5. Run the project and click the button.

Figure 6.4 shows a snippet of code using integer variables.

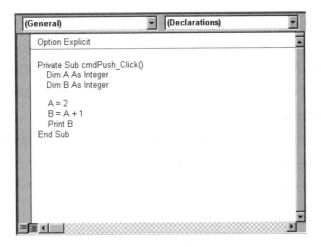

FIGURE 6.4: THE CODE WINDOW FOR THE SAMPLE APPLICATION

The last line of code prints the value of B (which should be 3) on the current form (see Figure 6.5).

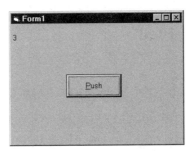

FIGURE 6.5: RUNNING THE SAMPLE APPLICATION

You will see more examples of integers in this skill as well as throughout the rest of this book.

Using Boolean Variables

The Boolean data type can be set to a value of either True or False. This value is often used to determine the "on" or "off" status of something within a program. Booleans are useful as return codes for wrapper functions. You can set the return code to True is the function was successful, or to False if the function failed. Let's use the Boolean data type to create a wrapper function that determines the existence of a file on the hard disk:

1. Start a new project by selecting File ➤ New Project.
2. For the project type select Standard EXE from the Project Wizard.
3. Add a Text Box control to the Form1. Set its Name property to **txtFilename**.
4. Blank the Caption property of the Text Box by double-clicking the Caption property in the Properties Window and deleting Text1.
5. Add a command button to the form. Using the Properties window, set its Name property to **cmdSearch** and its Caption to **&Search**.
6. Double-click Form1 to open the Code window.
7. Type the following code in the Code window to create a wrapper function called IsFile:

```
Private Function IsFile(Filename As String) As Boolean
  If Len(Dir$(Filename)) > 0 Then
    IsFile = True
  Else
    IsFile = False
  End If
End Function
```

8. Select cmdSearch from the object drop-down list (on the top left of the Code window). The event will set itself to Click.
9. Add the following code to the click event of cmdSearch:

```
Private Sub cmdSearch_Click()
    Dim filename As String
    Dim rc As Boolean

    filename = txtFilename.Text
    rc = IsFile(filename)
    If rc = True Then
        MsgBox "File exists!"
    Else
        MsgBox "File not found!"
    End If
End Sub
```

10. Run the project.

To test the wrapper function, type the name of a file in the text box. If the file exists, then the wrapper IsFile will return a boolean value of True. Otherwise it returns a False. Notice that the IsFile function also uses an string variable, filename, passed to it as a parameter. The value of filename is set in the Click event of cmdSearch.

Tip

If you want to test the existence of a file, you can use the Dir$() function nested within a Len() function, for example Len(Dir$(filename)). This will yield an integer value greater than zero if the file exists or a zero otherwise. To make this function a little simpler, you could create a wrapper function much like IsFile in the previous exercise.

Variants — The Bane of a Programmer's Existence

A variant is a general-purpose data type that can take any value—whether it be an integer, byte, string, or boolean—and convert it to another type without requiring you to keep track of the variable. If you use a variable implicitly, without dimensioning it with the Dim statement, Visual Basic will treat the variable as a variant.

The variant data type may sound handy, but heed my warning: don't use a Variant unless you have absolutely no other option. Visual Basic will attempt to convert the data type when necessary. Variants are slower because of the overhead that Visual Basic requires to interpret them, and they waste memory because they allocate enough memory to hold strings, when all you may require is a byte of memory.

Caution

Don't use a variant unless you absolutely have to. You can lose track of a data type and crash your program. Variants also make debugging more difficult.

Determining the Scope of a Variable

The explicit variables discussed so far are all declared with the Dim (short for "dimension") statement. You use Dim to declare variables in a procedure. However, you can only access that variable from the same procedure. In other words, you can't assign it a value or read its value from any other procedure, whether in the same form, or in another form, or in a standard module.

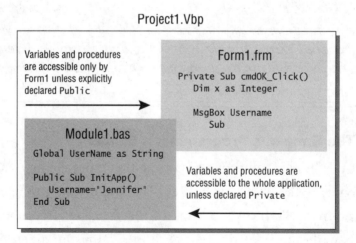

FIGURE 6.6: A VARIABLE'S SCOPE

The variable is a procedure-level (or local) variable. To make a variable visible throughout the whole module, you declare it slightly differently. First, you place the declaration in the (General) (Declarations) section of a form or standard module. Second, you declare it with Private rather than Dim (though Dim is still supported for compatibility with earlier versions of Visual Basic). The variable is now a module-level variable and can be accessed from any procedure in the module—its scope is larger than a procedure-level variable.

You can also have a variable that is application-wide in its scope. These are often called *public* or *global variables*. To declare a public variable, you use Public rather than Dim or Private, and it must be declared in the (General) (Declarations) section of a module. It's common practice to add a standard .BAS module and place all your public variables together in its declarations section.

To better understand how the various scopes work, try this example:

1. Create a new project.
2. Select Standard EXE from the Project Wizard.
3. Add a code module to the project by right-clicking in the Project Explorer and selecting Add ➤ Module.
4. Select Module from the Add Module dialog box. This will also open the Code window for Module1.
5. In the Code window, add the following statements:

```
Option Explicit

Global UserID As String
Global ACL As Integer
6. Add the following procedure to Module1:
Public Sub InitApp()
   UserID = "Joe"
   ACL = 255
End Sub
```

Before you continue, let's look at the two previous steps. By declaring UserID and ACL as Global, they can be accessed and modified by any procedure in any module or form within the application. Because the function InitApp resides in the code module and has the Public keyword in front of it, it becomes a global function that can be called from any procedure within the application. It will be called to initialize the application by setting the UserID variable to Joe and ACL to 255. Now let's create the logon form:

1. Double-click on Form1 in the Project Explorer to make it the active control in the Form Designer.

2. In the Properties window, set the Name property of Form1 to **frmLogon**. Set the Caption property to **User Logon**.

3. Add a Label control to the form. Set its Name to **lblUserID** and its Caption to **User ID:** .

4. Add another Label control below lblUserID and set the Name property to **lblPassword** and the Caption to **Password:**.

5. Add a Text Box control to the right of lblUserID. Set the Name property to **txtUserID**.

6. Add another Text Box control to the right of lblPassword. In the Properties window set the Name property to **txtPassword** and the PasswordChar property to the asterisk character (*).

7. Add a Command Button to the bottom centre of the form. Set its Name property to **cmdLogon** and the Caption to **&Logon**.

Once you have added all of the controls in the previous steps, your form should look like the one shown here.

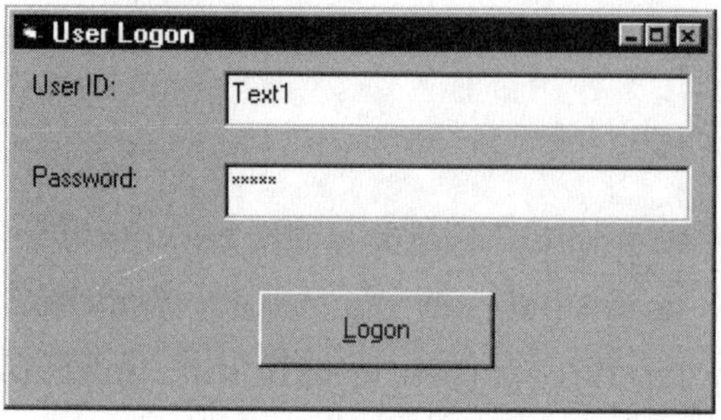

FIGURE 6.7: THE LOGON FORM

8. Next, double-click on Form1 to open the Code window.

9. Position the cursor to the left of Option Explicit in the (General)(Declarations) section of Form1.

10. Press the Enter key twice to insert two lines in front of Option Explicit.

11. Type the following line of code above Option Explicit:

```
Private Password As String
```

12. Open the Load event of the form and add the following code:

```
Private Sub Form_Load()
    InitApp
    txtUserID.Text = UserID
    txtPassword.Text = ""
End Sub
```

13. In the Code window, open the Click event for cmdLogon and add the following code:

```
Private Sub cmdLogon_Click()
 Dim msg As String

 UserID = txtUserID.Text
 Password = txtPassword.Text

 msg = "UserID: " & UserID & Chr$(13)
 msg = msg & "Password: " & Password & Chr$(13)
 msg = msg & "ACL: " & Str$(ACL)
 MsgBox msg
End Sub
```

14. Run the project by clicking on Run ➤ Start.

Notice that the Logon ID field has the name "Joe" in it. This value was retrieved from the global string variable called UserID. It was not declared in the Form_Load() event but was declared global in Module1.

Also worth noting is the password variable. This variable was declared in the (General)(Declarations) portion of the form. This allows any function within the form to access its value, but nothing else. This is important because you don't want code somewhere else in the program attempting to change the user's password. Password is said to be private to the form module. It is a module level variable.

15. Next, type anything in the password field and click the Logon button. The code in the Click event utilizes both module level and global variables to display your user information.

The Static Statement

There is one further way of declaring variables that's quite important and is used instead of Dim procedure-level variables. You use the command Static, as in:

```
Static X As Integer
```

This means the variable retains the last value assigned to it, even when the procedure has finished. Static variables are useful for accumulators, where you want to keep a running tally. If you omit Static (and just use Dim), the variable is reset to zero (for integer and other numeric variables) each time the procedure runs.

Here's another example for you try. It shows a static variable in action. Visit the Coffee Shop and order all you want. Coffees are free, but I warn you there's no restroom! Follow these steps if you are thirsty or just need a good caffeine jolt:

1. Start a new Standard EXE project.
2. Set the Caption property of Form1 to **The Coffee Shop**.
3. Add a label control to the upper centre of the form. In the Properties window set its Name property to **lblQuantity**. Set its Caption property to **Coffees Ordered: 0**.
4. Add a command button below the lblQuantity. Set the Name property to **cmdAdd** and the Caption to **&Give Me Another!**

5. Double-click on cmdAdd in the Form Designer to open the Code window.

6. Add the following code to the click event of cmdAdd:

```
Private Sub cmdAdd_Click()
    Static count As Integer

    count = count + 1
    lblQuantity = "Coffees Ordered:" & Str$(count)
End Sub
```

7. Run the project and click the command button to order as many coffees as you want.

The count variable in the click event procedure is declared as Static. This allows the count value to remain the same between events. The result is a counter-style variable that remembers how many coffees you ordered.

Tip

To make all the Dim variables in a procedure static, you can leave them as Dim and preface the name of the procedure with the Static keyword, as in Private Static Sub cmdAdd_Click()

Using Arrays

Arrays are a form of variable, but you use them to hold more than one value at a time. For example, a spreadsheet is an array of cells, with each column or row belonging to a particular group. You may use arrays to hold red, green, and blue values (RGB) in a bitmap, or possibly as a small database in memory. While they are not used as often, they do have an important role to play in program development. Let's look at an example of declaring an integer array and assigning values to the elements within the array:

```
Static X(2) As Integer
X(0) = 7
X(1) = 99
X(2) = 123
```

To process an array, use a For... Next loop that itself uses an integer variable as a counter (see Figure 6.8):

```
Dim Y As Integer
For Y = 0 To 2
    Print X(Y)
Next Y
```

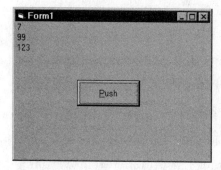

FIGURE 6.8: USING A FOR ... NEXT LOOP

This prints the values of each element (0, 1, and 2 are the references to the three elements) in the integer array X to the current form.

To create a module-level array, declare it with Dim in the declarations section of a module. To have an application-level array, declare it with Public in a declarations section.

To understand better how to work with an array, try this example:

1. Start a new Standard EXE project.
2. Remove Form1 from the project by right-clicking on Form1 in the Project Explorer and selecting Remove Form1 from the pop-up menu.
3. Add a code module to the project by right-clicking in the Project Explorer and select Add ➤ Module.
4. Select **Module** from the Add Module dialog box.
5. In the Code window for Module1, add the following procedure:

```
Sub Main()
 Dim x(7) As Integer
 Dim i As Integer
 Dim txt As String

 'Populate Array with Bit Values
 For i = 0 To 7
   x(i) = 2 ^ i
 Next

 'Print Array
 For i = 0 To 7
   txt = "Array Element" & Str$(i) & " = "
   txt = txt & x(i)
   Debug.Print txt
 Next
End Sub
```

6. Run the program and watch the Immediate window.

The first block of statements dimension the required variables for this program. The array x is dimensioned to hold eight elements (0 to 7). I is the counter for the For...Next loops, and txt is a string that is used to format the output.

The first For...Next loop populates the elements in the array. Using the formula:

```
x(i) = 2 ^ i
```

each element is set to the corresponding decimal value for that bit. Don't worry too much about binary. You will not use it much, if at all, as a beginner. This is just used as an example.

The last For...Next loop formats the txt variable so it can be printed to the Immediate window. The command Debug.Print actually send the value of txt to the window.

Dynamic Arrays

Often, you don't know how large (that is, how many elements) to make an array. If that's the case, then declare an empty array. An array that starts life with no elements is called a *dynamic array*. You declare it in the same way as a normal array, except that you can use Dim, as well as Static, in a procedure:

```
Dim Y() As Integer
```

It can be wasteful to allocate an array larger than you need. To prevent this, you can dimension the dynamic array with no elements (as shown above), and then add elements only when you need to. This technique is especially useful if you are working with a large number of elements.

Later you'll want to define some elements for the array to hold values. To do this, use ReDim, which can only appear in a procedure:

```
ReDim Y(5)
```

You can then assign values to elements within the array. You can also change the number of elements later, as in:

```
ReDim Y(7)
```

If you attempt that, then any values already in the array are lost. To keep existing values, use the Preserve keyword:

```
ReDim Preserve Y(7)
```

Caution

When you work with arrays, be sure you know exactly what is going on. Arrays can consume a lot of memory if you are not careful, so plan accordingly.

Using Constants

Constants are nonvariable variables. They resemble variables in that they are declared and assigned a value. Unlike variables, the values they hold remain fixed while the application is running. These are commonly used to make coding easier. For example, it is easier to understand and debug a variable with the name vbModal, rather than to track down an integer one (1) coded somewhere in your application. You declare and assign values to constants on the same line, using the keyword Const:

```
Const conPi = 3.142
```

To see the value of a constant in action, see the code in Figure 6.9 and this code here:

```
Const conPi = 3.142
Dim Radius As Integer
Dim Area As Double
Radius = 3
Area = conPi * (Radius ^ 2)
Print Area
```

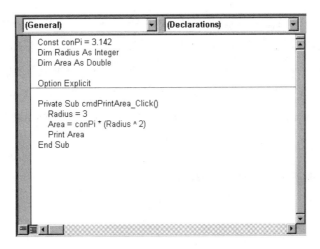

FIGURE 6.9: USING THE VALUE OF A CONSTANT

This code calculates the area of a circle using a constant called conPi (the con prefix is optional, though recommended). It prints the area of the circle to the current form (see Figure 6.10).

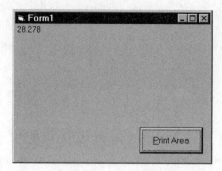

FIGURE 6.10: RESULTS OF THE AREA CALCULATION

You can declare constants both in procedures and in the declarations section of modules. To create an application-wide constant, preface the declaration and assignment with the term Public.

Choosing the right variable for the task at hand is of paramount importance. Not only will it will save you time debugging, it will help you create tighter code and will teach you good programming discipline. Construction workers don't build buildings with only a screwdriver. They use many tools, each with its own purpose. Variables are the same way. Remember to use the right tool for the job.

Summary of Skills Acquired

Now you can...

☑ use the appropriate variables for a given task

☑ use arrays to store information

☑ define and use constants in your programs

Storing and Retrieving Data

Featuring

- ❏ Working with ASCII files
- ❏ Understanding sequential mode
- ❏ Understanding random access mode
- ❏ Using binary access mode
- ❏ Using a data control
- ❏ The anatomy of a database
- ❏ Creating databases with Visual Data Manager

Working with ASCII Files

When you use data in Visual Basic that was stored on a disk, it will come in one of two forms: a database or an ASCII file. You will probably spend most of your time working with database files (discussed later in this chapter), but it is important to learn how ASCII files work as well. ASCII files contain data of all types and can be formatted in a comma-separated values (CSV) list, otherwise known as a *delimited ASCII file* (see Figure 7.1). They can also be listed one item per line, or they can be formatted in any other layout you can think of. Understanding how to work with these files is important, because it allows you to work with almost any type of data. You can use

your knowledge to retrieve information that describes your system from
initialization files.

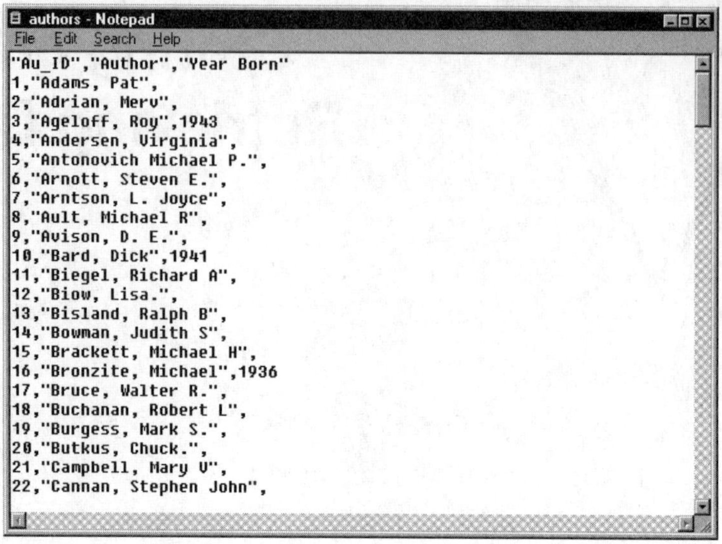

FIGURE 7.1: A DELIMITED ASCII FILE

Keeping the data you enter into your applications is considered normal
practice. For example, you might want to save to disk the entries you make
in text boxes. For example, game programmers often save players' high
scores so they can be loaded the next time a game is run. When you do need
to retrieve this data, Visual Basic gives you many options. You can do it the
hard way (which may be necessary in some cases) by hard-coding the writing
and retrieving of data. For this purpose, you will need to create your own
sequential, random, or binary files (these are described in the following
sections). In addition, the code to explicitly read and write to only that file is
added to the program. This *hard-coding* makes your code specific to the
application, but sometimes that's all you need to complete the job.

The first step in working with one of these types of files is to open it. In
Visual Basic, you use the Open statement to do this. You use this command

to open a specific file and prepare it for reading or writing. The minimum requirements for the Open statement are a filename, a mode to open the file, and a file number handle. The syntax is shown here:

```
Open filename For mode As fileno
```

You supply the name of a file in the filename parameter. The mode parameter specifies how you want to access the file. It can be set to Append, Input, Output, Binary, and Random. Finally, the fileno parameter specifies an integer, called a *handle*, that references the opened file. You use the handle to reference the file in your code. You will see this in the next section.

If the file specified by filename does not exist and you try to open the file in Append, Binary, Output, or Random modes, then Visual Basic will create an empty file for you. In addition, if you do not specify the mode parameter, the file will be opened in random access mode, which is the default. No particular file mode is better than the other. Each has its own specific advantages and they should be selected based on the format of your data file. For example, you would not want to open a delimited ASCII file in binary mode because you would only read the data in one byte at a time. You would then need to write code to put the values back together into discreet strings. Input mode is better suited for these type of files.

When you are done working with the file, you need to close it with the Close statement. You just follow the Close statement with the handle of the file:

```
Close fileno
```

You will see more of this in the following sections. In the meantime, let's take a more detailed look at the different file access modes.

Understanding Sequential Mode

When you want to store or retrieve data in Visual Basic, you may choose to create a sequential file. A sequential file is a series of lines of text in ASCII format, much like that shown in Figure 7.2.

FIGURE 7.2: A SAMPLE SEQUENTIAL FILE

To write data to a sequential file, you open it for Output or Append. If the file doesn't exist, then Visual Basic creates it automatically. If the file *does* exist, then Output overwrites existing data, while Append adds it to the end of the file. In most cases you will append data, but there are times when you may create a file to serve as a temporary workspace. In this case it would be acceptable to overwrite the contents of the file before each use. To read the data from a sequential file, you open it for Input. Whether you open for Input, Output, or Append, you must use a file handle (see below) with the file. And you should always close the file when you're finished by using a Close statement with the appropriate file number. One way of writing to the file is to use the Print # statement (or Write #). One way of reading from a file is with the Line Input # statement (or Input # statement or the Input function).

Below is the code that you could write to create a file in the C:\Data directory with two names in it:

```
Dim FileNo As Integer
FileNo = FreeFile
Open "C:\data\test.txt" For Append As FileNo
  Print #FileNo, "John"
  Print #FileNo, "Doe"
Close FileNo
```

The FreeFile function returns the next available file handle. This file handle or file number is used in all the Open, Print #, and Close statements. After trying the above code, you can see the results in WordPad or Notepad, as shown in Figure 7.3. To overwrite rather than append data—in other words, to delete data in your file and substitute it with new data, rather than just adding to the file—you substitute the keyword Output for Append.

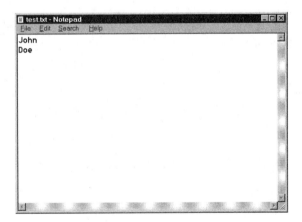

FIGURE 7.3: VIEWING THE RESULTS

One way of reading stored data is to read each line into an array. Just to refresh your memory, an array is a list of similar values that can be addressed using an index number with the variable name. You can learn more about these in Skill 6. The following example uses an array to store the values retrieved from the file c:\data\test.txt:

```
Dim FileNo As Integer
FileNo = FreeFile
Dim GetValues() As String
Dim Counter As Integer
Counter = 0
Open "c:\data\test.txt" For Input As FileNo
    Do Until EOF(FileNo)
        Counter = Counter + 1
        ReDim Preserve GetValues(Counter)
        Line Input #FileNo, GetValues(Counter)
    Loop
Close FileNo
```

The EOF function tests for the end of the file by detecting the End of File character. This is an ASCII character that is not displayed on screen and is added when you create or append to a file. Once you have retrieved the data, you can loop through the GetValues array and assign the data to controls on a form, or print the data:

```
Dim J As Integer
For J = 0 To UBound(GetValues)
    Print GetValues(J)
Next J
```

This works better, with the earlier code that reads the data, if you have Option Base 1 in the general section of your form. This command will start the index of the array at 1 instead of the default 0. If you do that, change the For ... Next to start at 1 rather than 0. The UBound function returns the highest index in an array. You can use this function to determine how many elements are actually in the array, or to determine where the array stops. The LBound function returns the lowest subscript in an array. Used with UBound, it enables you to work out the size of an array. You can process every element in a one-dimensional array with the following code:

```
Dim J As Integer
For J = LBound(arrayname) To UBound (arrayname)
    'your code goes here....
Next J
```

Understanding Random Access Mode

Random access mode also works to retrieve data from ASCII files, but you have greater flexibility when you use it instead of sequential mode. Random access allows you to position yourself anywhere within the file at any time to get the data you need. As a result, this works more like a database than a sequential file. Random access is also faster at retrieving data than sequential mode, because you tell it explicitly where to position the file pointer within the file.

To open a file for random access, use the Random parameter by typing the following:

```
Open "c:\data\test.txt" for Random as FileNo Len=10
```

Before you specify the Len parameter, you should know the length of each line of data. You can do this by adding up the length of the line in ASCII characters. This line of data is called a *record*, just like a database record. For the purpose of this section, we will reference each line of data as a record.

Let's assume that each record will contain a last name, a first name, and a description of the person. We can concatenate all of these parameters together and write it to the file, but it would be cumbersome to retrieve the data in a useable format. For example, if we used the code:

```
Private Sub SaveFile()
    Dim FileNo As Integer
    Dim RecNo As Integer
    Dim FName as String
    Dim LName as String
    Dim LineOut as String

    FName = "Jane"
    LName = "Doe"
    Desc = "Wife of John Doe"
    LineOut = LName & FName & Desc

    FileNo = FreeFile
    RecNo = 1
    Open "c:\test.txt" For Random As FileNo
```

```
            Put #FileNo, RecNo, LineOut
        Close FileNo
    End Sub
```

our record would look like this when we retrieve it:

```
    DoeJaneWife of John Doe
```

Now that is ugly! It would be impractical to write code to extract the names from this, because different people would have different length names. Instead, you could declare your own variable type for this situation using the Type…End Type keywords.

Now, the Type statement allows you to define your own variable type. This statement is especially useful in situations like the previous example. Before you can use the Type statement, however, you need to make sure there is a code module in the project. Visual Basic will not allow you to create a variable type within a form module. As a result, create the variable type within the (General)(Declarations) section of a code module. You could add the code:

```
    Type UserInfoRecord
        LName As String * 15
        FName As String * 15
        Desc As String * 50
    End Type
```

and change your procedure in the form to:

```
    Private Sub SaveFile()
        Dim FileNo As Integer
        Dim RecNo As Integer
        Dim usr As UserInfoRecord

        usr.FName = "Jane"
        usr.LName = "Doe"
        usr.Desc = "Wife of John Doe"

        FileNo = FreeFile
        RecNo = 1
        Open "c:\test.txt" For Random As FileNo Len = 80
            Put #FileNo, RecNo, usr
        Close FileNo
    End Sub
```

Let me explain the Type statement briefly. To create a variable type, you insert several variables and their declarations with the Type...End Type wrapping. In this example, we created a variable type that is broken into three separate string elements: LName, FName, and Desc. Notice that after they are declared, they are given a length. LName and FName are defined as strings with a fixed length of 15 characters each. Desc is defined to be 50 characters. If you add all of these lengths together you get 80 characters. This is the total length of your variable, and because this is the only variable you write to the file, it also becomes your record length.

To use the variable, UserInfoRecord, you need to Dim it, just as you do with all variables, so Visual Basic knows what data type the variable is. Then you can access each of the elements within the variable using the variable name followed by the dot "." operator and then the element name. You can then pass a value to it, or retrieve a value from it using the Get# statement. When the previous code is run it writes a record to a file. When viewed in Notepad, looks like Figure 7.4.

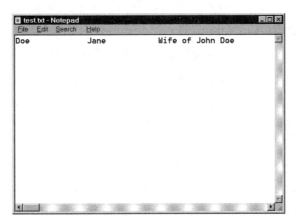

FIGURE 7.4: A RECORD IN A TEXT FILE

Random access mode is good for working with lists of data supplied in an ASCII file. However, most files will not fit neatly into this format. They might have headers of different lengths or other inconsistencies within the file. You may find that a relational database will work better for you. We will discuss these after examining binary access mode.

Understanding Binary Access Mode

Binary mode allows you the greatest amount of flexibility when working with files. When working with binary access mode, you retrieve data with the Get# command, and write data with the Put# command, just like you do with random access mode. The difference between binary and random access mode is that you cannot move around the file at random and get data. Instead, data is read sequentially and in chunks in the binary mode. The number of bytes read from the file equals the size of the string, in bytes, that you want to read data into. For example, the following statements read 10 bytes from a file:

```
Temp = String(10," ")
Get #FileNo, ,Temp
```

Notice that the RecNo parameter is missing. This is because binary files are read sequentially. Visual Basic remembers the current position within the file so you don't have to keep track of it. So without further delay, let's put this knowledge to use and write a file encryption program. I will describe the details of the program as we go along.

A Simple Encryption Program

To understand how to work with binary files, let's create an encryption program. Don't expect the application to create a file that cannot be hacked by a good programmer, however, because we are going to use the simplest of encryption algorithms. The purpose of this example is to show you how to work with a file in binary access mode. To encrypt a file, select Actions ➤ Encrypt from the menu. To decrypt a file, use Actions ➤ Decrypt. You will be asked to supply a text file for the encryption.

1. Start a new project. It will be a Standard EXE.
2. Make Form1 the active control and set its Name property to
    frmMain. Set its Caption property to **File Encrypter**.
3. Add a common dialog control to your form, and set its Name property
    to **dlgFile**.
4. Open the Menu Editor and create the following menu objects.

File Menu	
Caption:	**&File**
Name	**mnuFile**
File Menu Items	
Caption:	**&Exit**
Name:	**mnuFileExit**
Actions Menu	
Caption:	**&Actions**
Name:	**mnuAct**
Actions Menu Items	
Caption:	**&Encrypt**
Name:	**mnuActEncrypt**
Caption:	**&Decrypt**
Name:	**mnuActDecrypt**

When you're finished, your form should look like Figure 7.5.

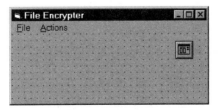

FIGURE 7.5: THE ENCRYPTION FORM

Note

The next step is to add the code behind the form. The only control used besides the menu is the common dialog control. The common dialog control is used to offer Open and Save dialog boxes, as well as font and printer settings. We will use it only to select a filename.

5. Next, open the Code window and set the object drop-down box to mnuFileExit.

6. Add an End statement to the mnuFileExit_Click() procedure.

7. You are going to add the encryption algorithm here, so open the (General)(Declarations) procedure and add the code below:

```
Function Encrypt(infile As String) As Boolean
  Dim fileno1 As Integer
  Dim fileno2 As Integer
  Dim outfile As String
  Dim xpos As Long
  Dim x As Byte

  'Show the hourglass
  MousePointer = 11

  xpos = 4
  outfile = "c:\temp.enc"
  fileno1 = FreeFile
  Open infile For Binary As fileno1
    fileno2 = FreeFile
    Open outfile For Binary As fileno2
      Put #fileno2, 1, 0
      Put #fileno2, 2, 128
      Put #fileno2, 3, 0
      Put #fileno2, 4, 128
      Do While Not EOF(fileno1)
        xpos = xpos + 1
        Get #fileno1, xpos, x
        Put #fileno2, xpos, x + 128
      Loop
    Close fileno2
  Close fileno1

  'Delete original file & replace with encrypted file
  Kill infile
  FileCopy outfile, infile
  Kill outfile
  Encrypt = True
```

```
'Reset the mouse pointer
MousePointer = 0
End Function
```

This code deserves some scrutiny because it does most of the work for the program. You'll notice instead of this procedure being a sub, it is a function. The purpose behind this is because the function will return a result code to its calling procedure. You should do this because you need to know if the process was successful before you actually notify the user or carry on with the program. This function simply returns a True if the encryption is successful, or a False if the process was unsuccessful. Notice that we also pass the infile parameter to the function. This is the fully qualified path and filename of the file you wish to encrypt. Infile is retrieved through the use of the GetFile() function.

After bypassing the standard variable declarations, you will notice that the mouse pointer is set to an hourglass. This will inform the user to wait, because the program is processing. Because you will be reading the file byte by byte, it could possibly be a slow process, so you should display the hourglass.

Tip

When the program will take a while to process, you should show an hourglass. This will let the user know the program is working. Without one, a user will not know if the program is running or if it crashed. You can display the hourglass by setting the form's MousePointer property to 11 - Hourglass.

As mentioned earlier, you use the FreeFile command to get the next available file handle. As I was creating this program, I had the two FreeFile statements next to each other in the code. I did this because I like to logically group commands whenever possible. When I ran the program, it kept giving me a "File Already Open" error. Why did it do this? I checked the values of infile and outfile in the debugger and they were both correct.

Neither of the files were opened by any other applications, so they couldn't be locked or causing a sharing violation. After some more scrutiny, I realized that FreeFile did not allocate a file handle for me. The Open statement allocates the handle for us. FreeFile just tells us what handles are available. What I had done was return the same file handle for both fileno1 and fileno2. Once I moved the FreeFile commands next to their corresponding Open statements, the program worked. The point of my rambling is that you need to keep FreeFile as close to Open as possible, especially when you are working with more than one file in a procedure. Also, even the simplest programs may need to be debugged!

Tip

Keep the FreeFile command as close to the Open command as possible when working with multiple files in the same procedure. FreeFile will not lock the file handle but just inform you it is available. Your best bet is to put the Open command right after the FreeFile command.

Before actually processing data, you'll want to add a sort of digital signature to the beginning of the encrypted file. This signature is used in the decryption algorithm to determine whether the file is encrypted. The signature should be a sequence of bytes that are not likely to appear in a file. For this example, I used a four-byte signature that consists of 0, 128, 0, 128. This is the exact data and sequence expected by the decryption algorithm. You could enhance the Encrypt and Decrypt functions by creating another function that generates and uses its own signature.

Notice that x is dimensioned as a byte, and not an integer. The reason for this is that its maximum value can be 255. When you add another number to it that makes the total value of x greater than 255, the value of x rolls over to 0 and continues adding. So when you add 128 to 128 we get 256. Since 256 is greater than 255, the value of x rolls over to 0. This is the key to the encryption. When you go to decrypt the file, you use the same algorithm to bring back the original values. If you add 128 to 0, you get 128, which was your original value. As a result, the encrypted character is restored to its original state.

Just before the end of the function you will notice some Kill statements. In Visual Basic, the Kill statement is the equivalent of delete. What this sequence of commands does is replace infile with outfile. This way you are left with one encrypted file and no temp file. Before you can rename a file, however, it must have a unique filename. This is why you delete infile before you rename outfile. Once the rename is successful, you delete outfile to clean up the mess.

Now that the function is complete, reset the mouse pointer to give the user a visual cue that the program is done running. You also want to send a True return code so the calling function can continue:

1. Now that you have written the meat of the program—the encryption function—you need a method to call it. You will do this through the mnuEncrypt_Click() event:

```
Private Sub mnuActEncrypt_Click()
 Dim filename As String

 filename = GetFile()
 If filename <> "" Then
   If Encrypt(filename) = False Then
     MsgBox "Error encrypting file!"
 End If
 End If
End Sub
```

2. Before the menu command can call the Encrypt function, it needs to call GetFile() to retrieve a filename:

```
Function GetFile() As String
 dlgFile.CancelError = True
 On Error GoTo filerr

 dlgFile.DialogTitle = "Select a File..."
```

```
      dlgFile.DefaultExt = "*.txt"
      dlgFile.Filter = "Text Files (*.txt)|*.txt| _
All Files (*.*)|*.*"
      dlgFile.FilterIndex = 1
      dlgFile.MaxFileSize = 32767
      dlgFile.ShowOpen
      GetFile = dlgFile.filename
      Exit Function

filerr:
 GetFile = ""
End Function
```

The GetFile function also deserves some examination. If you have read the Common Dialog section in Skill 3, then this function will be self-explanatory. At the heart of this function is the common dialog control. This control provides all of the functionality you need to retrieve a filename. As you may have learned, the Open dialog box that you have seen in other applications does not actually open the file. Rather, it retrieves a filename and passes it back to the application. Then another procedure uses this filename and opens the file for processing. This is exactly what this program does as well.

The first action we take is to set the CancelError property to True. When this property is set to True, the dialog box will send an error message if the user clicks the Cancel button. We trap this error so that we do not process any code if the user wants to cancel. The On Error command is what actually tells the procedure to skip the encryption algorithm.

For aesthetics you set the DialogTitle property to Select a File... This just makes the program a little more user-friendly. You can actually place any text here that you want.

Set the default extension to *.txt. For those of you familiar with DOS commands, the asterisk is a wildcard which tells the common dialog to filter out all files except those with a .txt extension. This makes it easier for the user to zero-in on files of interest. When you work with the common dialog control in your own applications, be sure to make it easier for your users.

Next define filters by setting the Filter property. You do this by alternating a description and the actual filter. You separate these with the pipe symbol (|). There are multiple filters, which you may have seen in other applications. You just need to separate everything with the pipe symbols. We can access these filters using the FilterIndex property.

FilterIndex is the index number of the filter to be displayed in the dialog box. The first filter has an index of 1, the next is 2, and so on. When you set this property, it only sets the starting index. You can change the filter from the actual dialog box, as in Figure 7.6.

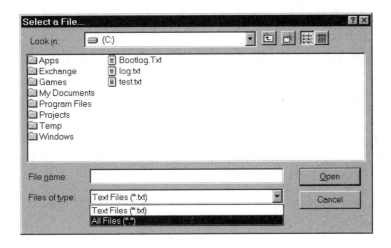

FIGURE 7.6: THE COMMON DIALOG BOX

Notice how I set the MaxFileSize property to 32767. Setting this property will cause the common dialog to only return filenames of files whose sizes are 32K or less. You can set this property to whatever you want, but it is important to make sure the files you open can fit into the controls you use. While we don't use anything with a size limitation on it, this property doesn't really matter for this application.

Tip

You can use the MaxFileSize property in the common dialog control to filter filenames based on file size. This is a great error-checking feature to implement when you use controls that have memory limitations imposed on them, for instance, a text box control.

Finally, set the ShowOpen property to display the dialog box. If the user clicks the Cancel button, then the dialog box returns an error message, and the function cancels itself. Otherwise it sets the FileName property to the filename that the user selected. You then pass this value back through the parameter. If you don't get a filename, then you return an empty string to the calling procedure.

Let's add the decryption algorithm so we can get our file back:

1. Add the following code:

```
Private Function Decrypt(infile As String) As Boolean
  Dim fileno1 As Integer
  Dim fileno2 As Integer
  Dim outfile As String
  Dim xpos As Long
  Dim x As Byte
  Dim t(3) As Byte

  'Show the hourglass
  MousePointer = 11

  xpos = 4
  outfile = "c:\temp.enc"
  fileno1 = FreeFile
  Open infile For Binary As fileno1
    fileno2 = FreeFile
    Get #fileno1, 1, t(0)
    Get #fileno1, 2, t(1)
    Get #fileno1, 3, t(2)
    Get #fileno1, 4, t(3)
    If (t(0)=0 And t(1)=128 And t(2)=0 And t(3)=128) Then
      Open outfile For Binary As fileno2
        Do While Not EOF(fileno1)
          xpos = xpos + 1
          Get #fileno1, xpos, x
          Put #fileno2, xpos - 4, x + 128
        Loop
      Close fileno2
```

```
      'Delete original file & replace with encrypted file
      Kill infile
      FileCopy outfile, infile
      Kill outfile
      Decrypt = True
    Else
      Decrypt = False
    End If
  Close fileno1

  'Reset the mouse pointer
  MousePointer = 0
End Function
```

You will notice the code is almost identical to the encryption algorithm. However, before deciphering a file, you need to check to see if it is started with your signature, the 0,128,0,128 sequence at the beginning. When a file is encrypted, the program inserts these four numbers in the beginning of the encrypted file. That way the program knows if a file is actually encrypted before it tries to decrypt it.

2. Now you need to add the code to call the Decrypt function from the decrypt menu item:

```
Private Sub mnuActDecrypt_Click()
  Dim filename As String

  filename = GetFile()
  If filename <> "" Then
    If Decrypt(filename) = False Then
      MsgBox "Error decrypting file!"
    End If
  End If
End Sub
```

Now that you have all of the code added, save your project and give it a test run. Although it does not do anything spectacular, it's a good lesson on how files can be stored and retrieved from a disk. Now you have enough knowledge to start working with files and you should be able to incorporate them in your programs.

Using Data Controls

Many Visual Basic developers choose to keep data in Microsoft Access tables or other databases because Visual Basic provides tools that make it relatively easy to access data within them. You can try this out by using the sample Access database supplied with Visual Basic—Biblio.mdb—it's in the Visual Basic directory by default. That database (and its component tables) is provided for you, but you'll probably need to create your own databases from time to time. To create an Access database, you could hard-code all the table, field, and index definitions, but that's not always very convenient. There are a couple of other avenues:

- If you already have Microsoft Access, you can use it to easily create databases that can be accessed by Visual Basic. This is the quickest and most efficient method of creating databases, but it is not the only solution.
- If you don't have Access, you can use the Visual Data Manager add-in of Visual Basic (see Figure 7.7). To start the Data Manager, select Add-Ins ➤ Data Manager.

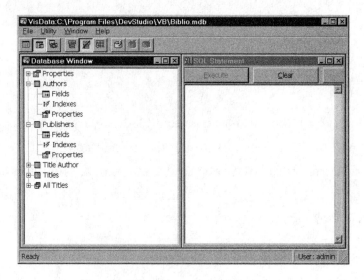

FIGURE 7.7: VISUAL DATA MANAGER

Once you have a database, you need a way to access it from within Visual Basic. You have a few ways to do this:

- One way is to write code and use Data Access Objects (DAO) to access your data. These are objects that allow you to access records, tables, and queries through code.
- You can also have an Access-style form wizard do all the hard work— the Visual Basic Data Form Designer. To install it, click Add-Ins ➤ Add-In Manager and select it from the list. From now on it appears under the Add-Ins menu.
- The last method is to use the data control that comes with Visual Basic. This is the method that will be covered in this section.

Adding the Data Control

To get you started using a data control, try the following example, which allows you to browse through a table in a database. It requires no programming at all:

1. Add two text boxes to the top of a form.
2. Double-click the data control in the Toolbox to add it to the form.
3. Drag the newly added data control to position it below the two text boxes.
4. Widen the data control so you can see its caption (shown below).

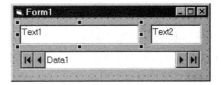

5. Set the properties for the data control as follows:

Caption:	**Authors Table**
Connect:	**Access (default)**
DatabaseName:	**c:\vb\biblio.mdb** (amend path if necessary)

RecordsetType: **1 - Dynaset** (default)

RecordSource: **Authors** (from drop-down list)

6. Set properties for the text box on the left as follows:

DataSource: **Data1**

DataField: **Author**

7. Set the properties for the text box on the right to:

DataSource: **Data1**

DataField: **Au_ID**

8. Run the program and scroll through the records with the navigation buttons on the data control. Note that any changes you make in the text boxes are written back to the database.

The following graphics show you some sample results that you may see when you browse through the database. If you go to the first record within the table, the author is Pat Adams. If you go to record 53 you will see Yair Alan Griver.

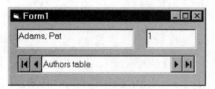
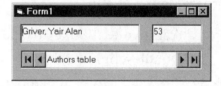

9. If you want to add new records, then set the EOFAction property of the data control to **2 - Add New**. To add a record, scroll to the last record, and then click the next record navigation button.

10. Type the author name **Doe, John** in the first text box and move to another record. The new author name is appended to the database (as shown here).

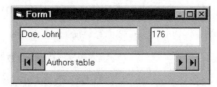

11. If you want to delete a record, then add a command button to the form. In its Click event procedure add the following code (shown below):

```
Data1.Recordset.Delete
Data1.Recordset.MoveFirst
```

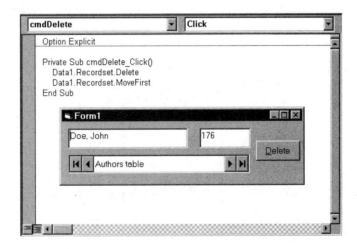

The above example gives you a simple, yet workable, database application. To repeat the process for another database, you need to be aware of some of the properties and what they mean.

The Data Control Properties

Let's start with the data control properties (see Figure 7.8). The Connect property specifies the type of database you want to use—the default is Access. The DatabaseName property specifies the actual filename of the database (strictly speaking, this is true only for Access databases; for non-Access databases you may have to set just the directory). The RecordsetType property determines whether the data you see is from a table, a dynaset, or a snapshot. Typically (though not always) a table is the most efficient if the data is from one table; a dynaset is needed if the data is a subset of a table or comes from more than one table, and a snapshot is sometimes best if the data is to be read only. In this example the RecordsetType property could be any one of the three available. The RecordSource property corresponds to the table in the database you want to access (at least, it does in Access; for non-Access databases you may have to set this property to a filename). To access multiple tables in a dynaset, you have to enter an SQL statement or create the dynaset first in code or in Access.

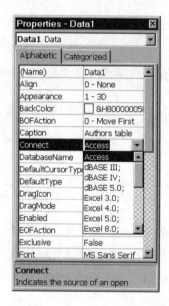

FIGURE 7.8: THE DATA CONTROL PROPERTIES

The data control does not actually display data—to do that, you must link another type of control to the data control. In the previous example two text boxes were used. For each text box you set the DataSource property to the name of the data control (here it's Data1). Next you set the DataField property equal to the name of a field in the recordset returned by the data control's RecordSource property.

This ability of the data control to extract data is one of the strongest features of Visual Basic. You can also hard-code data access. The latter is quite easy as well, but unfortunately beyond the scope of this book. However, it's possible to accomplish a great deal just through the data control.

The Anatomy of a Database

The possibilities for working with Visual Basic and Microsoft Access .MDB databases (and via Access to SQL Server and Oracle) are manifold. While there are many methods of bringing data into Visual Basic, only a couple are touched on here. Fortunately, you don't need a copy of Access to begin using Access databases, because the Access Jet Engine is provided with Visual Basic. All you require is an Access .MDB file. Although using Access is a better solution to designing database files, we will use the Visual Data Manager add-in for this skill because it comes with Visual Basic.

An Access database is a file that contains tables, indexes, and queries. A table is a collection of data that can be represented in rows and columns. In database terms, rows are called *records* and columns are called *fields*. An index is a linked list of pointers to records within a table. You use an index to rapidly search through a table. Queries are Structured Query Language (SQL) statements that you define to extract a subset of records from a table.

Database Tables

If you've used SQL before, then you know what a table is. If you are moving to Visual Basic or Access from one of the traditional PC-based database applications, then you might need some practice. What xBase users refer to as a database is actually a table in Access. In Visual Basic and Access the table is only one of potentially many components that will actually make up a database. A full-fledged Access database would typically contain other objects as well—other tables, queries, forms, and so on. A table is not saved as a separate file but rather is stored as an intrinsic part of a database. To open a table, you must open the parent database first. Tables are the starting point for any database and they are where data is stored. If this is your first visit to the world of databases, but if you've had experience working with spreadsheets, then think of a table as basically a worksheet. To extend the worksheet analogy, rows represent your records and columns your fields. I've reproduced a simple table here to illustrate this comparison.

TITLE	AUTHOR
C++ in 5 Easy Minutes	F. Bloggs
Astrophysics Simplified	J. Doe
How to Make a Billion	B. Gates

Apart from the column titles, there are three rows, each referring to a specific book. In other words, this table shows three records. Each record has various attributes or properties such as the title and author. These attributes are listed in columns, and each column represents a field. This table has only two fields—the title column and the author column. And that is all there is to a table—though, in reality, a table would typically include many more records than this one and have a larger number of fields.

Without a minimum of one table, a database would contain no data and be totally meaningless. Therefore the first step in creating a database is to define a table and add some data to it. As your requirements develop, you'll probably find yourself creating more tables for the same database. For example, you might want a second table that lists publishers of the books in the first table. It *is* possible to append publisher details to the first table by adding extra fields—but if a publisher supplies more than one book, then you would want a second table. The reason for this has to do with data integrity and sensible database design.

Database Queries

A query is a way of extracting or changing table data. After you create the database, you pose a query to it, and (if you ask the question correctly) it comes up with an answer—saving you a good deal of time rummaging around for the answer by other means. There are additional methods of extracting data, but a query is a good place to begin. There are also alternatives for altering data—you could edit a table directly, yet a query makes it easy to enact changes on multiple records and fields simultaneously. Suppose you wanted to see which books were written by F. Bloggs. In this case you'd define a query that selected or filtered only the relevant records using Structured Query Language (SQL). Try this example:

1. Open the previous example from the "Adding the Data Control" section.
2. In the Properties window, change the RecordSource property to the following: **select * from [Authors] where [Author] = "Doe, John"**
3. Select Run ➤ Start to view the results.

The result of the query is shown here:

AUTHOR	AUTHOR ID
Doe, John	176

This looks pretty much like a table, and in fact, it's a subset of the table. In Visual Basic and Access terminology it's called a *dynaset*. Dynaset means a "*dyna*mic *set* of records". The data in a dynaset does not actually exist— it's extracted from the underlying table or tables, and only the criteria for the query (here the criterion is books by the author John Doe) are saved. It's also dynamic in the sense that if you change the table, then different data could appear in the dynaset without your changing the query definition. Because it's a subset of an existing table, you can edit the data in the dynaset and this changes the original data back in the table. You should note that there are some restrictions on editing data in a dynaset—for example, you may not be able to edit data if it threatens referential integrity. For example, if you configure the table to only allow unique author names, then you could not add a new record for a book by the same author.

Queries are an extremely important part of Visual Basic and Access. Not only can you edit data directly in the dynaset, but you can then query the query itself, if you see what I mean. If the dynaset had included a number of separate titles by F. Bloggs, then you could narrow this down further by specifying a couple of titles. This leads me to an important observation on queries. Why not simply specify those titles in the first place and have just one query rather than two? That is, of course, perfectly possible and is often the approach to adopt. However, the great beauty of Access queries is that by querying another query you can progressively narrow down the dynaset and see the results of all intermediate queries. This allows a layered approach to queries and is sometimes exactly what's required.

You might raise another equally important point. Why bother to extract the data from the original table in the first place, when it's easy to spot the book by F. Bloggs and all its details? With just three records, that might be a valid objection. But with tens, hundreds, or even thousands of records, the use of a suitable query lets you concentrate on only those records you want. Queries really come into their own when you add more than one table to the query definition—this allows you to view and edit data from related, though separate, tables from a Visual Basic form.

Creating Databases with Visual Data Manager

Databases provide an easier format to store and retrieve data. They include tables, queries, and indexes that make record searching faster. Without these features, you would have to write your own code, which is very difficult and impractical since you don't have to. Visual Basic and Access provide everything you need to make fast and efficient databases that can be used by your applications.

The first step in creating a database is to specify a filename. The database is saved as a single file with a .MDB extension. Once this is accomplished you then go on to create the objects (tables, queries, and so on) that are going to be part of your database. As a reminder, these are held within the .MDB file and not as separate files.

Let's create a database designed for a bookshop named Read Only, which suggests a suitable name for the database.

Creating a database is straightforward; just follow these steps:

1. Select Tools ➤ Visual Data Manager... to start Visual Data Manager.
2. Click File ➤ Microsoft Access ➤ Version 3.0 MDB to see the Select Microsoft Access Database to Create dialog box.
3. Type in a name for your database; here let's use ReadOnly (the case is unimportant). There is no need to provide the .MDB extension, as Access does this for you automatically.
4. Click OK.

A database window will appear with the name of the database in its title bar.

There are two windows that are visible right now. The first window is the Database window (see Figure 7.9), and the other window is the SQL Statement window. In the Database window is a list of the properties for the newly created database. There are no tables or queries defined in the database at this moment. The toolbar offers you some buttons to manipulate the database. The button for tables is already pressed down, but the list under Tables is empty, indicating the database contains no tables at the moment.

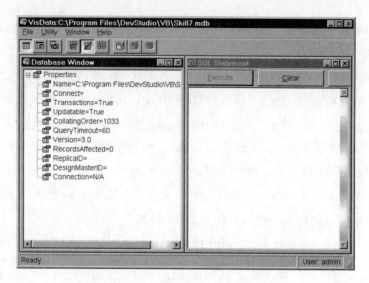

FIGURE 7.9: THE DATABASE WINDOW

Before adding the first table object to this database, let's see how to close and reopen it:

1. Click File ➤ Close. You could also use Close from the database window's Control menu or double-click this menu. Double-clicking the Visual Data Manager Control menu not only closes your database but Visual Data Manager as well.

2. Click File ➤ Open Database ➤ Microsoft Access to see the Open Microsoft Access Database dialog box. In this dialog box select ReadOnly.mdb and click Open. If you are not sharing your database across a network, then you can ignore the Open as Read-Only check box in the dialog box. You are back to the empty database window.

Now it's time to add the first object to the database.

Creating a Database Table

The sample table is simply a list of books. Each row (or *record*) in the table is to represent one book, though there may be more than one copy of an individual book in stock. The table is also to have three columns (or *fields*) to represent the properties of the books. To begin with, we only want to see the title and author of each book. Later you'll append more detail. Here's a table showing the books in stock:

TITLE	AUTHOR
A Philosophy of Solitude	John Cowper Powys
The Art of Growing Old	John Cowper Powys
Soliloquies of a Hermit	Theodore Francis Powys
Glory of Life	Llewelyn Powys
Windows—The Definitive Book	Emma Radek
Access—The Definitive Book	Emma Radek

This is fine as far as it goes. But book lists are often sorted by author surname. So you need to split the author field into two—surname and forename. Now the table looks like this, and this is how it's going to be entered:

TITLE	SURNAME	FORENAME
A Philosophy of Solitude	Powys	John Cowper
The Art of Growing Old	Powys	John Cowper
Soliloquies of a Hermit	Powys	Theodore Francis
Glory of Life	Powys	Llewelyn
Windows—The Definitive Book	Radek	Emma
Access—The Definitive Book	Radek	Emma

Before you can enter any data into the table, you must design the table. It's important to get the design stage right, though you can always modify the design later. There a few questions to ask before you begin the design. You must ask yourself what data you want to put in the table; in particular you must decide on the properties (fields) for the data. Once you've done this, the next question to ask yourself is what type of data is it. In the book list example the answers are quite straightforward. You need to have fields for the title of each book, plus two fields showing the surname and forename of the author. These fields contain text, so the data type for all three fields is text.

Defining a Table

The table is part of the ReadOnly database, so make sure you can see the Database window (use File ➤ Open Database if necessary). As it stands the window only has the properties list of the database. Select the Table button before creating a new table:

1. Click the Table button, if necessary, to display an empty Tables list in the database window.

2. Right-click in the Database window and select New Table to begin a new table. You are presented with an empty table window in design view. This is where you specify your fields and the data type—it is not where you enter the actual data (see Figure 7.10).

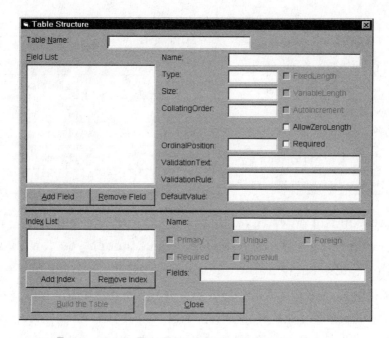

FIGURE 7.10: THE TABLE STRUCTURE DIALOG BOX

The left side of the dialog box contains an empty list of cells. When you open a database that already has a table definition, you will see the database field names listed here. The right side contains the cells that describe the properties for each database field. Finally, the bottom of the dialog box contains the list of indexes within the database.

3. The field at the top of the dialog box is where you enter the name of the table. Enter **Book List** as the table name.

Adding Fields

Now you can add the three fields for this table:

1. Click the Add Field button to add the first field. You will see the Add Field dialog box shown in Figure 7.11.

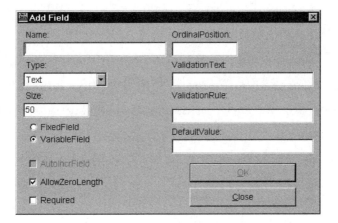

FIGURE 7.11: THE ADD FIELD DIALOG BOX

2. Type **TITLE** in the Name cell. The cursor should be in the Name cell by default—if you've been experimenting, click in this cell to reposition the cursor.
3. Press Tab to jump to the next cell. Note how Access inserts a default data type (Text) for you.
4. Press Tab to jump to the Size cell. Type **40** in this box.

5. Click the OK button to commit the field definition to the table.

6. Type **SURNAME** for the second field name.

7. Press Tab twice to accept Text for the data type and type **20** for the field size.

8. Click the OK button to commit the field definition to the table.

9. Type **FORENAME** as the next field name.

10. Press Tab twice to accept Text as the data type and enter **20** for the field size.

11. Click the Close button. The table design is now complete.

12. Click the Build the Table button in the Table Structure dialog box to have the Data Manager add the table structure to the database.

You have just added the first table to the database. From here you can re-open the table to modify it or you can open it to add records. In addition you can delete it, or you can copy the table's structure:

1. Right-click on the Book List object in the Database window. Select Open from the pop-up menu. This displays your table in a row and column format ready for data entry—or editing or browsing if there were some data already there.

2. Close the Table Structure dialog box by clicking on the Close button.

Entering Data

As you enter data into the Book List table, all the standard Windows editing techniques apply. The one you may not be familiar with is the F2 key, which selects all the data in a cell. You can, of course, simply double-click, but that only selects one word and is not enough if your field contains two or more words. But the first step is to re-open the table:

1. Make sure the Table object type button is selected.

2. In the list of tables select Book List.

3. Right-click and select Open from the pop-up menu. A quicker way to open the table is to double-click the table name.

The cursor should be positioned ready for the first data in the first field of the first record.

Type the relevant data in each field and record. To move from field to field click it with the mouse. When you move the cursor to the next record, you will be asked if you want to commit the changes. Answer Yes to save the record. Here are the steps for the first record:

1. Type **A Philosophy of Solitude** as the Title for the first record and click the mouse in the Surname field.
2. Type **Powys** as the Surname and click in the Forename field.
3. Type John Cowper in the Forename field and click in the first field of the next record.
4. When prompted to commit changes, answer Yes.

The cursor is now in the first field of the second record. Continue data entry, using the rest of the data that is reproduced below.

TITLE	SURNAME	FORENAME
The Art of Growing Old	Powys	John Cowper
Soliloquies of a Hermit	Powys	Theodore Francis
Glory of Life	Powys	Llewelyn
Windows—The Definitive Book	Radek	Emma
Access—The Definitive Book	Radek	Emma

Some of the entries are too long to fit in their grid cells. Note the pencil icon in the left-hand border. This indicates a record is being entered (or edited) and has not been saved yet. The asterisk (*) symbol indicates a new record.

As you tab out of the second entry for Emma, you have finished creating the table. If you can't quite see all the data in each column, you can drag column dividers to make them wider. For example, to increase the width of the Title column, do the following.

1. Position the mouse pointer over the divide between the Title and Surname columns in the top border. The mouse pointer changes to a two-way arrow.

2. Drag the divide to the right to increase the width of the Title column.

As indicated earlier, a table is the basis for all the other objects in a database. We'll use this simple table to build a query. Later we'll go back and modify this table in order to look at some of the other features involved in constructing a table. For now, we'll base a simple query on this Book List table.

Creating a Query

A *query* is an SQL statement that recalls a subset of records that match the criteria in the SQL statement. In this section you'll consider some very basic queries that filter the Book List table and carry out some sorting of data. Before running a query, however, you must define it first:

1. Right-click the Database window and select New Query from the pop-up menu. You could also select Utility ➤ Query Builder from the Visual Data Manager menu. You will see the Query Builder dialog box shown in Figure 7.12.

2. Select the Book List table from the Tables list in the dialog box. This will expose all of the fields within the table. Notice that the Field Name cell defaults to the first field in the table. Change this cell to [Book List].Surname.

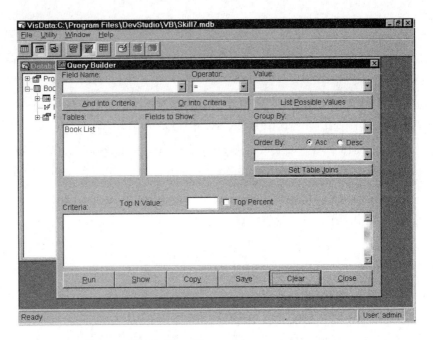

FIGURE 7.12: THE QUERY BUILDER DIALOG BOX

3. Leave the Operator cell intact. We are going to query on the authors' surnames, so we want exact matches.

4. In the Value cell, you can type **Powys**, or you can click the List Possible Values button and select Powys from the list. This button queries all of the values entered in the selected field of the current table. This can be a time saver if you have many values to search through.

5. Select each field in the Fields to Show list by clicking each one. We want to show every field for any matching records.

6. You can preview the SQL statement by clicking the Show button. This will display a message box with the complete SQL statement required to extract all authors with the surname Powys from the Book List table.

7. Click the Add into Criteria button to add the SQL statement to the Criteria cell. You can continue making more queries to add to the current statement by clicking the Add into Criteria or the Or into Criteria buttons. For this example, we just want to search for Powys.

8. To test the query, click the Run button. The Data Manager will ask you if this is a SQLPassThrough Query. (Click the No button. SQL Passthrough is used to access databases on SQL database servers such as Microsoft SQL Server.) If your query is built correctly, you will see a subset of records that all have the surname of Powys (see Figure 7.13).

9. After you have browsed the query results, click the Close button to close the dialog box.

10. Click the Save button on the Query Builder dialog box. You will be prompted to enter a query name. Type **Powys**. After a brief pause the query will be added to the database.

11. Click the Close button to close the Query Builder.

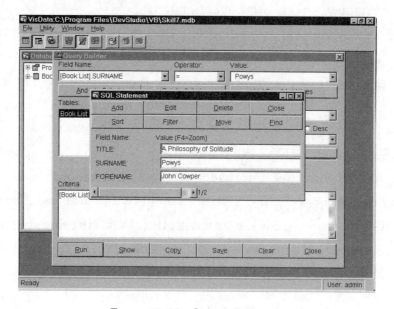

FIGURE 7.13: QUERY RESULTS

The query results are also known as a *dynaset*. The data is dynamic and can be edited—any changes are reflected in the underlying Book List table. There is little point, however, in designing a query like this—you can only see books from one author name. It would be impractical to create a separate query for every author in the database. As soon as you add a new author to the inventory, you would have to create a new query as well. Queries embedded within a database should be more general than this.

If you wanted a more generic query, you could use the Visual Data Manager to design the query. When you are satisfied with the query, you copy the SQL statement to your Visual Basic application. Using some string concatenation you could selectively replace a value with that which was entered in a field by the user. For example, you could create a SQL query like this:

```
SQL = "Select * From [Book List] Where [Book List].Surname = '"
SQL = SQL & txtAuthorName.Text & "'"
```

Then you create a field on the form called txtAuthorName. The user can enter a value in this field and when you call your query, it will extract the name entered in the field and place it in the SQL string. Then you just create a dynaset based on SQL.

Now let's consider what extra data the bookshop might find appropriate in the Book List table.

Primary Keys

A primary key is one that uniquely identifies each record in a table, such as a part number in a stock file. A primary key is advisable in tables, because it speeds up operations like searching, sorting, and filtering. Furthermore, if you want to relate two tables together, you must have a primary key in one of the tables. None of the existing fields in the Book List table would work as a primary key. A quick glance at the data reveals that both author surname and forename are duplicated across records—for example, there are four records for Powys and two for Radek. You might be tempted to nominate the book title as a primary key. However, two different books with the same title might be stocked. For example, if the bookshop were to expand on its Powys titles, it would find there are two books by John Cowper Powys called *The Art of Happiness*. And, given the nature of the bookshop, there is a further objection to using the title field as a primary key. Out-of-print and rare books (which the Powys books are) would warrant an entry for each individual copy (unlike the modern computer books), because book collectors are concerned about the edition and condition of each book. For a bookshop the ISBN (International Standard Book Number, which uniquely identifies every book published) of each book might be an obvious candidate for a primary key. Unfortunately the ReadOnly bookshop stocks older, out-of-print books. This means many of its titles do not have an ISBN number. And it's no good simply leaving the ISBN entry for these books blank (a null value), for two blanks contravene the rule that every single entry in the primary key field must be unique. A solution to this problem is to create a counter field, described next.

Counter Fields

A counter field has two main benefits: It enables you to define a primary key when there is no other suitable candidate field and it automatically inserts data that increments by one for each record. The latter is ideal if you want to create part numbers (or invoice numbers and the like) in a table. To create a counter field in Visual Data Manager, you can add a field and set its data type to Long. Then you check the Auto Increment option. Create an index and set this field as Required and set it as the Primary Key.

In the Book List table a counter field is a viable alternative to an ISBN number, but it also assigns a unique identifier to all the books, not just those that are likely to have an ISBN. A suitable name for this counter is BOOK CODE. The information it contains is largely notional, and it's unlikely that the number would mean that much to employees. Still, you could argue that some customers might order books using this book code. In a real-world situation you would also include the ISBN number for the modern computer books, but you couldn't use it as a primary key. Here, we're dispensing with the ISBN altogether. However, the book code information is not notional to Access internally—it will speed up queries and so on, based on the table (the faster queries would be particularly noticeable with a larger table, though with the small amount of data in the Book List table, it's of little practical value here). The book code is also vital for relating tables together. When you design your own tables it's good practice to have a primary key from the beginning—as your table grows, you'll reap the benefits.

Number Fields

The three existing fields in the Book List table are text fields. Such fields are not suitable for storing numeric values. With numeric values you may want to control how many decimal places are displayed and perform totalling and other calculations. A typical calculation is to add up the value of all items in stock for an inventory.

There are two distinct possibilities for numeric fields—the number of copies of each book, and the price. However, Access has a dedicated data type for prices, called a *currency field*. Therefore, you need only one numeric field—for the quantity in stock. This is particularly useful for the computer book side of the business. When the quantities in stock begin to run a little low, it shows it's time to place fresh orders with publishers. The out-of-print side of the business is handled slightly differently. Here the quantity of each book is always one. Duplicate copies are given their own entries—each copy of the same book has a separate entry, as the price varies according to the edition and condition of the book. Thus the default number of copies is one. You'll instruct Access to enter this default amount for you shortly.

It's important to realize there are various subtypes to a number data type. These subtypes are defined in the Field Size row of the field's property sheet and include Byte, Integer, Long Integer, Single, and Double. The subtype you choose determines the range of values you can enter, the maximum number of decimal places the field can accommodate, and the amount of disk space (and hence processing time) the field requires. Here's a list of the number data type subtypes:

FIELD SIZE PROPERTY	ACCEPTED NUMBERS	DECIMAL PLACES	STORAGE REQUIREMENTS
Byte	0 to 255	0	1 byte
Integer	−32,768 to 32,767	0	2 bytes
Long Integer	−2,147,483,648 to 2,147,483,647	0	4 bytes
Single	-3.4×10^{38} to 3.4×10^{38}	7	4 bytes
Double	-1.797×10^{38} to 1.797×10^{38}	15	8 bytes

The list is in ascending size of the range, decimal places, and storage requirements of the subtype. If you can visualize your number fields holding decimal places, then you need to specify single or double (except for monetary values, which should be assigned to a separate currency data type field). Try to choose a subtype from as high up the list as possible, since this can cut down on disk space used to hold the data and thus improve processing times. In our example, the bookshop is never going to carry more than 255 copies of a book, so the byte subtype is fine. The field is called QUANTITY. For larger (or negative) whole numbers (integers), you should specify integer or long integer.

Currency Fields

Currency fields take as much room as double number fields. However, they're ideal for holding prices and values. First, they automatically display two decimal places for cents. Second, for values of more than one thousand they show a thousands separator. Third, they are right aligned. Fourth, they are automatically prefixed with your default currency symbol, such as a dollar sign—you can simply type in the number during data entry. The Book List table would benefit from a field that gave the price of each book in stock. This, unsurprisingly, is to be called PRICE. As a safeguard, this field is going to be validated to prevent the possibility of entering negative prices—you presumably don't want the bookshop to pay its clients when they take a book!

Yes/No Fields

Yes/No fields are sometimes referred to as boolean or logical fields and contain only one of two possible values (typically Yes/No, True/False, or On/Off). The bookshop has two businesses—computer books and out-of-print rare editions. It would be nice to be able to distinguish the books at a glance. One way of doing this is to have a Yes/No field indicating if a particular book is (or is not) an out-of-print one. Using that field as a basis, it's then a straightforward matter to produce two separate book catalogues (by designing a query), one for computer book readers and another for out-of-print book readers. A good title for such a field might be RARE BOOK? (note the question mark).

Memo Fields

Memo fields are ideal for holding free-form text such as explanatory notes. This type of text often fits uncomfortably into normal text fields where there frequently are restrictions on the field length and formatting. In addition, it's difficult to apply validation to free-form text. If you want to validate normal text entries, then it makes little sense to place memo text in one of the normal text fields. The memo data type is specifically designed to accommodate free-form text. It allows you to input more characters than a text data-type field, but at the expense of more storage space on disk. The maximum capacity of a text field is 255 bytes (255 characters, or about 40 words), while a memo field holds up to 64,000 bytes.

A memo field would be ideal to hold information that describes in considerably more detail an out-of-print book. For example, you could mention whether it's a first edition, what its condition is, and whether it still has its original dust jacket or even an author's autograph. These are all of interest to the potential out-of-print book customer. The memo field is to be called NOTES.

Date/Time Fields

Date/Time fields are specifically designed to hold data that shows a date, or time, or both. Dates and times are stored internally by Access as numbers, making it possible to use them in calculations. However, both Visual Basic and Access display them as dates and times and both give you various formats from which to choose. There's also a degree of flexibility in how you enter dates. For example, to enter April 27, 1996, all the following are acceptable:

- 4 27 96
- 27 Apr
- April 27
- 04/27/1996

No matter how you enter the date, it always displays in the format you chose for the date field. Notice that omitting the year from the date results in the current year being stored and displayed. To enter April 27, 1989, you need to explicitly type 89 or 1989.

The Book List table might benefit from a date/time field. This is to hold the date when a book first arrived in stock—as a result, it only has to show the date and not the time. This information is more useful for the out-of-print business, because it lets you see how long you've been holding a particular item. Perhaps you might want to consider a price reduction for a rare book that's been sitting on the shelves for more than a year. You can ask Visual Basic or Access to list those books for you and to perform a price reduction automatically. The field is to be called ACQUIRED.

Modifying a Table

The preceding discussion suggested a number of fields and data types that would improve the usefulness of the Book List table. Here's a summary of those fields and the data types:

FIELD NAME	DATA TYPE
BOOK CODE	Counter (also to be a primary key)
QUANTITY	Number (Byte)
PRICE	Currency
RARE BOOK?	Yes/No
NOTES	Memo
ACQUIRED	Date/Time

To modify the table design to accommodate these new fields follow these steps:

1. If you don't have the Book List table open in design view, right-click the Book List table and click the Design item on the pop-up menu.

2. Click the Add Field button to add another field. In the Name cell type **BOOK CODE**. Press Tab to move into the Type cell. Open the drop-down list in the cell and select Long. To make this a counter field,

click the check boxes next to **AutoIncrField** and **Required**. Click the OK button.

3. Type **QUANTITY** for the next field name and press Tab. This field is a number field. In the Type field select **Byte**. Press the OK button to begin defining the next field.

4. Type **PRICE** in the Name field. Tab down to the Type list and type the letter **c**. This will select the Currency data type for this field. Click OK to save the field definition and start a new one.

5. For the next field type **RARE BOOK?**. Select **Boolean** for the field type. This is the equivalent of a Yes/No field. Again, click the OK button to save this definition.

6. The next field name should be labelled **NOTES**. Set the data type for this field to **Memo**. Click OK.

7. This is the last field for the table. Type **ACQUIRED** in the Name cell. Select **Date/Time** for the data type. Click OK to save. Click the Close button to close the Add Field dialog box.

8. From the Table Structure dialog box, click the Add Index button. Type **BOOK CODE** in the Name field. Click **BOOK CODE** in the Available Fields list to add the filed to the Indexed Fields list.

Also notice that the Primary and Unique options are checked. This establishes BOOK CODE as the primary key field. In some cases you may not want to create a counter field to be the primary key field. In the absence of any other suitable field, you might want to nominate two or more fields as a single primary key.

For example, in a library neither the date of borrowing or the book number is satisfactory. The date would be repeated (that is, not unique) for each reader borrowing books on the same day. The book number would be repeated, since the same book is borrowed on different dates. However, the two fields together are unique—this is assuming that the same book is not borrowed, returned, and borrowed again all in the same day.

To nominate a double field primary key, click the names of the fields in the list to add them to the Index Fields list. With both fields selected click the OK button to add this index to the database as the primary key. If you look at the Index properties in the Database window you can see that the properties UNIQUE, PRIMARY, and REQUIRED are set to true. The table is now indexed on the book code field and each entry into the field must be unique. With a counter field each entry is automatically made by the Access engine, and you can be sure that they are all unique. With, say, a text field, you must make sure that you enter unique values into each record. If you don't, then Access won't let you save the duplicate record until you change your entry.

9. Now to index on some other fields. Type **TITLE** in the Name field and then click TITLE in the Available Fields list. Remove the checks from the Unique and Primary options. Clearing these two check boxes cause the index to allow duplicate values in the field—here it allows books with the same title to be entered. Click the OK button to save the index.

Tip

Setting an index, like a primary key, helps speed up many processes in Access. If you define a field with a unique index, then you're building in a form of validation—you can't enter duplicate values. A unique index is the same as a primary key except that a primary key is the controlling index for the table and can also be used to establish relations into other tables.

---

10. Repeat the previous step to index by surname—be careful, though, not to set a unique index.

11. When you are done adding the indexes, click the Close button to close the dialog box.

12. In the Field List, select QUANTITY to make it the current field. Enter **1** in the DefaultValue cell. This is the default number of books in stock.

    When you enter a new record, Access inserts this value automatically. This is handy for the out-of-print books that are usually bought and sold in single copies. When the bookshop acquires multiple copies of modern computer books, then the amount must be entered manually to override the default. Default values are very useful and can be used with all data types except counters and OLE objects.

13. In the Field List, select PRICE to make it the current field. As well as defaults, you can set validation rules for fields. One idea might be to validate the quantity field to ensure that negative amounts are not entered accidentally. However, the Byte subtype only accepts integer values between 0 and 255, so validation is not really necessary.

    Incidentally, if you enter decimal places in an amount in a byte number field, the amount is rounded up or down to the nearest integer. Instead of validating the quantity field, try validating the price field.

14. In the ValidationRule cell row and type >0 and **<1000**. The price field is a currency one. Therefore it's possible to enter negative prices. This validation rule prevents negative prices and at the same time stops the accidental entry of prices over one thousand dollars (or pounds or whatever currency you're working in). This assumes that the bookshop is not going to stock books with a value of more than $1,000.

15. Click in the ValidationText cell and type Price between zero and one thousand dollars. If you try to enter a price that fails the validation rule, then a warning dialog box appears. This dialog box contains a

message that tells you that your entry is not valid. However, to provide a more meaningful message (perhaps explaining which values are allowed), you make an entry under Validation Text.

16. Click the Close button to save the table definition.

When you're finished, try creating some Visual Basic projects that access your new database. From Visual Basic you can click Add-Ins ➤ Data Form Designer to create an instantaneous form based on the table or one of the queries. Alternatively, you can add a data control to a new form and add text boxes or any of the other data-bound controls to link to with the data control. The important properties for the data control are DatabaseName, which points to your Access .MDB, and RecordSource, which points to a table *or* a query in your .MDB. With text boxes, set the DataSource property to point to the data control and the DataField property to point to the fields in the table or query that's the RecordSource for the data control. For data-bound combo or list boxes, use the RowSource property (with ListField) to bring data from the data control. To write data back to the database, via the data control, use the DataSource property (and DataField) as well.

You now have experience creating an Access database. As you develop your applications, you can create new databases using the methods described in this skill. Although Visual Data Manager has many improvements over previous versions, you might want to consider purchasing Microsoft Access if you don't already have it. This application has many features that make database design even easier than what you have done to create the previous database. Access also has more features and functionality built into it that can further define your database. Best of all, the database will still be compatible with you Visual Basic application

Now that you can work with files and databases, you can take the data from your applications and store it for retrieval, printing, or even use the data to store and retrieve application configuration settings. Spend some time experimenting with Visual Data Manager. There are many features that we have not covered in this Skill (it could take a small book to cover them). You can use Visual Basic to access your database and can actually create some sophisticated applications when you couple these two tools together. The next skill deals with the third important feature of an application: printing.

Summary of Skills Acquired

Now you can...

- ☑ open and work with an ASCII file
- ☑ work with files using sequential, random, and binary access
- ☑ use the Data Control too access information in a database
- ☑ use the Visual Data Manager
- ☑ create Tables and Queries

SKILL
8

Printing

Featuring

❏ Making the ultimate use of your data
❏ Understanding the Print method
❏ Printing to the Debug window
❏ Understanding the PrintForm method
❏ Using Crystal Reports for Visual Basic
❏ Using a report in your application
❏ Printing your source code

Making the Ultimate Use of Your Data

During the life of your project, you will input data, manipulate it in memory, and possibly store it on disk. These are all very important functions required by many applications, but it is perhaps most important to be able to print these values. In Visual Basic, you have many options to print. You can do any of the following:

- Print the current form
- Print line by line to a form or a printer
- Print to the Debug window
- Print reports from Crystal Reports (bundled with Visual Basic)

- Print via another application, such as Word for Windows, using DDE or OLE Automation

Understanding the *Print* Method

The Print method is the first example you will examine in this skill. This method is handy for displaying the values contained in variables so you can examine how they've changed up until the Print statement. You can check the values printed to the Debug window by breaking the project while it's running (with Run ➤ Break). The Print method also works for printing to both a form and a printer. To print to the printer, use Printer.Print—to print to the current form just Print is sufficient, though it's good practice to preface the method with the object name (for example, frmMyForm.Print).

Note

If you want to clear the text on a form before printing to it, use the Cls method. Otherwise, a series of many Print methods causes the output to disappear off the bottom of the form.

When you do print to a printer, you have to tell the printer *when* to print. The Print method alone only places the output in memory—making it ready to print but not actually printing it. The reason for that is you may want to print a series of lines on a single page and if Print caused the printer to start, you'd end up printing lots of pages with only one line on each one. To actually send the Print command to the printer, use the EndDoc method. For multi-page documents the NewPage method is also available.

Try the following code (perhaps in a form's Click event) to print a multi-page document:

```
Printer.Print "This is on page one"
Printer.Print "This is a second line on page one"
Printer.NewPage
Printer.Print "And this is on page two"
Printer.EndDoc
```

Viewing Values in the Immediate Window

While you are developing your application, you may find yourself spending time tracking down those pesky pieces of renegade code that programmers so fondly refer to as *bugs*. What you will find out when you are *debugging*—or fixing the erroneous code—is that you spend much of your time checking the values of variables. You have many options to display these values: You can place MsgBox commands strategically throughout your code, use trial and error (not a very efficient use of your time), or display values to the Debug window.

A cumbersome, but operational way to view variables at run time is to place a message box in the code after the variable's value has been set. Then you tell the message box to display this value.

Although this works, it is bad practice because you must continually add the MsgBox statements in the code, re-run the application, stop it, debug the code, and then remove the MsgBox statements. This is an awful way to track down bugs and is time consuming.

Trial and error is basically experimenting with variables and their values until the program works. You can get an idea for where the program is causing problems and then try to fix that code, but often the data gets mangled long before it appears to the user or the application. These are the worst types of bugs to track down because they appear intermittently.

Note

The Debug window in Visual Basic has been replaced by the Immediate, Watch, and Locals windows. However, Debug and Immediate are used interchangeably to describe the Immediate window.

To print to the Debug window, you need to use the Debug object. You simply tell Debug to print a value, as in the following example:

```
.
.
.
x = x + 1
Debug.Print x
.
.
.
```

This will display the current value of the variable *x* in the Debug window. Although this is very simple code, it is also very powerful.

Viewing an Error in the Debug Window

To give you a better idea of how you can implement this feature, let's create a small program with a bug in it; you can then use the Debug window to view the error:

1. Start a new project with a form.
2. Open the Code window and add the following code:

```
Private Sub Form_Click()
  Dim x As Integer

  On Error GoTo looperr
  Do While x < 100000
    x = x + 1
  Loop

looperr:
  Debug.Print "Error!"
  Debug.Print "x = " & trim$(str$(x))
End Sub
```

The program will create an error when you run it. Can you figure out what causes the error?

3. Run the code, click the form, and see what happens. You should see the results in the Immediate window, as shown in Figure 8.1.

If you haven't read Skill 6, or you are unfamiliar with the different variable types, the cause of the error will probably not be obvious to you. We caused an error by trying to force an integer to count beyond its own limitations. An integer can hold a value between -32768 and 32767. Since

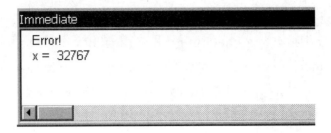

FIGURE 8.1: THE IMMEDIATE WINDOW

this example tries to count to 100,000 it will create an error when the value of the variable "x" equals 32768. In a situation like this, it would be better for us to dimension the variable *x* as a long integer (Long).

Fixing a Bug

Once you find a bug when you are debugging you need to fix it. You can fix this particular bug by following these steps:

1. Stop the program if you have not already done so.
2. In the Code window, change the Dim statement in the Click event from:

```
Dim x As Integer
```

to:

```
Dim x As Long
```

3. Run the program again (Run ➤ Start) and see what happens.

This time the program worked because a long integer can count much higher than a standard integer. Notice that the code is syntactically correct. Visual Basic recognizes all of the commands and even let's you try to run the program. Sometimes syntax is the cause of an error, and this is easy to fix. Unfortunately many bugs are the result of mismatched data types or invalid calculations. You can use the debug window to track the values of suspicious variables.

Debugging is an important process to learn, and the Print method is a handy tool to use when checking the values of variables at run time. Not only is this method useful in debugging, but you can use it for prototyping programs as well as creating simple reports. Before your results can print to paper though, you must print the contents of the printer's buffer with the PrintForm method.

Understanding the *PrintForm* Method

The PrintForm method prints the active form, unless another form is explicitly named, to the default printer. It does this by sending a pixel-by-pixel image of a form object to the printer. This is a handy method if you want to make simple screen dumps.

If you add Me.PrintForm to the Form_Click() event in the previous example, the form picture will be sent to the printer before the error message is printed in the Immediate window. To explicitly name a form to be printed, use a command similar to the following:

```
frmReport.PrintForm
```

In this example, the code instructs Visual Basic to print the contents of frmReport. You could also specify names like frmMain, frmAbout, or any other form name in your project.

Using Crystal Reports Pro for Visual Basic

Visual Basic comes with a companion product called Crystal Reports Pro. This powerful application allows you to visually design and lay out a report and then link it to your database. The result is a professional-looking report of the data you want to print.

Crystal Reports follows Visual Basic's lead by presenting you with a Report Wizard (see Figure 8.2), much like the Project Wizard you are already familiar with.

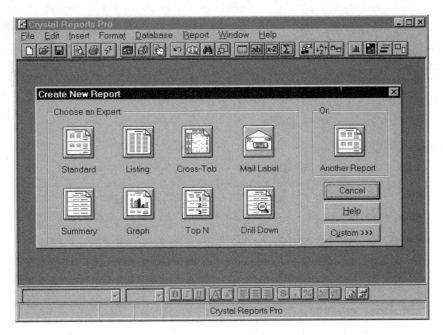

FIGURE 8.2: THE REPORT WIZARD IN CRYSTAL REPORTS

The Report Wizard offers several enhancements to versions that have come with previous versions of Visual Basic. Because it is beyond the scope of this book to cover every detail of Crystal Reports, we will cover a few of the procedures to create and use a report in your application.

After you select a report type (the options are shown in Figure 8.2), Crystal Reports will step you through a wizard that allows you to select a database and choose the appropriate fields required to create a complete report. The final step in the Report Wizard allows you to select from a predefined layout for the report type you select. This is a very nice feature and is a great time-saver!

After you have defined your report, you can either preview the report or work with it further in Design view (see Figure 8.3). You can create, delete, and move the fields around the report to get the exact layout that you desire. After you test your report, you can save it so it can be called from your application.

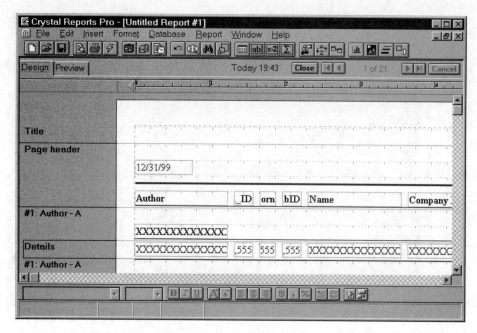

FIGURE 8.3: CRYSTAL REPORTS' DESIGN VIEW

Using a Report in Your Application

To use a report created by Crystal Reports in your application, you need to add the Crystal Reports custom control to your project. Once the control is added to the project, you must also add the control to the form you want to print from.

If you are planning to use only one report and one database, you can probably get away with setting the report properties from the Custom property entry in the Properties window. Figure 8.4 shows you the Custom Property Pages dialog box for the report control. By navigating through the tabs you can define what report to use with a database and where to print it. Notice that you can print to a window, a printer, a file, or even various e-mail systems such as MAPI, VIM, and Lotus Notes.

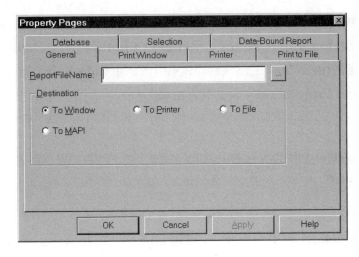

FIGURE 8.4: THE CRYSTAL REPORTS PROPERTY PAGE DIALOG BOX

Printing Your Source Code

It can become quite hard to keep track of all the properties you've set for your forms and controls. To check all of them, you could open each form in turn and click on each control with the Properties window open. But this would be very time consuming. Is there an easier way to keep a record of objects, properties, and code that's easy to read and check? By far the best way is to use File ➤ Print. Clicking File ➤ Print opens the Print dialog box (see Figure 8.5).

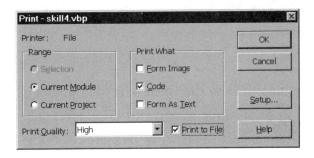

FIGURE 8.5: THE PRINT DIALOG BOX

Using the Print Dialog Box

The Print dialog box contains a number of options in two main sections, Range and Print What. The Range options include Selection, Current Module, and Project; they are discussed next.

Selection

This only prints out code, and *then* only the code you've selected in the Code window.

Current Module

This prints details of the form you're currently working on in the Design window. What details it actually does print depends on the settings in the Print What section (described shortly). There are other modules apart from form modules, and you can print their code if one of those modules is current.

Project

Choosing this option prints details of all the form modules in your project. It also prints details of other modules (standard and class modules). Again, the amount of data printed is determined by the settings in the Print What section.

The Print What section of the Print dialog box has the choices: Form Image, Form As Text, and Code; they are discussed in the following sections.

Form Image

This prints a bitmap of how the form will look at run time. You might want to use this option to produce a series of GUI screenshots for end user evaluation. It also serves (together with the next Form As Text option) as a way of documenting the whole of your interface design. It's not so handy as a method of producing a user manual—each form image prints on a separate page, and there's no easy way of inserting the form image into a document. All the screenshots of forms in this book were produced by a different method.

If you're interested—you might want forms to appear in a help file or in a manual you're preparing for users—the forms can be captured as Windows screenshots onto the Clipboard. You do this by holding the Alt button and pressing Print Screen. From there they can be pasted into and saved as .BMP files. Most word processing and DTP (desktop publishing) applications that are likely to be the choice for preparing manuals support the insertion of .PCX or .BMP files. To include the screenshot in a help file, you can simply reference the bitmap in your .RTF source file.

Form As Text

This prints a listing of the properties of your form and the properties for all the controls placed on the form. As such, it's a valuable reference—it's actually easier to re-create and debug a Visual Basic application from a list of properties than it is by simply referring to a form image. Be aware that not every single property for every single object is listed. In a complex application, that could easily run into a hundred pages or more. The only properties listed are those you've changed from the defaults (typically, the Name and Caption properties), those that give an indication of the position and size of the object (Left, Top, Height, and Width), those that correspond to the internal measurements and measuring system of objects (Scale... properties), the TabIndex property if it's appropriate, and the LinkTopic property for forms. You can safely ignore the latter for now. The listing also contains the menu controls, detailing their Shortcut property as well as the expected Caption property.

Code

Now we're getting closer to a traditional program listing. The Code option prints all the event procedures for a form and its controls. If you select Project under the Print Range section, it prints all the event procedures for all the forms and controls in your application. If you're debugging or documenting code for colleagues or for later referral, this is the one you want. The code is arranged form by form. Within each form code listing, the event procedures are arranged in the alphabetical order of the object Name property. Form event procedures always begin with Form, no matter how you change the Name property of the form. This means it's unlikely that the form procedures are listed before those of all other controls on the form. For example, the event procedure cmdOK_Click comes before that of Form_Load. This assumes that you have a control called cmdOK and that you've entered code into both procedures. If an event procedure contains no code at all, then the blank procedure template is not printed. A Visual Basic application often includes other procedures apart from event procedures. These other procedures might be user-defined Sub and Function procedures that you've created in form or standard modules. These too will be in the printout.

Commenting Your Code

Commenting your code is an important discipline to learn. Comments are lines of text preceded by an apostrophe, they are not actual program code. You should add comments to your programs when the code may be difficult to understand or when it requires special consideration during the development process. The comments in your source code are for the use of the programmer. Visual Basic ignores all your comments when you run the application. Commented code also prints. It's often tempting to dispense with comments, because surely all the code you type is obvious! But will it be so to colleagues, or even to you in a few weeks' time? Adding a few simple comments now could save hours of frustration down the road. Comments are especially important before and in between complex lines of code.

To place a comment in a procedure, type an apostrophe character (') at the start of the line. The following example is a comment:

```
'This line is a comment
```

You can also add comments at the end of a line, again preceded by an apostrophe:

```
cmdOK.Enabled = True      'Turns on the OK button
```

Viewing the Results

Another useful aspect of printing source code is that you might find it helpful to incorporate property or code listings in another document. Coming shortly is a sample property and code listing from Skill 4. It was not necessary to type all the listing out for the purposes of this book. Instead, a text file was created and inserted into the rest of the text. To do this I chose to print to file and used the Generic/Text printer driver supplied with Windows.

Tip

To create a text file containing properties and code for a project, first install the Generic/Text printer driver that comes with your copy of Windows. During the configuration, select FILE as the printer port. Then after selecting File ➤ Print in Visual Basic, turn on the Print to File check box. You can view the finished text file in WordPad. If you wish, you can incorporate this text file into a word processed document.

Below is the source code listing of the menu and toolbar example from Skill 4. Don't worry if your version is slightly different—some of the properties are not too important.

Form1 - 1

```vb
Option Explicit

Private Sub mnuFileExit_Click()
  End
End Sub

Private Sub tbrToolbar_ButtonClick(ByVal Button As ComctlLib.Button)
  Select Case Button.Key
    Case Is = "New"
      MsgBox "You clicked the New button."
    Case Is = "Open"
      MsgBox "You clicked the Open button."
    Case Is = "Save"
      MsgBox "You clicked the Save button."
    End Select
End Sub
```

Form1 - 1

```vb
VERSION 5.00
Object = "{6B7E6392-850A-101B-AFC0-4210102A8DA7}#1.1#0"; "COMCTL32.OCX"
Begin VB.Form Form1
  Caption        =    "Form1"
  ClientHeight   =    1572
  ClientLeft     =    3084
  ClientTop      =    2556
  ClientWidth    =    3744
  LinkTopic      =    "Form1"
  ScaleHeight    =    1572
  ScaleWidth     =    3744
  Begin ComctlLib.Toolbar tbrToolbar
    Align        =    1    'Align Top
    Height       =    336
    Left         =    0
    TabIndex     =    0
    Top          =    0
    Width        =    3744
    _ExtentX     =    6604
    _ExtentY     =    593
    ButtonWidth  =    487
    Appearance   =    1
    ImageList    =    "imlToolbar"
    BeginProperty Buttons {0713E452-850A-101B-AFC0-4210102A8DA7}
      NumButtons       =    4
      BeginProperty Button1 {0713F354-850A-101B-AFC0-4210102A8DA7}
        Key            =       ""
        Object.Tag        =          ""
        Style          =    3
        Value          =    1
        MixedState     =    -1    'True
      EndProperty
      BeginProperty Button2 {0713F354-850A-101B-AFC0-4210102A8DA7}
        Key            =    "New"
```

```
        Object.Tag           =      ""
        ImageIndex       =    1
      EndProperty
      BeginProperty Button3 {0713F354-850A-101B-AFC0-4210102A8DA7}
        Key            =    "Open"
        Object.Tag           =      ""
        ImageIndex       =    2
      EndProperty
      BeginProperty Button4 {0713F354-850A-101B-AFC0-4210102A8DA7}
        Key            =    "Save"
        Object.Tag           =      ""
        ImageIndex       =    3
      EndProperty
    EndProperty
    MouseIcon          =    {Binary}
  End
  Begin ComctlLib.ImageList imlToolbar
    Left             =    2520
    Top              =    720
    _ExtentX         =    804
    _ExtentY         =    804
    BackColor        =    -2147483643
    ImageWidth       =    16
    ImageHeight      =    16
    MaskColor        =    12632256
    BeginProperty Images {0713E8C2-850A-101B-AFC0-4210102A8DA7}
      NumListImages   =    3
      BeginProperty ListImage1 {0713E8C3-850A-101B-AFC0-4210102A8DA7}
        Picture          =    {Binary}
        Key              =      ""
```

Form1 - 2

```
      EndProperty
      BeginProperty ListImage2 {0713E8C3-850A-101B-AFC0-4210102A8DA7}
        Picture          =    {Binary}
        Key              =      ""
      EndProperty
      BeginProperty ListImage3 {0713E8C3-850A-101B-AFC0-4210102A8DA7}
        Picture          =    {Binary}
        Key              =      ""
      EndProperty
    EndProperty
  End
  Begin VB.Menu mnuFile
    Caption          =    "&File"
    Begin VB.Menu mnuFileExit
      Caption          =    "E&xit"
    End
  End
  Begin VB.Menu mnuEdit
    Caption          =    "&Edit"
    Begin VB.Menu mnuEditCut
      Caption          =     "Cu&t"
    End
```

```
    Begin VB.Menu mnuEditCopy
      Caption          =    "&Copy"
    End
    Begin VB.Menu mnuEditPaste
      Caption          =    "&Paste"
    End
  End
  Begin VB.Menu mnuHelp
    Caption          =    "&Help"
    Begin VB.Menu mnuHelpAbout
      Caption          =    "&About"
    End
  End
End
```

Deciphering the Code Listing

The code and properties of a form appear on separate pages. Each is headed by the name of the form and a page number. The latter is useful if a form's code or properties extend over more than one page. The code page is a listing of all the event procedures for that form module. The properties page lists all the relevant properties for the form and all the controls it contains. The separate pages have been run together for the purposes of this book. However, you can see a heading Form1 - 1 for the page of code for the Form1 form. There's also another frmData - 1 for the first page of properties for that form.

The code pages are, I trust, straightforward. The property pages require a little by way of explanation: Each form starts with a Begin Visual Basic.Form and finishes with an End. Indented one level is a list of the form's properties and a number of further Begin...End blocks. Each of these indented Begin...End blocks corresponds to a control on the form. The Begin is followed by the object type, then by the Name property. Indented yet one more level are the properties for each control.

Now you have the basic foundation to print from your application. I encourage you to practise using Crystal Reports to design reports. It is a very powerful tool that can save you time and simplify your development efforts.

Summary of Skills Acquired

Now you can...

- ☑ use the Print method to send data to the printer
- ☑ display data in the Debug window
- ☑ use the PrintForm method to print a form's image
- ☑ start using Crystal Reports to print data from a database
- ☑ print out your source code

SKILL 9

Using Dialog Boxes

Featuring

- ❏ Using predefined dialog boxes
- ❏ Creating your own dialog boxes
- ❏ Creating a dialogs class
- ❏ Using the dialogs class

Using Predefined Dialog Boxes

Two dialog boxes are often used in Visual Basic projects: the message box and the input box. They are built into Visual Basic, and thus if these built-in ones are adequate, you don't have to design your own forms as dialog boxes. A message box (MsgBox) allows you to provide the end user with simple messages. In contrast, an input box (InputBox) elicits information from the user.

Creating a Message Dialog Box

Here's a partial syntax for a message box statement:

```
MsgBox Prompt, DlgDef, Title
```

Prompt is the text the user sees in the message box. *Title* is the caption in the message box's title bar. The DlgDef parameter is used to set the Dialog

Definition. That is, it defines which icons and buttons you will see on the message box. The following table lists the values and constants you can use to define your dialog box.

CONSTANT	VALUE	STYLE
vbOKOnly	0	Display OK button only
vbOKCancel	1	Display OK and Cancel buttons
vbAbortRetryIgnore	2	Display Abort, Retry, and Ignore buttons
vbYesNoCancel	3	Display Yes, No, and Cancel buttons
vbYesNo	4	Display Yes and No buttons
vbRetryCancel	5	Display Retry and Cancel buttons
vbCritical	16	Display Critical Message icon
vbQuestion	32	Display Warning Query icon
vbExclamation	48	Display Warning Message icon
vbInformation	64	Display Information Message icon

You can add these together to get the desired effect. For example, to see an OK and a Cancel button with an information icon, you would add the appropriate values in either format listed below:

```
DlgDef = vbOKCancel + vbInformation
DlgDef = 1 + 64
```

Then you would pass DlgDef to the MsgBox command.

The message box can also act as a function by returning a value that depends on the button clicked by the user. The syntax is virtually the same as for the message box statement:

```
Dim rc As Integer 'Return Code
rc = MsgBox(prompt, buttons, title)
```

Note the parentheses when it's a function. The possible values returned to rc are listed in the following table.

CONSTANT	VALUE	BUTTON CHOSEN
vbOK	1	OK
vbCancel	2	Cancel
vbAbort	3	Abort
vbRetry	4	Retry
vbIgnore	5	Ignore
vbYes	6	Yes
vbNo	7	No

Creating an Input Dialog Box

As with a message box, an input box can also be shown using a statement or a function. A partial syntax for it as a function is:

```
Dim rc As String
rc = InputBox(prompt, title, default)
```

There is no DlgDef parameter this time, but the additional default parameter lets you specify the default text to display in the entry text box. If the user clicks OK, any entry is returned to the variable (rc in the example). If the user clicks Cancel, a zero-length string is returned. Note that the InputBox function returns a string, while a MsgBox function returns an integer.

To try out the InputBox, try this example:

1. Start a new project by selecting File ➤ New Project.
2. Select **Standard EXE** from the Project Wizard.
3. Add a command button to Form1.
4. In the Properties window, set the Name property of the command button to **cmdTryMe**.
5. Set the Caption property of cmdTryMe to **&Try Me**.
6. Double-click on cmdTryMe to open its Code window.
7. Add the following code to the Click event of cmdTryMe:

```
Private Sub cmdTryMe_Click()
 Dim rc As String

 rc = InputBox("Enter your name below:")
 MsgBox "Hello, " & rc & "!"
End Sub
```

8. Run your project by selecting Run ➤ Start.

9. Click the Try Me button to test the InputBox dialog box.

10. When the InputBox appears, enter your name and click the OK button to see what happens.

This small example shows you briefly how an InputBox dialog box and a MsgBox dialog work. If all goes well, you should be asked to enter your name in the InputBox dialog box. After you do that, Visual Basic should say "Hello, Steve!" (shown below) or whatever name you typed in the dialog box.

Creating Your Own Dialog Boxes

In addition to the MsgBox and InputBox, you may find that you want or need a custom dialog box of your own to include in several of your applications. In my software business, I have dialog boxes that I use to give all of my applications the same look and feel. In the this section I will show you how to create your own dialog box objects that you can reuse in any of your applications.

If you do not remember all of the constants and parameters required to create your own dialog boxes, you can create simple functions, called *wrappers*, and put them in a separate dialogs code module. You can then include this module in your projects so you can call up the dialog boxes without having to remember too many specifics.

A *wrapper* is a function that encompasses one or more function and statement for the purpose of creating a simple and reusable module of code.

You can call the wrapper function with all of the appropriate parameters and it will do most of your work for you. The beauty of a wrapper is that the code only needs to be written once. Afterward, the wrapper can be used over and over without you needing to rewrite its code for every program. Let's look at a quick example:

1. Open the Code window for the previous example.

2. Add the following code in the Code window:

```
Private Sub LoginBox()
 Dim rc As String

 rc = InputBox("Enter your name below:")
 If rc = "ADMINISTRATOR" Then
   MsgBox "Welcome, master!"
 Else
   MsgBox "Hello, " & rc & "!"
 End If
End Sub
```

3. Change the code in the Click event of cmdTryMe:

```
Private Sub cmdTryMe_Click()
 LoginBox
End Sub
```

4. Run the application.

5. When the InputBox dialog appears, type **ADMINISTRATOR** in the field and click the OK button.

Although much the same as the previous example, the dialog box code has been placed in a wrapper called LoginBox. Instead of placing all of the dialog code in the Click event, you just call the LoginBox function and it performs the same tasks.

Notice that you also added another task to the function. It checks to see if the login name is "ADMINISTRATOR". The LoginBox function checks for this name, and when it is entered Visual Basic greets the user appropriately. This is an example of how you can encapsulate all of the functionality necessary to perform a complete task within one logical function. You will learn to take this a step further in the next section, as well as in Skill 13, "Object-Oriented Programming."

In you want to take this a step further, you can combine this module with a class module and create your own dialogs class. However, this doesn't make sense unless you want to add custom dialog boxes that Visual Basic cannot provide. For example, much of the software I write is distributed as shareware. Because Visual Basic cannot provide "nag" and registration code dialog boxes found in many shareware applications, I created a simple ShareLib class that I use in all of my shareware projects. In the next example, you will create a simple dialogs class that you can further modify to suit your needs.

Tip

If you have several tasks that you perform over and over within your programs, you can "wrap" them up in your own function, called a wrapper, and then call the wrapper function from your code. This not only saves you programming and debugging time, but it also saves memory!

Doing Dialog Boxes with Class

We are now going to create a simple dialogs class that you can use in your future projects. If you are confused as to the purpose of some of the properties and techniques, don't worry. We will cover object-oriented programming (OOP) and ActiveX in Skills 13 and 14.

To create a dialogs class, follow these steps:

1. Start a new project by selecting File ➤ New Project.
2. Select ActiveX DLL as the project type, and press OK.
3. Add a code module to your project and set its name property to **modDialogs**.
4. Open the Code window for modDialogs and add the following procedure:

```
Sub Main()
 'No code is required here. However,
 'this sub is required for
 'the DLL to start.
End Sub
```

5. Double-click on Class1 in the Project Explorer to make it active.
6. Set the following properties for the class:

    Name: **clsDialogs**

    Instancing: **5 - MultiUse**

The first dialog box you are going to add is a simple Yes/No dialog box. This type is handy for "Are you sure?" type questions. I use them before I ever call a critical piece of code, such as closing an app with unsaved data or formatting a disk. All you have to do is create a title and a message and pass them to the YNBox function. Then just check to see if the return code is vbYes or 6.

7. Open the Code window for clsDialogs and add the following function:

```
Public Function YNBox(title As String, msg As String) As _ Integer
 Dim rc As Integer
 Dim DlgDef As Long

 DlgDef = vbYesNo + vbQuestion
 rc = MsgBox(msg, DlgDef, title)
 YNBox = rc
End Function
```

The next subroutine we are going to add is an error message dialog box. You can call this from your error-trapping routines so your error messages have a similar look and feel.

8. Create the following sub:

```
Public Sub ErrMsg(title As String, msg As String)
  Dim rc As Integer
  Dim DlgDef As Long

  DlgDef = vbOKCancel + vbCritical
  rc = MsgBox(msg, DlgDef, title)
End Sub
```

To use this subroutine you just pass a title and a message, and the procedure will do the rest of the work for you.

The last function we are going to add is a login dialog box. I am not going to create a complex dialog box with password masking and UserID and password verification. This dialog box's only purpose is to prompt you to enter your UserID. However, at a later time, you can add a login dialog form with text boxes that mask password characters, check for password lengths, and any other rules you may define. Then you can call this form instead of calling the InputBox function.

9. Add the following code:

```
Public Function LoginBox(title As String, msg As String,_
   default As String) As String
  Dim rc As String

  rc = InputBox(msg, title)
  LoginBox = rc
End Function
```

10. Finally, save your project as **dialogs.vbp.**

11. Open the Project Properties dialog box, and type **Dialogs** in the Project Name field. Then, type **A Sample Dialogs Class** in the Project Description field.

12. Select the Make tab and type **Dialogs** in the Application Title field.

13. Now that we have added the code to our dialogs class, we need to compile it so we can use it in our application. Select File ➤ Make Dialogs.Dll. Click the OK button.

After a short pause, you will have a fully compiled DLL that you can use in other programs. You will learn more about the details of using ActiveX DLLs in Skill 14. The next example shows you specifically how to use the dialogs class.

Using the Dialogs Class

In the previous example you created a simple dialogs class that you can reuse in your own applications. Once you work through the following example you will understand how to incorporate ActiveX DLLs in your applications. Then you can go back and tailor the dialogs class to meet your own needs.

Let's start a sample application to test our dialogs class:

1. Start a new project with File ➤ New Project. Select **Standard EXE** from the Project Wizard.

2. Set the following properties for Form1:

    Name: **frmDialogs**
    Caption: **Doing Dialogs With Class**

3. Add two labels to frmDialogs. Set their properties as follows:

    Name: **lblTitle**
    Caption: **Title Text:**
    Name: **lblMsg**
    Caption: **Message:**

4. Add two text boxes. Set their properties as follows:

Name:	**txtTitle**
Text:	**no text**
Name:	**txtMsg**
Text:	**no text**

5. Add three command buttons to your form. Set their properties as follows:

Name:	**cmdYN**
Caption:	**&Yes/No**
Name:	**cmdErr**
Caption:	**&Error**
Name:	**cmdLogin**
Caption:	**&Login**

Your form should now resemble the form displayed in Figure 9.1.

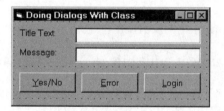

FIGURE 9.1: THE SAMPLE DIALOGS CLASS FORM

6. Next, select Project ➤ References.

7. Add **A Sample Dialogs Class** by checking the box to the left of it, as shown in Figure 9.2; then click OK.

8. Open the Code window and enter the following lines in the (General) (Declarations) sub:

```
Dim dlg As clsDialogs
Option Explicit
```

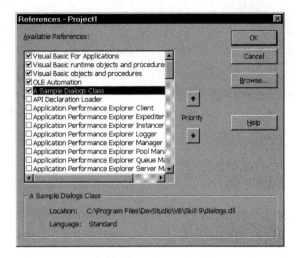

FIGURE 9.2: REFERENCING THE DIALOGS CLASS

9. The first thing you need to do to use the dialogs class is to create an instance of the dialogs object. You can do this by adding the following code to the Form_Load() sub:

```
Private Sub Form_Load()
  Set dlg = New clsDialogs
End Sub
```

10. Whenever you create an instance of an object, you must destroy it when you are done using it. Because you will use the dialogs class throughout the program, you will destroy it when you exit the application. Add the following code to the Form_Unload() sub:

```
Private Sub Form_Unload(Cancel As Integer)
  Set dlg = Nothing
End Sub
```

11. Add the following code to test the Yes/No dialog box (YNBox):

```
Private Sub cmdYN_Click()
 Dim rc As Integer

 rc = dlg.YNBox(txtTitle.Text, txtMsg.Text)
 If rc = vbYes Then
   MsgBox "The user selected Yes"
```

```
      Else
        MsgBox "The user selected No"
      End If
    End Sub
```

12. Add the following code to test the error dialog box (ErrMsg):

```
    Private Sub cmdError_Click()
    dlg.ErrMsg txtTitle.Text, txtMsg.Text
    End Sub
```

13. Add the following code to test the Login dialog box (LoginBox):

```
    Private Sub cmdLogin_Click()
    Dim UserID As String

    UserID = dlg.LoginBox(txtTitle.Text, txtMsg.Text)
    If UserID <> "" Then
      MsgBox UserID & " logged in successfully!"
    End If
    End Sub
```

14. Save and run your project.

If you have no typos or errors in your code, you should be able to type text into the Title Text and the Message fields. To test the YNBox dialog box:

1. Type **Quit?** in the Title Text field.
2. Type **Wanna Quit?** in the Message field.
3. Press the Yes/No button.

You should see a dialog box similar to that shown in Figure 9.3.

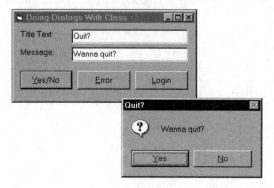

FIGURE 9.3: THE YNBOX DIALOG BOX

We will now use the ErrMsg to display a fake error message. You can call this dialog box from your error-trapping routines in your own applications. To test the ErrMsg dialog box:

1. Type **System Error** in the Title Text field.
2. Type **The Disk Cannot Be Formatted!** in the Message field.
3. Press the Error button.

You should see a dialog box similar to the one presented in Figure 9.4.

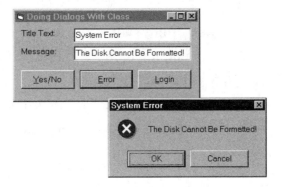

FIGURE 9.4: THE ERRMSG DIALOG BOX

Although the LoginBox dialog box needs some serious improvements to be really useful, the simple test in this example will show you how the InputBox works. To test the LoginBox dialog box:

1. Type **Login** in the Title Text field.
2. Type **Please Enter Your UserID:** in the Message field.
3. Press the Login button.

You should see a dialog box similar to the one shown in Figure 9.5.

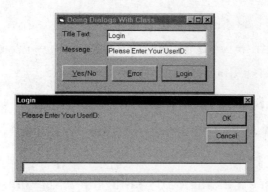

FIGURE 9.5: A SAMPLE LOGIN DIALOG BOX

This is a simple example of how you can use a custom dialogs class in your applications. You can add many more dialog boxes as you develop more standardized applications in the future.

In this example, you not only learned how to use dialog boxes, but you got a brief taste of how to create your own object in Visual Basic. Again, we will cover objects in more detail in Skills 13 and 14.

Summary of Skills Acquired

Now you can...

- ☑ use the message box provided by Visual Basic to convey information to your users
- ☑ use the input box to receive simple information from the user
- ☑ create your own dialog boxes
- ☑ integrate a custom dialogs class into future applications

Working with the Mouse

Featuring

❑ Detecting mouse events

❑ Using drag-and-drop

❑ Creating an Easter egg

Detecting Mouse Events

So far you've met two mouse events, Click and DblClick (double-click). In this skill you'll learn there are many more mouse events that Visual Basic recognizes. These include the use of any button on the mouse, a movement of the mouse, and holding down the Shift, Alt, or Ctrl keys as a mouse button is pressed. The three event procedures you can use to carry out processing based on these actions are MouseDown, MouseUp, and MouseMove. The latter is handy for showing and hiding messages as the mouse passes over buttons on a toolbar.

Different controls have different mouse events. This skill will show you the basic events and how they are used. Then you will create a small drag-and-drop program sample. You will then have a good understanding of which mouse events to specify for your controls.

The *Click* Event

The Click() event is generated when you rapidly click on a control. Almost all controls in Visual Basic that are visible at run time support the Click() event. You will use this event primarily for a command button control. You place code in the button's Click() event, and it is executed when you click the button with the mouse. For example:

```
Private Sub cmdOK_Click()
  Unload Me
End Sub
```

The *DblClick* Event

The DblClick(), or double-click, event is called when you rapidly click a control twice in succession. The sensitivity of the double-click is set in the Mouse item of the Windows Control Panel. This event is useful for list boxes, enabling the user to view properties of an item, or to add or remove an item from the selection. For example:

```
Private Sub lstMembers_DblClick()
  Dim m as clsMember

  Set m = New clsMember
    m.MemberName = lstMembers.Text
    m.ShowMemberProperties
  Set m = Nothing
End Sub
```

Typically, you use this event to provide a quicker alternative to a command button or menu item that does the same thing.

The *DragDrop* Event

The DragDrop() event is generated when you drop an object that was dragged from a form in the application. The DragDrop() event has the following syntax:

```
Private Sub target_DragDrop(Source As Control, X As Single, _
  Y As Single)
```

Notice that this event takes three parameters that you can check before you perform any actions. The Source parameter contains the name of the control that has been dropped on the current control. The parameters X and Y specify the coordinates of the mouse when the DragDrop() event was generated. You can use these to specify the placement of the control on its target. We will look at drag-and-drop functionality in more detail in the next section of this skill.

The *DragOver* Event

The DragOver() event is generated when you drag an object over a control with your mouse. The syntax for this event is:

```
Private Sub target_DragOver(Source As Control, X As Single, _
    Y As Single, State As Integer)
```

Source is the name of the control being dragged over the target. The parameters X and Y are the coordinates of the mouse. State is an integer that represents the state of the control being dragged in relation to a target:

State Parameter	Purpose
0	The control is entering the boundary of the target
1	The control is leaving the boundary of the target
2	The control is being dragged within the target's boundaries

This is a useful event if you want to show users when they can and cannot drop the item on a control. For example, you may not want your user to drop an object on a command button; when the command button's DragOver() event is generated, you can check the Source parameter and change the DragIcon property to a No Drop icon.

The *MouseDown* Event

When you click a mouse button and hold it down, a MouseDown() event is generated. The MouseDown() event syntax is:

```
Private Sub target_MouseDown(Button As Integer, Shift As Integer, _
    X As Single, Y As Single)
```

As with other mouse events, the parameters X and Y are the coordinates of the mouse. The Button parameter is an integer that represents one of three values:

Button Parameter	Description
1	Left Mouse button
2	Right Mouse button
4	Middle Mouse button

You can check this parameter to see which button was pressed. This is handy if you want to use one of the buttons to display a pop-up menu on a control. For example:

```
Private Sub lstMembers_MouseDown(Button As Integer, Shift As Integer, _
    X As Single, Y As Single)
    If Button = 2 then
        PopupMenu mnuMembers
    End If
End Sub
```

The Shift parameter contains an integer that describes which of the Shift, Ctrl, and Alt keys were pressed while the mouse button was held down. The values correspond to:

Shift Parameter	Key Pressed
1	Shift key
2	Ctrl key
4	Alt key

The above values can be added together to indicate key combinations. For example, the integer 6 indicates the Ctrl and Alt keys were pressed simultaneously, while a 7 indicates all three keys were pressed simultaneously.

The *MouseMove* Event

The MouseMove() event is generated when you move the mouse over a control. You can use this event if you want to change the status of the control currently under the mouse. For instance, you can make a command button under the mouse turn green if it is enabled and the mouse is over it. The syntax is as follows:

```
Private Sub target_MouseMove(Button As Integer, Shift As Integer, _
    X As Single, Y As Single)
```

The parameters for this event are identical to those in the MouseDown() event. Here is a MouseMove() example that changes the form's caption if the mouse moves over the Exit button:

```
Private Sub cmdExit_MouseMove(Button As Integer, Shift As Integer, _
     X As Single, Y As Single)
  Me.Caption = "Click me to close the application"
End Sub
```

You can place a similar line of code in other controls' MouseMove() events to provide relevant captions for them. Before tool tips were readily available, I used this event to display status messages in the status bars of my applications.

The *MouseUp* Event

When you release the mouse button on a control, it generates a MouseUp() event. The syntax for this event is:

```
Private Sub target_MouseUp(Button As Integer, Shift As Integer, _
     X As Single, Y As Single)
```

The parameters are the same as those for the MouseDown() and MouseMove() events.

Many Windows applications use this event, rather than the Click() event, to execute functions. For example, you can place the End statement in the MouseUp() event so the user has a chance to abort even after clicking the exit button while the mouse button is still being pressed. Once the Exit button is clicked, the user can abort by moving the mouse away from the button and then releasing the mouse button. Then the End command is completely bypassed.

Using Drag-and-Drop Operations

Increasingly, drag-and-drop operations are used in Windows applications (to adjust the splitter bar in Windows Explorer, for example). They make many operations fast and simple. It's quite straightforward to add drag-and-drop capabilities to a Visual Basic application. Try the following small project to see how it's done:

1. Start a new project. Select Standard EXE for the project type.
2. Set the Name property of Form1 to **frmMain**. Set its Caption property to **Drag-N-Drop**.
3. Add two equally sized list boxes. Place one on the top of the form, and the other on the bottom of the form.
4. Set the Name property of the top list box to **lstA**. Set its DragIcon property to **\Graphics\Icons\DragDrop\Drag1pg.ico**.
5. Set the Name property of the bottom list box to **lstB**. Set its DragIcon property to **\Graphics\Icons\DragDrop\Drag1pg.ico**. Your form should look like that displayed in Figure 10.1.

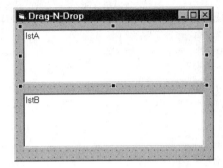

FIGURE 10.1: THE DRAG-AND-DROP APPLICATION

6. Add the following code to the Form_Load() event:

```
Private Sub Form_Load()
 lstA.AddItem "Apples"
 lstA.AddItem "Peaches"
 lstA.AddItem "Oranges"
End Sub
```

7. Now add the following code to the lstA_MouseDown() event:

```
Private Sub lstA_MouseDown(Button As Integer, Shift As Integer, _
    X As Single, Y As Single)
 If lstA.ListCount > 0 Then
   lstA.Drag 1
 End If
End Sub
```

8. Add this code to the lstA_DragDrop() method:

```
Private Sub lstA_DragDrop(Source As Control, X As Single, _
    Y As Single)
 If Source = lstB Then
   lstA.AddItem lstB.Text
   lstB.RemoveItem lstB.ListIndex
 End If
End Sub
```

9. Add this code to the lstB_MouseDown() event:

```
Private Sub lstB_MouseDown(Button As Integer, _
    Shift As Integer, X As Single, Y As Single)
 If lstB.ListCount > 0 Then
   lstB.Drag 1
 End If
End Sub
```

10. And add this code to the lstB_DragDrop() method:

```
Private Sub lstB_DragDrop(Source As Control, X As Single, _
    Y As Single)
  If Source = lstA Then
    lstB.AddItem lstA.Text
    lstA.RemoveItem lstA.ListIndex
  End If
End Sub
```

11. Save and run the project.

The list box on the top of the screen will have apples, peaches, and oranges in it. You can click on any of these items and drag it to the list box on the bottom. When the mouse pointer is over the list box, you can drop the item in it. You can also drag these items back to the top list box (see Figure 10.2).

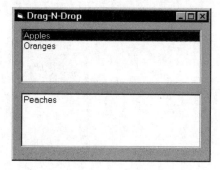

FIGURE 10.2: DRAGGING AND DROPPING FRUIT

The key to this program is the Drag method. Notice that in the MouseDown() event we use the Drag method with the 1 parameter. The 1 tells the control to perform a manual drag. By coding a Drag 0, the object will stop dragging. In other words, if you want to drop a control, you set the Top and Left properties to the x and y coordinates of the mouse pointer, and add a Drag 0 method. This will give the object the appearance of moving, whereas you actually perform the move in the DragDrop() event.

I'll leave you to have fun with this and to work out what's happening. You may want to adapt this approach for your own projects. Notice the

DragMode property for the source control—that is, the one being dragged. If you don't set DragIcon properties, then you see the outline of the control being dragged.

Creating an Easter Egg

For our sample application, we will create a simple Easter egg. If you are not familiar with what this signifies in computer terms, let me explain. Many Windows applications have hidden functions in them that display information or show a picture. The messages usually list the members of the programming team who worked on the program. Sometimes the Easter egg is a nasty animation about a competitor's product. Other times, the Easter egg will display a digitized photograph of the development team.

The reason they are called Easter eggs is because you have to hunt for them. They usually reside in a program's About dialog box and can only be discovered through a specific sequence of mouse clicks and key presses. We will use the About dialog box created by the Form Wizard and add a simple Easter egg to it. With a little clever programming, you can reuse this dialog box with the embedded Easter egg in other applications.

1. Start a new Standard EXE project.
2. Set the Caption property of Form1 to **Easter Egg**.
3. Add a simple menu to Form1. Set its Caption property to **&About**, and its Name property to **mnuAbout**.
4. Right-click the Project Explorer and select Add ➤ Form. When the Form Wizard appears, select About Dialog and click the Open button (see Figure 10.3).
5. Double-click the icon in the upper left corner of the About dialog to open the Code window.
6. Select the picIcon_MouseUp() event in the Code window. Add the following code:

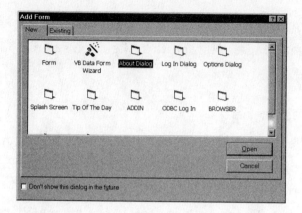

FIGURE 10.3: ADDING A FORM TO ABOUT DIALOG

```
Private Sub picIcon_MouseUp(Button As Integer, _
Shift As Integer, X As Single, Y As Single)
  If Button = 2 And Shift = 6 Then
    MsgBox "You found the Easter egg!"
  End If
End Sub
```

7. Double-click on Form1 in the Project Explorer to open the Code window for Form1.

8. In the mnuAbout_Click() event, add the following code:

```
Private Sub mnuAbout_Click()
  frmAbout.Show vbModal
End Sub
```

9. Save and run the program.

10. Find the Easter egg by...

No, I won't tell you how to get to the Easter egg. If you understand the code in this example, it should be quite obvious. When you actually uncover the egg, you will see something like the Easter egg shown in Figure 10.4. This egg is actually quite boring. If you really want to razzle-dazzle your users, you can create a custom form with graphics and even sound. If you want to learn how to play a .wav file, read Skill 15. It has all the code you will need.

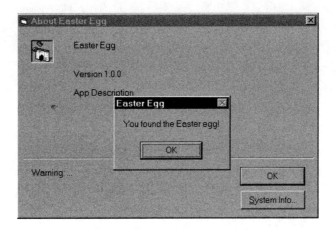

FIGURE 10.4: THE EASTER EGG UNCOVERED

Summary of Skills Acquired

Now you can...

- ☑ programmatically control the mouse
- ☑ add drag-and-drop functionality to your application
- ☑ create an Easter egg for your About dialog box

**SKILL
11**

Creating and
Using Help Files

Featuring

❑ Using help files in your applications

❑ Creating help files

❑ Designing and creating a contents file

❑ Writing topic files

❑ Creating help project files

❑ Linking your applications to your help files

Using Help Files in Your Application

Before you distribute your application, you should create an on-line help system to distribute with it. This is the user's first line of technical support if something about the application is unclear or needs explaining. Your help file should be well designed and should integrate well with your application. A context-sensitive help system allows the user to call up the on-line help from virtually any control on any form and display the help information for that particular control. We will make a simple help file that explains how to create a help file in this skill. You can look at this help file when creating your own help files in the future.

Although there are numerous commercial and shareware applications available to create help files, for this skill you will use the tools that come with Visual Basic.

Note

Contrary to popular belief, help files are not difficult to create. The difficult part is understanding the documentation. As a result, this skill clarifies a lot of the grey areas of help file creation.

To create a help file you will need a word processor that accommodates footnotes and can save .RTF (Rich Text Format) files. Many developers use Word for Windows for this purpose, and that is what we will use for the exercise in this skill. If you do not have Word, you can use another word processor. The methods for creating the files should be easy to understand and adapt to your personal word processor. In addition, you will need a help compiler that generates a .HLP file from a .RTF file (and from bitmaps if you wish). Fortunately, Visual Basic comes complete with its own help compilers. We will use the Help Workshop found on the Visual Basic CD (see Figure 11.1).

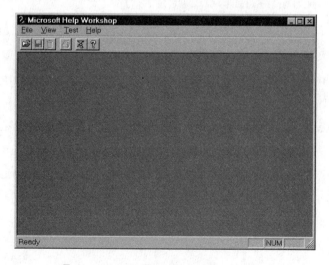

FIGURE 11.1: THE HELP WORKSHOP

> ### Note
>
> *In addition to this skill, see the Help Compiler Guide that is part of the Visual Basic documentation set. This will provide you with additional information on how to set up the .RTF files and how to make .HLP files.*

Creating Your First Help File

To create any help file, you need to create a contents file, a topic file, and a project file. The contents file is an ASCII file that defines the layout and appearance of the Contents tab of the help file. The topic file is where you write the text and add the graphics that make up the actual help document. Finally, the project file links the topic and contents files, as well as other files that may be required to complete the project. It also defines the layout, appearance, and position of the help file when someone runs it. Figure 11.2 shows what a contents file looks like in a compiled help file.

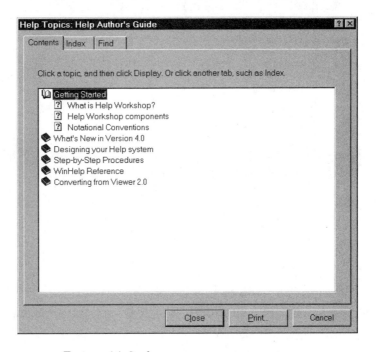

FIGURE 11.2: A SAMPLE HELP CONTENTS FILE

Designing and Creating a Contents File

Although many help manuals say to create the topic file first, I prefer to create a visual outline of the help system with the assistance of the contents file. I find it easier to create the outline on the computer because it allows you to easily make changes and it saves paper. After all, the computer is a tool, so let's use it as such. Fortunately, the Help Compiler Workshop provides a graphical layout of the topics within the project (see Figure 11.3), much like the Menu Editor in the Visual Basic IDE. During development it looks exactly like a normal Contents tab on other help files. It is a great way to lay out your help project.

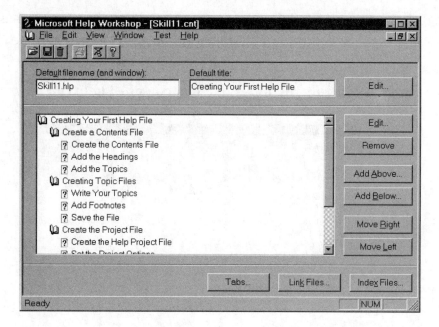

FIGURE 11.3: CREATING A CONTENTS FILE

It is a good idea to write down the topic IDs and titles when you lay out your help contents file. Topic IDs are used by the Help Compiler to provide a numeric "hook" to your application. These will come in handy when you define the footnotes within your topic file. Let's start the help file project by creating the contents file:

1. If you have not already done so, copy the Help Workshop, found in the \Tools subdirectory on the Visual Basic CD, to a directory on your hard disk.

2. Start the Help Workshop.

3. Create a new contents file by selecting **File ➤ New** from the menu. Select **Help Contents** from the dialog box and click OK.

4. The first thing you want to do is define the name of the help file. Type **Skill11.hlp** in the Default Filename field.

5. In the Default Title field, type **Creating Your First Help File**.

6. The first step to creating your outline is to add a heading to the list. Click the Add Above button and select the Heading option. In the Title field, type **Creating Your First Help File**.

7. Click Add Below to add another heading below the first. Select the Heading option and type **Create a Contents File** in the Title field. When you are done, click the OK button.

8. Click the Move Right button to indent this heading. Much like the Menu Editor in Visual Basic, indenting makes the selected item a subitem of the item above it. Now the heading "Create a Contents File" is a subheading of "Creating Your First Help File."

9. Again, click Add Below. This time, select the Topic option. In the Title field type **Create the Contents File**. In the Topic ID field type **IDH_CreateContentsFile**. Leave the Help File and Window Type fields blank.

10. Add the following topics using the topic text and topic IDs:

Topic ID	Topic Text
IDH_AddHeadings	Add the Headings
IDH_AddTopics	Add the Topics

11. Add another heading by clicking the Add Below button. Type **Creating Topic Files** in the Title field and click the OK button.

12. You don't want this heading to be a subheading of the one above it so click the Move Left button and it becomes a subheading of the main heading.

13. Add the following topics under the Creating Topic Files heading:

Topic ID	Topic Text
IDH_WriteTopics	Write Your Topics
IDH_AddFootnotes	Add Footnotes
IDH_SaveRTF	Save the File

14. Add the last subheading. Type **Create the Project File** in the Title field and click the OK button.

15. Outdent the heading by clicking the Move Left button. This will make it a subheading of the main heading.

16. Add the following topics under the Create the Project File heading:

Topic ID	Topic Text
IDH_CreateProjectFile	Create the Help Project File
IDH_SetOptions	Set the Project Options
IDH_SaveRTF	Save the File
IDH_AddFiles	Add Files to the Project
IDH_DefineWindow	Define the Help Window
IDH_Compile	Save and Compile Your Project
IDH_Test	Test Your Help File

17. Save the file as **Skill11.cnt**.

Now that you have created your first contents file, you can start creating your topic file. I hope you wrote down the topic IDs and topic titles. You will need them when you add the footnotes to your topic file. If you didn't write them down, now would be a good time to do so.

Writing a Topic File

After you create the contents file, you can start writing the topic file. This is a Rich Text Format (RTF) document that contains the text, graphics, links, and macros that appear when you actually run the help file. For this example I used Microsoft Word. You can read through and adapt the commands to work with your word processor.

1. The first step is to start your word processor and create a new document.

2. Take the first topic title you entered in the contents file and type it on the first line of the document: **Create the Contents File**.

3. Type the following text on the first page, under the topic title:

   ```
   I believe that you should create the contents file first. I do this
   because the Help Compiler Workshop provides a graphical framework to
   do this. It is much like the Menu Editor in Visual Basic, allowing
   you to create a hierarchical list of headings and topics.

   From the Help Compiler Workshop, select File | New.
   Select Help Contents and click the OK button.
   ```

4. Before you can access this topic, you need to add a footnote. This footnote needs to be at the beginning of the topic. Place the cursor *before* the topic Create the Contents File.

5. Select Insert ➤ Footnote from the menu bar. In the numbering frame, select Custom Mark and enter the # sign.

6. When the word processor takes you to enter the footnote text, type **IDH_CreateContentsFile**. This is the topic ID for this topic.

7. Next, add a topic title. This is the text that appears when you search through the help file. Position the cursor between the # sign and the title at the top of the topic.

8. Insert another footnote by selecting Insert ➤ Footnote. Again, select Custom Mark. Enter a dollar sign ($) as the custom mark.

9. When the word processor takes you to enter the footnote text, type **Create the Contents File**. This is the topic title for this topic.

10. Finally, add the browse sequence footnote. Place the cursor in between the dollar sign and the title text. Insert another footnote (Insert ➤ Footnote). Select Custom Mark and enter a plus (+) sign in the field.

11. Enter **auto** as the footnote text. This will cause Windows Help to create an auto-browsing sequence throughout the help file.

12. If you have not already done so, you can enhance the title text at the top of the topic by raising the font size and adding a bold style to it. When you are done, your topic file should look similar to Figure 11.4.

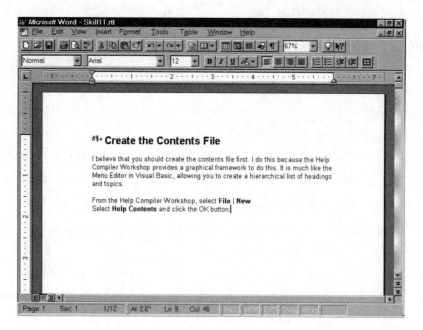

FIGURE 11.4: THE FIRST TOPIC TEXT

Before continuing, let's take a look at what you did for this topic. The first thing you did was to add a title. This lets the user know what they are supposed to be reading about. In this case the user is learning about creating the contents file. After you entered the title, you typed the body of the topic. Although you don't do it in this help file, you can add graphics and jumps to other topics. If you want to learn more about this, look at the on-line help for the Help Compiler Workshop. It gives you more information than you could ask for.

Finally you added the footnotes. These are required for the help file to work properly when it is compiled. You used three footnotes, however, there are more that you can use. The first was the topic ID footnote. After that you added the topic title footnote. Finally you added the browse sequence footnote. If you think that you will have a difficult time remembering these footnote characters, remember that the topic ID comes first, and it is a # sign. Most IDs that we think of are numbers. Even though the topic IDs in your help file are not numeric, remember that IDs are usually numeric. You used the dollar sign ($) for the topic title footnote. Obviously the topic title is, in programming terms, a string. You can use the dollar sign to represent strings in Visual Basic. Finally you added the plus sign (+) as the footnote for the browse sequence. Just remember that since many programs use the plus and minus keys to navigate through numbers, you can use the plus symbol to navigate through the help file.

Here is a summary of how to add the appropriate footnotes to your help topics:

- Footnotes belong at the beginning of the topic, before any text.
- Add the topic ID footnote (#) first. Then type in the topic ID. This is required.
- Add the topic title footnote ($) next. Then type in the topic text. This is optional but recommended.

- Add the browse sequence footnote (+). Then you can enter a browse number or simply the word *auto* to let the help compiler worry about it.

Be sure to save your work between topics. Now that you know the basics of creating a topic with footnotes, let's finish the topic file:

1. Add a hard page break by pressing the Enter key while holding down the Ctrl key at the bottom of the topic text. Before you can add another topic, you need to add a hard page break below the current topic. This causes the word processor to keep topics on their own pages.

2. Type the following text as the next topic:

   Add the Headings

   ```
   You add the headings by clicking the Add Above and Add Below
   buttons. When the Edit Contents Tab Entry dialog appears, select the
   Heading radio button. Then enter the description of the heading.

   You can use headings to categorize the topics within the help file.
   For instance, this help file will have three headings, one for each
   step in building the help file. Under each of these headings we will
   add the topics describing the operations that complete each step.
   ```

3. Create the following footnotes:

   ```
   #    IDH_AddHeadings
   $    Add the Headings
   +    auto
   ```

4. Type the next topic:

   Add the Topics

   ```
   You create a topic for each subject you wish to discuss in the help
   file. This page you are typing is a topic within the help file.

   To add a topic, click either the Add Below or Add Above buttons and
   select the Topic radio button on the Edit Contents Tab Entry dialog.

   For each topic, you need at least a Topic ID. The Help Compiler
   Workshop prefers to have Topic IDs prefixed with IDH_. Notice that
   ```

this is what we have been doing. This prefix makes it easier to compile the topic file.

In addition, you should give the topic a title. Enter this in the Title field. Don't worry about the other fields for this exercise. They are used when you execute help macros or utilize multiple help files within one contents file.

5. Add these footnotes:

```
#    IDH_AddTopics
$    Add the Topics
+    auto
```

6. Type the next topic:

Write Your Topics

The next step to creating your help file is to write your help topics. You need a word processor that can save in Rich Text Format (RTF) to do this.

Start by creating a new document.
Write each topic on its own page. If you are writing multiple topic files, separate each with a hard page break. In Word you do this by pressing Ctrl-Enter.

When you are done you can add the footnotes that link the topics together.

7. Add these footnotes:

```
#    IDH_WriteTopics
$    Write Your Topics
+    auto
```

8. Type the next topic:

Add the Footnotes

After the topics have been created, you need to add the footnotes to each page. The only required footnote is the Topic ID. You define the Topic ID by inserting a footnote, and using the **#** sign as the footnote character.

Add the Topic ID footnote:

Go to the top of the topic page and click the mouse. The footnotes must be entered at the beginning of the topic. In Word, select Insert > Footnote. Set the Custom Mark field to the **#** sign. When you go to write the footnote text, type the Topic ID. This should be prefixed with the string "IDH_". This helps the help compiler process the file.

9. Add these footnotes:

```
#IDH_AddFootnotes
$Add the Footnotes
+auto
```

10. Add the next topic:

Save the File

When you are done authoring your topics and defining the footnotes, you need to save the file as an RTF file. Then you can go back to the Help Compiler Workshop and start the project file.

11. Add the footnotes:

```
#IDH_SaveRTF
$Save the File
+auto
```

12. Add the next topic:

Create The Project File

The final element of the help file is the project file. This defines the characteristics of the help file, links to your topic file and contents file, and everything else that is needed to build the help file.

From the Help Compiler Workshop, select File | New.
Select Help Contents and click the OK button.

Type the name of the help file in the Help File field. For this example I used Skill11.Hlp.

13. Add the footnotes:

```
#    IDH_CreateProjectFile
$    Create the Project File
+    auto
```

14. Add the next topic:

Set Help File Options

Click the options button to set the project options.

General Tab
Set the Help Title to a description of the help file.

Compression Tab
Select **Custom** and **Hall Compression**. Selecting these allows your help file to perform keyword searches.

Files
Select the RTF topic file that you created. Set the contents file field to the name of the contents file you created for this project.

15. Add the footnotes:

```
#    IDH_SetOptions
$    Set Help File Options
+    auto
```

16. Add the next topic:

Add Files to the Project

Once you have set the project options, you add the topic file, and graphics, and the contents file to the project.

17. Add the footnotes:

```
#    IDH_AddFiles
$    Add Files to the Project
+    auto
```

18. Add the next topic:

Define the Help Window Appearance

To allow your help window to have navigation buttons, you need to define a custom window style.

Click the Window button. In the Window Properties dialog, click the Add button. Enter a name for the window style and base it on a standard procedure window.

Next, click the Buttons tab and check the Browse check box. This will allow the help window to display the browse buttons.

Finally, click the OK button to close the dialog.

19. Add the footnotes:

```
#    IDH_DefineWindow
$    Define the Help Window Appearance
+    auto
```

20. Add the next topic:

Save and Compile Your Help File

Before you do anything else, you need to save your project and contents files. You can do this by clicking the Save and Test button on the bottom of the project dialog.

The Help Compiler will process your topic, contents, and project files. Once they are processed, the results will be displayed in the window. If you have no errors, you can test the help file.

21. Add the footnotes:

```
#    IDH_Compile
$    Save and Compile Your Help File
+    auto
```

22. Finally, add the last topic to your help file:

Test Your Help File

This is the last and most important step. Test your help file to make sure you can successfully navigate between topics. Check for typos and layout problems. Basically, test it as you would your application.

When everything works, you can link the help file to your application!

23. Add the footnotes:

```
#IDH_Test
$Test Your Help File
+auto
```

You have just created your first topic file. Remember that this is a very basic topic file, but it shows you what you need to do. If you typed in every topic and footnote section, then this process should be stuck in your memory for quite a long time. After all, the best way to learn is to practise. Let's move on to the final stage of help file development: the project file.

Creating a Help Project File

Before you can link your contents and topic files together, you need to create a help project file:

1. If it is not already open, open the Help Compiler Workshop.
2. Create a new project file by selecting **File ➤ New** from the menu. Select Help Project and click OK.
3. When the Help Compiler asks you for a project name, type **Skill11** as the project name and click the Save button. You should see something like Figure 11.5.

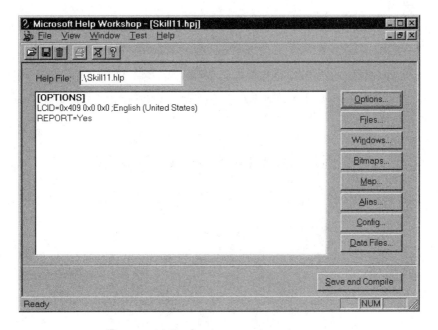

FIGURE 11.5: A NEW HELP PROJECT FILE

4. Click the Options button to open the Options dialog box (see Figure 11.6).
5. When the Options dialog box appears, type **Creating Your First Help File** in the Help Title field.
6. Click the Compression tab. Select the Custom option and check the box next to Hall Compression.

7. Select the Files tab. In the Help File field, type **Skill11.hlp**.

8. Click the Change button next to the RTF Files field.

9. When the Topic Files dialog box appears, click the Add button. Select Skill11.rtf. This adds your topic file to the help project. Click the Open button.

10. If Skill11.rtf is listed in the Topic Files list, click the OK button to close the Topic Files dialog box.

11. Click the Browse button next to the Contents field. Select Skill11.cnt from the dialog box. This binds the contents file you created to the project file.

12. Click the OK button to close the Options dialog box.

You will notice there are several tabs in the Options dialog box (see Figure 11.6) that have not been selected. You can learn more about the options on the tabs from the on-line help for the Help Compiler Workshop.

FIGURE 11.6: THE OPTIONS DIALOG BOX

13. Click the Windows button to bring up the Window Properties dialog box (see Figure 11.7).

14. On the Window Properties dialog box, click the Add button to create a new window style.

15. In the Add New Window Type dialog box, type **Main** in the Create a Window Named field. Set the Based on this Standard Window field to **Procedure**. Click the OK button when the options are set.

FIGURE 11.7: HELP WINDOW PROPERTIES DIALOG BOX

16. Click the Buttons tab and check the **Browse** option. This adds the browse buttons to the help window. Leave the other options as they are.

    Click the OK button to close the Window Properties dialog box. Your help project should look similar to Figure 11.8.

17. Click the Map button. From this dialog box we will make your help context-sensitive.

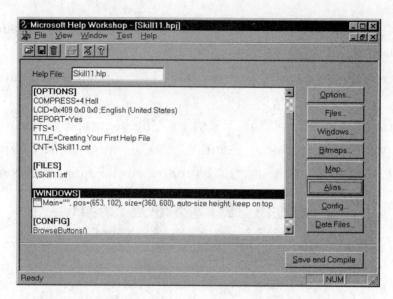

FIGURE 11.8: YOUR HELP PROJECT FILE

18. For each of the topics below, click the Add button and enter the appropriate topic ID in the Topic ID field and the context ID in the Mapped Numeric Value field:

Topic ID	Context ID
IDH_CreateContentsFile	100
IDH_AddHeadings	200
IDH_AddTopics	300
IDH_WriteTopics	400
IDH_AddFootnotes	500
IDH_SaveRTF	600
IDH_CreateProjectFile	700
IDH_SetOptions	800
IDH_AddFiles	900
IDH_DefineWindow	1000
IDH_Compile	1100
IDH_Test	1200

19. Click the Save and Compile button. The Workshop will minimize while it compiles. If all goes well, the Workshop will restore itself and display the compiler results (see Figure 11.9).

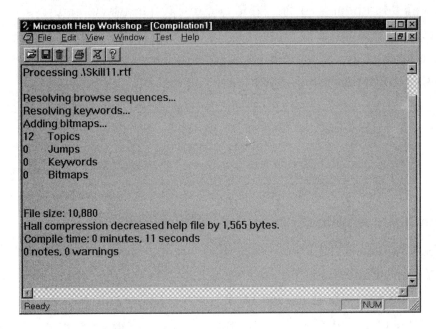

FIGURE 11.9: THE COMPILER RESULTS FOR YOUR PROJECT FILE

After making your complete help file, you'll want to test it right away to make sure it works. To do this, follow these steps:

1. To test the help file, click the Help button (the yellow question mark) on the toolbar.

2. When the View Help File dialog box appears, it should already be defaulted to Skill11.hlp. If it's not, click the browse button and select Skill11.hlp. When this file is selected, click the View Help button.

3. When you see the Contents tab of your help file, expand the headings to see how your help file looks. Click the topics to view them.

That's all there is to creating a simple help file. You now have a summarised version of this skill in help file format. You can open this file whenever you want to create a help file in the future. If you are adventurous, you can add updates to the topic file to explain other features of the help system, like jumps and graphics. If I were to explain all of the features and procedures to create a sophisticated help file, I would need to write another book on only that topic. So, I leave the rest up to you.

Tip

Be sure to check out the on-line help of the Help Compiler Workshop. It includes step-by-step instructions on implementing the other Windows help features.

Linking Your Application to Your Help File

Once you have a .HLP help file, there are a number of ways it can be used with your application. You can set a help file for the whole application, you can set up help files for each form, or you can set up context-sensitive help for forms and controls. To implement context-sensitive help, you must map Context IDs to the Topic IDs in your help project file.

You can set the help file for the whole application by opening the Project Properties dialog box and typing the name of the help file in the Help File field, or you can set the HelpFile property of the App (application) object at run time.

To access the help file from your code, you can use the Windows API or the Common Dialog control. We will use the latter for this example. If you want to learn how to use the Windows API functions for help, read Skill 15 to get familiar with accessing the API, and read the on-line documentation to learn the parameters and commands you must use. Aside from that, let's hook your help file to a sample application:

1. Start a new project in Visual Basic. Select Standard EXE as the project type.
2. Change the Name property of Form1 to **frmMain**. Set its Caption property to **My First Help Application**.
3. Right-click on Project1 in the Project Explorer and select **Project1 Properties**.
4. From the Project Properties dialog box, set the Help File field to the help file you created in the previous exercise, then click the OK button.
5. Add a menu to the form. Define its menus and menu items as follows:

File Menu	
Caption:	**&File**
Name:	**mnuFile**
File Menu Items	
Caption:	**E&xit**
Name:	**mnuFileExit**
Help Menu	
Caption:	**&Help**
Name:	**mnuHelp**
Help Menu Items	
Caption:	**&Contents Files**
Name:	**mnuHelpContentsFile**
Caption:	**&Topic Files**
Name	**mnuHelpTopicFiles**
Caption:	**&Project Files**
Name:	**mnuHelpProject**

6. When the menus are defined, click the OK button to close the Menu Editor.

7. Add a Common Dialog control to your project. Set its Name property to **dlgHelp**. This is what you will use to call up your help file.

8. Open the Code window and add an **End** statement to the mnuFileExit_Click() procedure.

9. In the Form_Load() event, add the following line of code:

    ```
    dlgHelp.HelpFile = App.HelpFile
    ```

10. Add the following code to the mnuHelpContentsFile_Click() event:

    ```
    Private Sub mnuHelpContentsFile_Click()
      dlgHelp.HelpContext = "100"
      dlgHelp.HelpCommand = cdlHelpContext
      dlgHelp.ShowHelp
    End Sub
    ```

11. Add the following code to the mnuHelpTopicFiles_Click() event:

    ```
    Private Sub mnuHelpTopicFiles_Click()
      dlgHelp.HelpContext = "400"
      dlgHelp.HelpCommand = cdlHelpContext
      dlgHelp.ShowHelp
    End Sub
    ```

12. Add the following code to the mnuHelpProject_Click() event:

    ```
    Private Sub mnuHelpProject_Click()
      dlgHelp.HelpContext = "700"
      dlgHelp.HelpCommand = cdlHelpContext
      dlgHelp.ShowHelp
    End Sub
    ```

13. Save the project and run it.

When you click on the menu items, it will bring up the appropriate help topic from your help file. This is done because you mapped the topic IDs to context IDs. You told the Common Dialog which context to show by setting the HelpContext property to the corresponding context ID within the help file.

If you want to have context-sensitive help that is called up when you press the F1 key, you set the HelpContextID property in the Properties window or by code in run mode. Let's show you this in action:

1. Add a text box to frmMain. Set its Name property to **txtHelp**. Clear its Text property, and set its HelpContextID property to **1200**.
2. Save and run the program.
3. Click the mouse in the text box to make it the active control. Press the F1 button.

Visual Basic may give you an error message saying "The window name 'LangRef' was not defined in your project file." If you get this message, click the OK button to clear it. This error will go away when you further modify the help project file. If all goes well, you should see the topic Test Your Help File (see Figure 11.10).

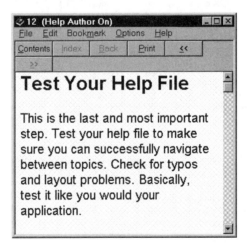

FIGURE 11.10: YOUR HELP FILE

Documentation for an application is just as important as the application itself. Fortunately, Windows provides an on-line help system that allows you to display your own help files from your application. The trick is writing the help file in the first place. Now you have enough information to start creating help systems for your applications.

Summary of Skills Acquired

Now you can...

- ☑ create help contents files
- ☑ create help topic files
- ☑ create help project files
- ☑ compile your contents, topic, and project files into a help file
- ☑ call a help file from your application

SKILL
12

Compiling and Distributing Your Application

Featuring

☐ Compiling your project
☐ Using the Make tab
☐ Setting the Compiler options
☐ Using the Setup Wizard
☐ Notes on distributing your program

Compiling Your Project

It's a great feeling when you finish your application. You may have spent hundreds of hours designing, coding, testing, and debugging. Everything appears to be in working order. The first step is to save your work! You should save your work as you go, but make sure you save this latest build. Your next step is to compile your project into an executable (EXE), dynamic link library (DLL), or ActiveX control (OCX) This will allow you or others to use your software without having to buy and Install Visual Basic for themselves. For this skill, you will learn how to compile your project by working with the VB Terminal sample application.

When your program is compiled, you'll need to create a setup program to distribute your application and associated files. Fortunately, Visual Basic comes with the Setup Wizard. This handy utility allows you to build a fully functional setup program by answering a few simple questions. There are also other professional as well as shareware utilities that allow you to build good setup programs, but for this example we will assume the Setup Wizard is all you have.

Let's assume that you just finished your application and you want to compile it and start testing. Open the VB Terminal project. It is saved as Vbterm.vbp and can be found in the \Samples\CompTool\MSComm subdirectory. Then follow these steps:

1. If you haven't already done so, load the \Samples\CompTool\MSComm\Vbterm.vbp project.
2. Select File ➤ Make vbterm.exe… from the Visual Basic menu.
3. When the Make Project dialog box appears, the File Name field should say vbterm.exe. Click the Options… button.

You will see a slim version of the Project Properties dialog box. It contains a Make tab and a Compile tab; each is discussed in the following sections.

Using the Make Tab

You can go to the Make tab to change various options that will affect how your program is built. You can change such options as version numbers, copyright information, and many others. The Make tab is broken down into four sections: Version Number, Application, Version Information, and finally, you have two text boxes labelled Command Line Arguments and Conditional Compilation (see Figure 12.1). The VBTerm dialog box also includes a Compile tab, which provides you with options to compile your application to P-Code or Native Code.

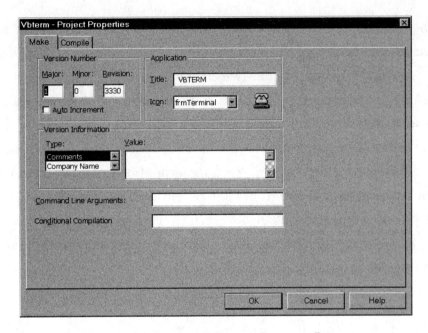

FIGURE 12.1: THE MAKE TAB OF THE VBTERM - PROJECT PROPERTIES DIALOG BOX

Version Number

The Version Number frame contains three fields and one check box. In this section you can set the version number of your application. A version number consists of a major version, minor version, and a revision number, otherwise known as a *build number*. When you set the version number for your application, you will usually start at version 1.0.0. This indicates the very first build of the first version. Notice that the Revision field in Figure 12.1 says 3330. I doubt this sample application has had that many separate builds, but that is what it says. By checking the Auto Increment check box at the bottom of the frame, you can have Visual Basic automatically increment the revision number of your application every time you compile it.

Version and revision numbers are important to include in your project. They enable you and your users to distinguish executables between builds. You can view these numbers and other program properties by right-clicking on the executable in Windows Explorer, selecting Properties from the pop-up menu, and selecting the Version tab in the Properties dialog box. Revision numbers are especially useful when users call for technical support. If you have distributed several different builds to your users and each has its own set of bugs, you can check their revision number to determine if they have the latest bug-free build.

In addition to checking the Auto Increment box, I recommend you write down a description of program changes for each build. You might even be well served to put these change descriptions in a database and sort them by version and revision numbers. This will help you later on when you need to support your product.

Tip

Document the changes your program goes through between builds. You can refer back to this information when you are dealing with trouble calls, or when you want to implement new features.

Application

The Application frame contains two fields: Title and Icon. The Title field contains the name of the application. This will be the same as the name with which you saved the project. The Icon field is a list box that allows you to select a form from the project that has the icon you want to use to represent your application. You can set the application icon in the startup form which by now you know I name frmMain. Then you set the Icon field to frmMain. When you choose a form containing the desired icon, the icon will be displayed to the right of this field.

Version Information

The Version Information section contains a Type list box and a Value text box. This is a very handy section because from here you can embed all of the legal notices and company information for your program. You can select from a number of options in the Type list and then you can type the text in the Value field. The Type list contains values for comments, company name, file description, legal copyright, legal trademarks, and the product name.

By selecting Comments from the Type list, you can enter any comments about the current version. Maybe you would include a notice that the program is a beta version. You could place any other information here not covered in the other sections. If you want to indicate the company that your application belongs to you can select Company Name in the Type list and type it in the Value field. Select File Description to enter any information specific to the compiled file.

Copyrighting Your Application

The Legal Copyright value is probably one of the most important properties of your compiled application. Let me first brief you on copyrights: When you create a work (in other words, a program, artwork, etc.) you have an automatic copyright to it. You can relinquish this copyright by explicitly stating that the work, in this case the application, is in the public domain. It is beyond the scope of this book to discuss this much further, but if you are planning to sell your programs, you will want to pick up a book on copyrights and trademarks. It will serve you well to include a copyright notice in this property so users will know who owns the title to the product. For the copyright notice to be legal, you need to indicate the application name, the word "Copyright" (spelled out), and the year of first release. If you want to reserve copyright privileges overseas, you should also include the words "All Rights Reserved." For example, you could enter something like:

MyApp Version 1.0.5 Copyright 1996 - Steve Brown
All Rights Reserved

Again, don't just take my word for it, pick up some good literature on the copyright process or even consult a lawyer.

Tip

Be sure to include a copyright notice in your application. This will allow your users to know who owns the legal title to the application.

If your program contains any trademarks, for example a company logo, or any artwork that is known to represent you, your company, or your product, you should include these notices in the Legal Trademarks property.

Type the full name of your application in the Product Name property. For example, "VBTerm" is not very descriptive, so you could type in **Visual Basic Terminal** in the Value field. This is also a good way to distinguish between two applications of the same name. Maybe you have two applications named Hello.exe. The first one is the Hello World application that you created at the beginning of the book. The second application is a greeting program that plays an automated message when you boot up your computer. It is just called Hello. You can see the importance of spelling out the complete name of an application in this property.

When you re-compile your application you do not need to continuously type text in these fields. Visual Basic will remember them and use them for each compile. You only need to change the information in these fields when it is necessary to reflect it in the program's executable file.

Command Line Arguments

You can enter values in this field to trigger your application to perform special functions. As an example, some programs allow you to specify a file name after the program name, and the program will automatically load the file you specified. Entering a value in this field simulates typing a program name and file name in the Run dialog box from the Start menu. For example:

```
MyApp.Exe  C:\Files\MyDoc.Doc
```

You can intercept any parameters passed to your applications through the reserved variable Command$. Anything typed after the program name will be passed to your application through this variable. You can then parse the information using functions such as InStr() and Mid$(). For example:

```
Private Sub Form_Load()
  If Command$ <> "" Then
    If InStr(Command$,"/?") > 0 Then
      ShowHelp
    End If
  End If
End Sub
```

The variable Command$ is an intrinsic part of Visual Basic. It can only be used to retrieve the values passed to an application before it starts. You can check for these parameters by checking the value of Command$ in the Load event of the startup form.

The example above first checks to see if any parameters were passed to the program. If there weren't any, then the If..Then command is bypassed and the program continues normally. If there is a parameter passed to the application, then the code checks to see what parameter was passed.

This sample only checks for the parameter /?, which you may be familiar with if you have ever tried to view on-line help for some DOS commands. You can check for any parameter you like.

The Instr() function checks for the presence of a value in a string. If it finds the value, the Instr() returns the first position in the string for which the string your searching for occurs. So if you passed the parameter /? To this application, then Instr() would return a value greater than zero. From the code above, you can see that if this return code is greater than zero, then the If...Then condition is satisfied, and the program calls the ShowHelp procedure.

The Command Line Arguments option allows you to enter a parameter in the field, which will then be passed to your application when you run it. This allows you to test your code without performing a complete build on your application.

Conditional Compilation

You can enter constant declarations in this field for conditional compilation. For example, if you check for WINDOWS_NT in your conditional compilation, you can enter WINDOWS_NT in this field.

Compiler Settings

The Compile tab contains the options available to you to compile your application (see Figure 12.2). You can compile your application using either P-Code or native code, otherwise known as machine code or machine language.

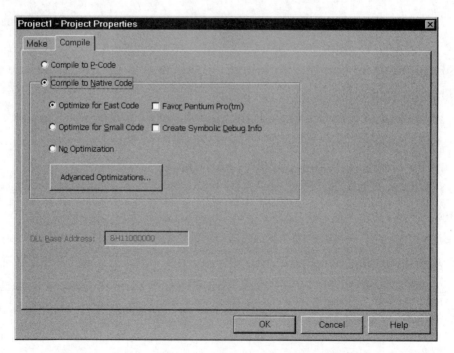

FIGURE 12.2: THE COMPILE TAB OF THE PROJECT PROPERTIES DIALOG BOX

Compile to P-Code

When you select this option, Visual Basic will compile your application into an interpreted language. This is what the previous versions of Visual Basic have always done. Programs compiled in P-Code require a run-time interpreter to run, for example VBRUN300.DLL or VBRUN500.DLL. P-Code allows your program's executable file to be smaller, but it must be shipped with the interpreter DLLs and any other components. In addition, the program runs slower because it is interpreted to machine code as it is run. For example, if you run a P-Code application, then the runtime module VBRUN500.DLL will look at the first line P-Code. If it recognizes the code, it then compiles it to machine code on the fly, and then runs it. Any resulting values will then be converted back to P-Code for the next command to be executed. This means each line of code goes through a couple of conversions before it is even run. Then it is converted back. Native code just runs the code without any conversion.

This does not mean that P-Code is not the best option. It works well for interfaces and other applications that are not processor intensive. Database programs that depend on database engines to do most of the processing work well when compiled to P-Code. Simple utilities, such as data conversion utilities, will work well when compiled to P-Code. In addition, compiling to P-Code requires less compile time. So if you are in a hurry to try out your application, and speed is not a major concern, you can compile to P-Code.

Compile to Native Code

Selecting this option will make Visual Basic compile your program to machine code. This is probably one of the biggest and most anticipated enhancements to Visual Basic. Now you can compile your application to run without the requirement and overhead of other DLLs. If you select this option to compile your application, you can select from further compiler options.

Optimize for Fast Code

If you select **Optimize for Fast Code**, Visual Basic will attempt to maximize the speed of your application by trading off program size for speed. The result is a possibly bigger executable program size, but the code should run faster on the computer.

Optimize for Small Code

Selecting this option will make Visual Basic trade off program execution speed for program size. Select this option if program size is a primary concern. If disk space is more of a concern than execution speed, this option will create a smaller executable file, but it could possibly run a little bit slower.

Favor Pentium Pro™

Selecting this option will make Visual Basic generate code for your program that utilizes the advanced features of the Pentium Pro™ processor. Don't select this option if your program is not specifically designed for the Pentium Pro™. Your program can still run, but it will be slower overall.

Create Symbolic Debug Info

This option will generate symbolic debug information about your program. If you use this option, your program can be debugged using Visual C++ or other debuggers that use the CodeView style of debugging. Visual Basic will create a .PDB file that can be used by CodeView compliant debuggers.

No Optimization

This option will make Visual Basic compile your program with no optimisations whatsoever. If you select this option, your compile time will be slightly shorter.

Advanced Optimizations

Clicking this button will display the Advanced Optimizations dialog box (see Figure 12.3). Do not enable any of these options without checking the Visual Basic on-line help first.

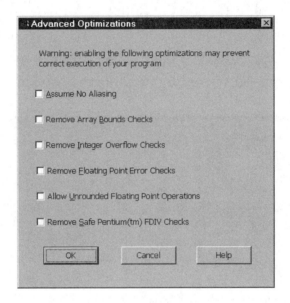

FIGURE 12.3: THE ADVANCED OPTIMIZATIONS TAB

Now that you know all of the compiler options available to you, you can tailor your program's executable to suit any preference you may require. For most of your applications you will only need to set the options on the Make tab. You probably won't need to set anything on the Compile tab until it comes time to test and debug your application. After you have set all of the preferences for your application, you can click the OK button and finally build it. Now let's take a look at distributing your application with the Setup Wizard.

Using the Setup Wizard

The Setup Wizard is a setup utility that comes with Visual Basic. It allows you to quickly and easily create set up programs to help distribute and install your application. When you use the Setup Wizard you have your choice of creating a standard installation to floppy or hard disk or an Internet download setup. When you start the Setup Wizard it will present you with an introduction dialog box (see Figure 12.4). You can navigate forward and backward through the Wizard by pressing the Next and Back buttons.

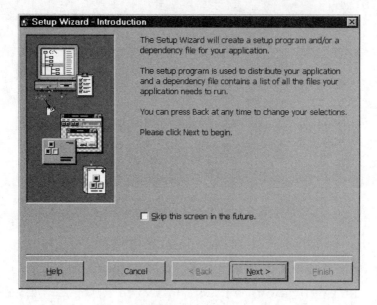

FIGURE 12.4: THE SETUP WIZARD INTRODUCTION DIALOG BOX

For this example, you will compile and create a setup program for the VB Terminal application:

1. Close Visual Basic if it is open, and start the Setup Wizard.
2. If you do not want to see the dialog box shown in Figure 12.4, check the Skip This Screen in the Future box.
3. Click the Next button to move on.

4. The next step in the Wizard will prompt you for a project file or a Setup Wizard template file (see Figure 12.5). Click the Browse button and select the VBTerm.vbp project from the first section. It is in the \Samples\CompTool\MSComm subdirectory of Visual Basic.

5. Leave the check in the Rebuild the Project box. The Setup Wizard will start Visual Basic in compile mode and compile your project. The resulting executable file will be included in your setup program.

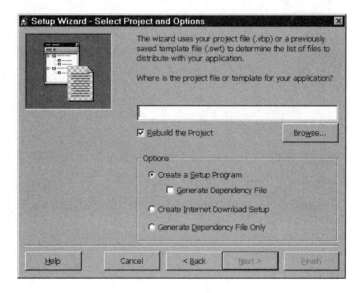

FIGURE 12.5 SELECTING A PROJECT

Note

If you wanted to, you could select the Create Internet Download Setup option to create an Internet-ready distributable. This is useful for distributing ActiveX controls. See Skill 14 for more information on ActiveX.

---

6. For this example, select the Create a Setup Program option.

7. Click the Next button. The Setup Wizard will compile the application. After a brief delay, you will arrive at the Distribution Method dialog box (see Figure 12.6).

8. We do not want to use floppies for this example, so select the Disk Directories option. The Setup Wizard will create disk images on your hard disk.

9. Click the Next button to move to the next step.

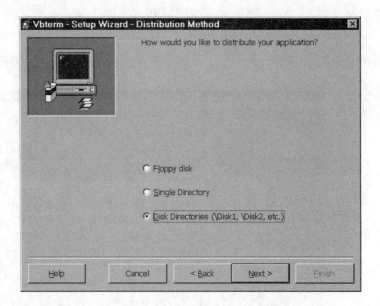

FIGURE 12.6: CHOOSING A DISTRIBUTION METHOD

10. Set the Destination to the drive and directory that you want to create your images in. I created the images in the \SWSetup subdirectory of my \Windows\Temp directory (see Figure 12.7).

11. Set the Disk Size to the appropriate size. For this example, choose 1.44MB. When you are satisfied with your settings, click the Next button.

If your application uses any ActiveX controls, they will be listed in the ActiveX Components dialog box (see Figure 12.8). From this dialog box, you can specify ActiveX components to add to or remove from your project. VB Terminal does not use any ActiveX components, so none are listed.

12. Click the Next button.

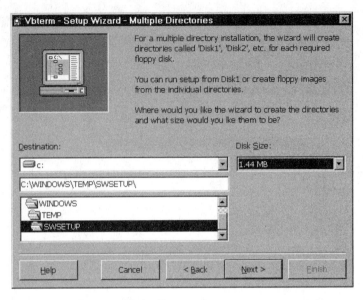

FIGURE 12.7: SELECTING DIRECTORIES

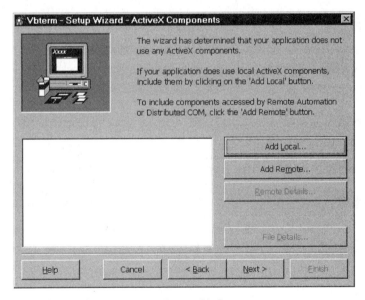

FIGURE 12.8: ACTIVEX COMPONENTS

The next dialog box allows you to confirm additional file dependencies for your application (see Figure 12.9). VB Terminal uses the ComDlg32, MSComm32, and ComCtl components.

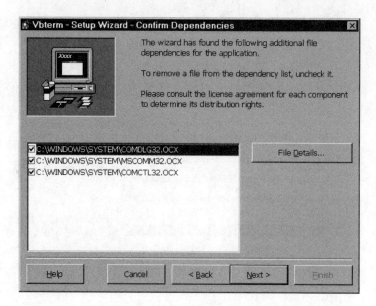

FIGURE 12.9: THE CONFIRM DEPENDENCIES DIALOG BOX

13. Make sure there is a check next to each OCX listed in the window. This will ensure that these controls are compressed and added to your setup. If you want to see more information on each file, click the File Details... button.

14. When you are ready to continue, click the Next button.

15. In the File Summary dialog box , make sure there is a check next to each file listed in the list box (see Figure 12.10).

When preparing the setup program for your own application, you may need to add or remove files from this dialog box. You can remove files by clearing the check box next to file you wish to remove. To add a file, press the Add button. The dialog box is self-explanatory.

16. We do not need to add or remove any files for VB Terminal. Click the Next button to continue.

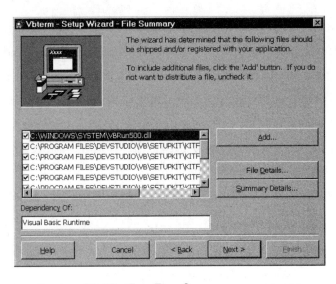

FIGURE 12.10: THE FILE SUMMARY DIALOG BOX

Saving a Template

You have set up all of the options that the Setup Wizard needs to create your setup program. As shown in Figure 12.11, you can save a template of this installation.

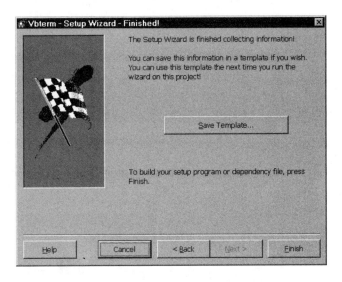

FIGURE 12.11: SETUP WIZARD IS READY TO GO

It is important to save a template of your setup program, especially for larger applications. Hopefully you won't have to come back and redo your setup program, but there may be instances when you will need to change something, perhaps because a file was not included in your setup, which is required on some machines. You can later come back to the Setup Wizard and instead of having to answer all of the Wizard's questions, you can simply open the template you saved previously, and then you can change only those options that need to be changed to fix your setup program:

1. Click the Save Template button to save your setup program settings.

2. You will be prompted for a filename for the template. Make sure the directory is set to the \Samples\CompTool\MSComm subdirectory of Visual Basic.

3. Type in the name **MSCommSetup** in the File Name field and click the Save button. When you save the template, Setup Wizard stores all of your settings in a template file. This is the file you will need to open if you need to modify the setup program in the future.

4. When you are ready to let the Setup Wizard finish your setup program, click the Finish button.

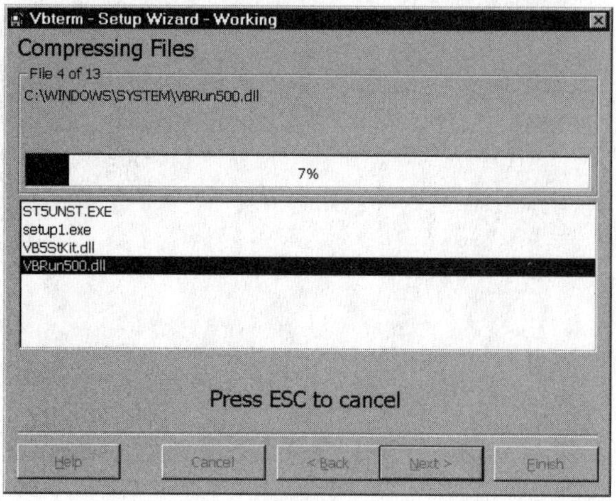

FIGURE 12.12: COMPRESSING THE FILES

After you've selected the Finish button, the Setup Wizard will start compressing the files that make up your application. This is a slow process, so be patient. The Wizard will display a status dialog box like the one in Figure 12.12. You can watch the Setup Wizard's progress as it compresses each file. You can press the Escape (Esc) button to cancel the process.

Scanning for Viruses

When the Setup Wizard is finished compressing the files and laying out the disk images, it will notify you that it is done (see Figure 12.13). It also reminds you to scan your setup disks for viruses. This is an important warning and should not be taken lightly. Nobody wants to get infected setup disks.

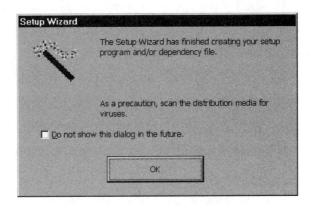

FIGURE 12.13: SCANNING FOR VIRUSES

That's all there is to creating a setup program. You can experiment with Internet setups and your own ActiveX controls to learn how it is done. Before you distribute your application, you should scan the distribution media for viruses. Then you should test the installation on another computer that does not have Visual Basic 5 installed on it. If there are any glitches in the setup routine, you can go back and fix them. Make absolutely sure that everything works before you do a widespread distribution. It will save you a lot of headaches from trouble calls.

Although there are other setup programs available, Setup Wizard is adequate for simple installations and you can't beat the price. If you want to modify your setup program in any way, you can modify the project in \SetupKit\Setup1 subdirectory of Visual Basic. This is a Visual Basic project that you can modify in the IDE to make it exactly the way you want it. This is also a good learning tool if you want to learn how to register files in the system registry. The best way to become proficient in the Setup Wizard, as it is with anything else, is to practise.

Distributing Your Program

Once you have finished your setup program, you have a variety of methods to distribute your application. If the program is to be used throughout your company and you have a Local Area Network, you can copy the disk images to a central file server that everybody has access to. Then each user can run the setup program from the server to install the program on their hard disks.

Another method is to distribute the application over the Internet. If the application is a stand-alone application that can be used by anybody, then you may want to combine all of the files into a zip file. This relieves the user from having to download each individual file and copying them to setup disks on their own.

Finally, you can copy the individual disk images to floppy disks. This is still the traditional method, and you should do it for each setup program you create. Then you can archive these master disk sets in case you need them again in the future. Again, be sure to scan them for viruses before you archive them.

Summary of Skills Acquired

Now you can...

- ☑ set your application's properties
- ☑ understand the difference between P-Code and Native Code
- ☑ compile your application to P-Code or Native Code
- ☑ use built-in version and build numbers
- ☑ add copyright and trademark notices to your executable files
- ☑ use the Setup Wizard to distribute your applications
- ☑ understand the various methods of software distribution

SKILL
13

Learning and Using Object-Oriented Programming (OOP)

Featuring

- ❑ Defining OOP
- ❑ Why should you use OOP?
- ❑ Learning about inheritance, encapsulation, and polymorphism
- ❑ Writing reusable code
- ❑ Creating a Human Resources class
- ❑ Using the Human Resources class

Defining OOP

Object-oriented programming, or OOP, is a method of analysing, designing, and writing applications using *objects*. So what is an object, you ask? An object is a piece of code, commonly referred to as a *class*, that contains properties and methods. Objects can mimic business rules, actions, or even physical objects.

OOP simplifies program development by encapsulating properties and methods within a simple security model. The security model of an object is defined by the keywords Private and Public. If you want an application to be able to access your object, the object must be accessed through a Public property or method. Private properties and methods are used only by the object itself. These object components cannot be seen or used by other procedures.

The most fundamental object in Visual Basic is the form object. Without it, your application would be hard pressed to be *visual*. The form has many properties including: Appearance, BorderStyle, Caption, Name, and WindowState. All of these properties are public and can be accessed by code that you write. The form also has many methods including: Load, Unload, Show, and Hide.

When you add a new form to your project, you are creating a "child" of the form class. It has the identical properties and methods as its parent form. However, as you change the properties and methods, it becomes its own form. This child form may perform many tasks similar to its parent, or it may not. That depends on how you program the form. You can add as many forms as your program can handle, and you can customize each of them differently.

Why Should You Use OOP?

Why would a programmer want to use OOP to develop a project? Simply put, the programmer can compartmentalise the functionality of a program into discreet objects. This will help make the program easier to design and develop. When you optimize your objects, you minimize the risk of one piece of code interfering with another piece of code. These objects basically mimic real-world situations.

Let us consider a large company with many departments. This company—we'll call it XYZ Corporation—will have an Administration department, a Human Resources department, an Information Technology department, and an Accounting department.

The Administration department is solely responsible to ensure that the other departments work together to produce the desired results. The employees in Administration are computer literate, but they are not computer-savvy enough to develop the company intranet. The administrators basically interact with the managers of different departments, but they do not directly deal with the rank-and-file employees within XYZ Corporation.

Human Resources (HR) is responsible for hiring, firing, and evaluating personnel within the company. HR manages several thousand personnel files that are considered confidential to other departments. Generally, people from other departments would not have free reign on the personnel files. A department must go through the proper channels to get the information required. Perhaps a manager will need to review an employee's file to determine eligibility for a promotion.

The Information Technology (IT) department makes sure all of the computer systems throughout the company function 100 percent of the time. The IT employees provide IT services to every other department within XYZ Corporation, as well as providing IT services that they need to do their job effectively.

Finally, the Accounting department handles all of the billing and invoicing for the company, maintains the inventory records, and balances the assets and liabilities. Some of the information that flows through Accounting deals with the financial situation of the company. This information is also highly confidential. If it got into the wrong hands, competitors could use it to gain an upper hand in the same market as XYZ Corporation.

Obviously, there are procedures to be followed for the departments to work together. If one department was to get hold of information it had no business seeing, it could cause turmoil within the company. If this turmoil got out of hand, it could possibly bring down XYZ Corporations a whole.

As a result, XYZ Corporation has established policies dealing with who can get what information and for what reasons. Only managers are allowed to view personnel documents. In addition, they can only view documents of employees who work under them. They are not allowed to access files of personnel they have no business dealing with. To be allowed this level of access could possibly expose a person to undue scrutiny or treatment. This is why it is necessary to have these controls in place.

OOP works in much the same way by providing controls that determine what code is used by other pieces of code. Objects are designed to do their own thing and to interact with other objects only when necessary.

While OOP is a different approach to programming, it has definite utility to programmers. OOP allows you to apply a single representation of a piece of code from program analysis, to design, and to the actual program code. An object in the real world can be represented almost exactly the same way in code using OOP.

If your objects are designed well, your code becomes reusable. For instance, if you create an object that processes data according to a specific method that your company uses, this object can be reused in another application, or even a new version, and still provide the same results.

OOP requires a new method of thinking to be effective. You must learn to think of your programs as a collection of objects, and each component is an object itself. Fortunately, visual programming gives you a head start to this method of thinking. Just remember that you *can* understand OOP, and you have actually used objects before. If you have read this book up to this point, you will have mastered using objects. Now it is time to learn to design and create your own.

Tip

Learn to think of your programs as objects. If you study the way objects interact with each other, you will start understanding another way to engineer your applications.

Characteristics of an Object

An object has characteristics that make it a discrete entity in the programming world. An object consists of properties and methods, just like other Visual Basic elements. However, objects are distinguished from procedures by having three characteristics: inheritance, encapsulation, and polymorphism.

Visual Basic employs inheritance and encapsulation, but not polymorphism. So technically, Visual Basic is not an object-oriented language, but it still presents a good environment to learn the basics of OOP. Let's take a closer look at the internals of an object.

The Properties of an Object

Properties, as mentioned in Skill 1, describe an object. Every object you use or create will have a *class name* to distinguish it from other objects. However, it will not necessarily have a Name property. Let's use properties to describe the Human Resources department mentioned earlier in this skill. First, you must be a manager in a department to access a personnel file. You can describe this with the following code:

```
Public IsManager as Integer
```

In addition, a manager can only access personnel files of people within his or her department. Therefore, you need to define a property to describe the department:

```
Public Department as Integer
```

You also need to a way to tell the HR clerk who we want information on. We can do this by creating a EmployeeID property:

```
Public EmployeeID as Long
```

Figure 13.1 shows you en example of the HR class. Notice that the name and department lines are represented by their equivalent properties in the class. Properties alone will not make a good object. They need to be used by methods within the same object.

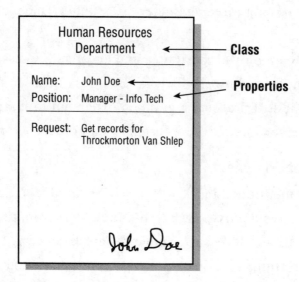

FIGURE 13.1: PROPERTIES OF THE HR CLASS

The Methods of an Object

Methods are the actions that an object can perform. For example, a Window object can show itself, hide itself, and even resize itself. So what can the HR department do? A simple function is to retrieve a personnel file, as shown in Figure 13.2. However, before the clerk, our HR class, can retrieve a personnel file, the clerk must make sure the requester is a manager in the correct department. You can create the method using the following code:

```
Public Function GetFile() as String
   If IsManager and Department = "Administration" Then
     GetFile = "John Doe"
   Else
     GetFile=""
   End If
End Function
```

Within this method, you first check to see if it is even appropriate to give the personnel file to the requester. In this example, the requester must be a manager from Administration. Shop workers and propeller-heads are not allowed to gain access to personnel files.

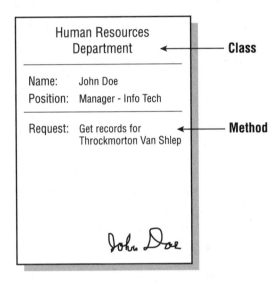

FIGURE 13.2: METHODS OF THE HR CLASS

The Inheritance Characteristic

Inheritance is the ability of an object to assume the characteristics of its parent class. For example, when you create a new form object, it inherits the properties and methods of its parent class. It has a Name property, WindowState property, and a BorderStyle property. In addition, it has the Load, Unload, and Hide methods.

In Visual Basic, you instantiate a new object by dimensioning an object of a particular class and then using the New keyword to create a new object. The new object will inherit the properties and methods of its parent.

If you look back at the dialogs class you created in Skill 9, you will see the methods contained in the clsDialogs object: YNBox, ErrMsg, and

LoginBox. The sample application also showed you how to create a new dialog.

First, you used Dim to allocate space for the object:

```
Dim dlg as clsDialog
```

Then you used the New keyword to create the object:

```
Set dlg=New clsDialog
```

The new object, dlg, has three members: YNBox, ErrMsg, and LoginBox. These are the same methods that were created in the original clsDialogs class.

Applying this same principle to your HR class, using the New keyword in Visual Basic is the equivalent of tearing off a form to fill out a request for the Human Resources Department.

The Encapsulation Characteristic

Encapsulation is a mechanism that hides data and methods from the programmer. It is used to shield the programmer from the complexities of the object. This is one of the major strengths of OOP.

Encapsulation is what prevents unauthorized employees from viewing personnel files. Each department encapsulates its business and only reveals it to the appropriate personnel under the appropriate conditions. Objects work the same way.

The Human Resources Department encapsulates its personnel files by keeping them locked in a filing cabinet. The only way you can get access to them is to fill out the request form. In Visual Basic encapsulation is performed using the Private keyword. You may have noticed that most procedures in code modules are prefixed with the word Private. This prevents these methods from being accessed by procedures in other forms and code modules. If you want to expose a particular procedure, prefix the Sub or Function statement with the keyword Public:

```
Public Function Format_Disk(Drive as String)
```

Note

When creating an object, be sure to expose only the essential properties. Encapsulate everything that will not be manipulated by the programmer. This will help ensure that no bugs can be introduced into your object by another programmer.

The Polymorphism Characteristic

Polymorphism is the ability of an object to assume many forms. You know that objects can be derived from other objects. The new object inherits the methods and properties from the other. Using polymorphism you can add, modify, or even remove functionality from the derived object. Although Visual Basic does not provide polymorphism functionality, the Human Resources department will give you a practical example.

Suppose the IT department wanted to maintain its own Human Resources section. This section would follow many of the same rules as the HR department but would incorporate special policies used only in IT. For instance, HR likes to keep their files on paper, whereas Information Technology likes to maintain its personnel information on a computer. Perhaps the IT Department would give special awards to the programmers who meet deadlines on time. Maybe IT would informally handle disciplinary actions internally so they would not have to go to the company-wide HR department.

IT could create its own personnel request form based on the form used by HR. In OOP, this would be done by creating an instance of the HR class and modifying it to suit the needs of IT. Fortunately, the only difference is that

IT stores file of only its employees, and on computers (see Figure 13.3). As a result, but IT and HR classes would have the same properties and methods, but if you asked HR to get a file, they would go pull it from their filing cabinet. If you asked for the same information from IT, someone would pull the information off of a computer. Polymorphism is the vehicle by which this is achieved in OOP.

FIGURE 13.3: POLYMORPHISM

Writing Reusable Code

Perhaps the biggest benefit of OOP is that you can write reusable code. Think of how you started writing in Visual Basic. Immediately you started working with objects, and you probably didn't even know it—which is exactly the point. You never touched the code to actually create a command button or a form. Visual Basic supplied you with objects and exposed only those properties and events you needed to make your application work. Visual Basic prevented you from dealing with the intricacies that lie deep within the bowels of the object. You also did not need to create your own command button from scratch.

Creating a Human Resources Class

To give you a taste of object design and development, let's create a more sophisticated version of the Human Resources class.

1. Start a new project and select Standard EXE as the project type.

2. Add a class module by right-clicking the Project Explorer and selecting Add ➤ Class Module from the pop-up menu.

3. In the Properties window, set the Name property to **clsHR**.

4. In the (General)(Declarations) section of the code window, add the following properties:

```
Option Explicit

Public Manager As Boolean
Public Dept As Integer
Public EmpID As Integer
Public EmpName As String
Public EmpDept As Integer
Public EmpPerformance As String
Public Reason As String
```

5. You want to be able to request personnel files so add a public method to do this:

```
Public Function GetRecord() As Boolean
  If Manager = True Then
    If Dept = GetDept() Then
      EmpName = GetEmpName()
      EmpPerformance = GetPerfEval()
      Reason = ""
      GetRecord = True
    Else
      Reason = "You cannot access files _
        from another department."
      GetRecord = False
    End If
  Else
    Reason = "You must be a manager to _
      access personnel files."
    GetRecord = False
  End If
End Function
```

6. You must add a method to verify the department of the employee:

```
Private Function GetDept() As Integer
  Select Case EmpID
    Case Is =  1
      GetDept = 1
    Case Is =  2
      GetDept = 1
    Case Is =  3
      GetDept = 2
    Case Else
      GetDept = 0
  End Select
End Function
```

7. Add a method to retrieve the employee name:

```
Private Function GetEmpName() As String
  Select Case EmpID
    Case Is =  1
      GetEmpName = "John Doe"
    Case Is =  2
      GetEmpName = "Jane Doe"
    Case Is =  3
      GetEmpName = "Throckmorton Van Shlep"
    Case Else
      GetEmpName = ""
  End Select
End Function
```

Note

This is a rudimentary example of how you can use a class to restrict and permit the retrieval of data. You will probably want to access a database and compare the values in the fields rather than hard-coding data in the class itself.

---

8. Now you need to add a method to retrieve the performance evaluation.

```
Private Function GetPerfEval() As String
  Select Case EmpID
  Case Is =  1
    GetPerfEval = "I've seen better!"
  Case Is =  2
    GetPerfEval = "Works well with others."
  Case Is =  3
```

```
    GetPerfEval = "Satisfactory."
  Case Else
    GetPerfEval = "Unknown."
  End Select
End Function
```

9. Finally, you need to make sure the properties of this class are initialized. Add the code:

```
Private Sub Class_Initialize()
  Manager = False
  Dept = 1
  EmpID = 0
  EmpName = ""
  EmpDept = 0
  EmpPerformance = ""
  Reason = ""
End Sub
```

That is all that is required to create the HR class. You created seven properties: Manager, Dept, EmpID, EmpName, EmpDept, EmpPerformance, and Reason. Manager is a boolean value that determines if the requester is a manager. Dept is set to the department that the requester belongs to. You set the EmpID property to the employee ID of the employee whose file you want to retrieve. If the file is retrieved, EmpName gets set to the name of the employee. EmpDept is the department that the employee belongs to. EmpPerformance gets set to the performance of the employee requested. Finally, an error message and a reason are returned via the Reason property if the request fails.

In addition to the properties, you created four methods for the HR class. Notice that only the GetRecord method is public. We don't want anyone to access personnel files without going through the proper channels. The class object now has all of the functionality to be used by an application. Let's create the Human Resources interface.

Using the Human Resources Class

1. Make Form1 the active form. Set the its Name property to **frmHR**. Set its Caption property to **Human Resources Dept.**

2. Add three labels and set their properties:

   ```
   Name:       lblDept
   Text:       Department
   Name:       lblManager
   Text:       Are you a manager?
   Name:       lblEmpID
   Text:       Employee ID
   ```

3. Add combo box and place it next to lblDept. Set its properties as follows:

   ```
   Name:       cboDept
   Style:      2 - Dropdown List
   ```

4. Add two option buttons and set their properties:

   ```
   Name:       optYes
   Caption:    &Yes
   Value:      True
   Name:       optNo
   Caption:    &No
   ```

5. Now you need to provide a way to enter the employee ID. Add a text box control and set its properties.

   ```
   Name:       txtEmpID
   Text:       -
   ```

6. Finally, add the following command button:

   ```
   Name:       cmdgetPE
   Caption:    Get Performance &Evaluation
   ```

Arrange the controls so it looks like Figure 13.4.

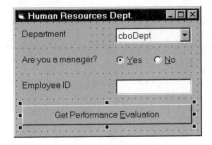

FIGURE 13.4: THE HUMAN RESOURCES DEPT. DIALOG BOX

7. Open the Code window for the form and place the following code in the (General)(Declarations) section:

```
Private hr As clsHR
Option Explicit
```

8. Add the following code to the Form_Load() event:

```
Private Sub Form_Load()
 'Instantiate HR Object
 Set hr = New clsHR

 'Add Departments to Combo Box
 cboDept.AddItem "1"
 cboDept.AddItem "2"
End Sub
```

Let's pause for a moment to examine the code in step 8. The New command is used to create a new instance of the clsHR class. In this single command, Visual Basic creates a new object of type clsHRc, your Human Resources class. You must create a new instance of an object before you can start using it.

9. Proceed to the Form_Unload() event and attach the following code:

```
Private Sub Form_Unload(Cancel As Integer)
 Set hr = Nothing
End Sub
```

Note

Whenever you create an object, you must destroy it when you are done. Forgetting to do so will leave the object in memory.

---

10. Add the code for the cmdGetPE button:

```
Private Sub cmdGetPE_Click()
 Dim rc As Boolean
 Dim msg As String

 hr.Dept = Val(cboDept.Text)
 hr.Manager = optYes.Value
 hr.EmpID = Val(txtEmpID.Text)
 If hr.GetRecord = True Then
   msg = "Employee ID: " & _
     Trim$(Str$(hr.EmpID)) & Chr$(13)
   msg = msg & "Employee Name: " _
     & hr.EmpName & Chr$(13)
   msg = msg & "Evaluation: " & _
     hr.EmpPerformance
   MsgBox msg
 Else
   msg = "I could not retrieve that _
     record!" & Chr$(13)
   msg = msg & hr.Reason
   MsgBox msg
 End If
End Sub
```

Save your project and give it a test run. You can select an employee number between one and three. If you want to see how the company's employees are doing, make sure you say you are a manager as well. Play with the parameters and check the results. You should see a dialog box that either says you have been denied access, or you will see the employee name and performance evaluation (see Figure 13.5).

You have created a simple object in Visual Basic. You will notice that the object itself is not visible, but you used an interface to make use of it. Some objects will have forms built into them, but most are formless. It is very easy to create a class as long as you take time to design it properly before you start coding.

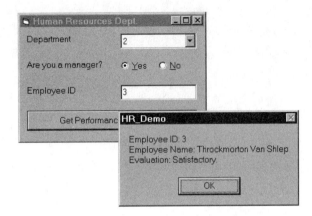

FIGURE 13.5: THE HR CLASS IN ACTION

Summary of Skills Acquired

Now you can...

- ☑ understand OOP and its use
- ☑ create, use, and destroy objects
- ☑ design and create your own object classes in Visual Basic
- ☑ write reusable code using objects

SKILL
14

Using ActiveX

Featuring

❏ Understanding the Active Platform
❏ Understanding the role of ActiveX in software development
❏ Using ActiveX with Visual Basic

Understanding the Active Platform

Briefly stated, Microsoft's Active Platform is a set of client/server development technologies used to integrate the Internet with the PC. It supports HTML 3.2, VBScript, Microsoft's Visual Basic scripting language, and JScript, or JavaScript. One of the major components of the Active platform is a framework called *ActiveX*.

ActiveX is a set of reusable components that can be created and utilized by several applications. In particular, ActiveX uses Internet technology to assist in creating compact and reusable applications that can be deployed via the Internet or a corporate intranet.

If you have been following the examples throughout this book, then you have already been using ActiveX controls. You can use ActiveX to create fancy command buttons or specialized data-bound controls. The limit is only your imagination.

Although you have been using ActiveX, this skill will teach you how to design and create ActiveX components that you can reuse in your own applications, as well as offer to other programmers. Figure 14.1 shows you can write an ActiveX document in Visual Basic and run it in the Internet Explorer Web browser. You will create this application in the section "ActiveX Documents" later in this skill.

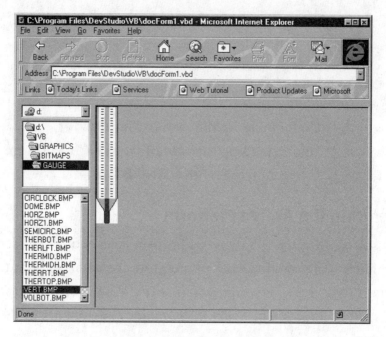

FIGURE 14.1: SAMPLE ACTIVEX DOCUMENT

The Role of ActiveX

ActiveX leverages Internet technology for several reasons. It provides a familiar client/server infrastructure to run your applications. Stand-alone Visual Basic applications can be ported over to ActiveX documents so they can then be downloaded via Internet Explorer. You can use this same technology to update ActiveX programs on clients' computers. As the application runs from the browser, the document can be configured to request updates when they are available. Then the control can be automatically installed on the clients' computers. It's all done without disks and without installation programs.

ActiveX Requirements

So what about viruses? Is it possible to send nasty and destructive code to someone's PC? Of course it is possible. If anyone is set on doing something destructive on a computer, they can do it. However, ActiveX takes steps to avoid guerrilla software, including the following:

- A digital signature is required
- ActiveX components must be marked as safe for scripting and initialization
- Each control must employ run-time licensing
- ActiveX components must be packaged in a format that enables progressive downloading

Let's look at the ramifications of these requirements.

First, each component must be digitally signed. This digital signature is received from an authorized certification company. When you distribute your control, the signature is embedded in the control so it can be reliably traced back to its originator should something go terribly wrong on the installation PC.

Second, your code must be designated as safe for scripting. Since ActiveX controls are used in Web pages through scripts, people can inadvertently or intentionally write scripts that can cause damage to your system. Although a control may be harmless under proper usage conditions, a malicious programmer can use it to cause harm. Remember, it's not technology in and of itself that's bad. It's the misuse of technology that's bad. If your control is legitimate, but someone uses it for malicious intent, the users will track you, the programmer, down. Remember that your control is digitally signed.

Your recourse is to create controls that cannot be scripted in such a way that can cause harm on a user's computer. If you receive a control that has not been marked as safe for scripting, Internet Explorer will display a warning message stating so. It is then up to you to decide to accept the control.

Third, each control must employ run-time licensing. You must include a pointer to a licence file on a server somewhere on the network. The reason this is done is because all of the code used to drive the control resides on the Web page. Any proficient Web surfer can view the source code of an HTML document and use your code. The pointer to the licence file ensures users don't download your control and create their own applications with it. This is very similar to how custom controls are licensed in Visual Basic. Controls are usually distributed with a licence file that allows the control to work in the IDE. When an application is distributed, the licence file does not go with the control. This way users cannot use controls in their own IDE.

Last, ActiveX controls must be packaged in a format that provides progressive downloading. This is basically using a Web browser as a replacement for an installation program. Let's look at how Web pages work within a browser. This will give you a better idea of how progressive download works.

How Web Pages Work

When you surf the Web, a Hypertext Markup Language (HTML) document is retrieved from the Web server. This document contains all of the information about the graphics, form layout, and content of the document. Before the page is displayed, the browser looks through a directory on your hard disk that maintains copies of Web pages, called a cache, to determine if the page or any of its graphics have been loaded onto your computer in the past. If they haven't, the browser requests the graphics from the Web server and the server will upload them to your computer. The browser then takes these components and stores them in the cache. This allows the browser to get the information from your hard disk instead of from the Internet. The primary purpose for this is speed. It is much faster to load a Web page from your hard disk than it is to get one using a modem. Finally, the browser displays the Web page on your screen. The next time you visit the same site it will appear on your browser much faster because the browser searches the cache first.

Progressive downloading uses this same type of process to prevent your browser from bogging down while on-line. This is especially important if you pay for your connect time by the hour! Instead of looking in a cache to see if a control exists, it compares the Class ID of an ActiveX control in the HTML document with the system registry. If the browser finds a match, then it knows your computer already has the control. If there is no match, then the browser starts the download and subsequent registration. Once the control is registered, the browser will not have to download it again.

These are some strict requirements for your ActiveX controls, but they are very important if you want to distribute your controls on a global basis. It should help you to sleep better at night knowing that you are also protected by this multilevel security model.

Understanding the Role of ActiveX in Software Development

Now that you understand how ActiveX fits into Microsoft's Internet strategy, you can start examining the tools Visual Basic gives us to utilize this technology. You can create sophisticated ActiveX controls that can be used in your Visual Basic applications, Web pages, and even in other Microsoft products such as Excel or Word. When you start up Visual Basic and examine the Project Wizard, you will notice several ActiveX component templates that you can choose from (see Figure 14.2). These include the ActiveX EXE, ActiveX DLL, ActiveX Control, ActiveX Document DLL, and ActiveX Document EXE. An ActiveX control can be added to the Visual Basic Toolbox. From there, it can be added to your project just like any other control, and it will operate and behave the same way. When you add an ActiveX control to a program, it becomes part of the IDE and provides new functionality for your application. ActiveX documents are basically Visual Basic applications that run in a Web browser, Internet Explorer in particular.

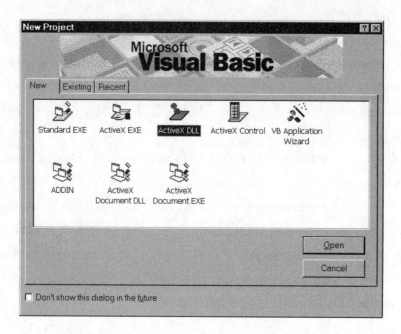

FIGURE 14.2: AVAILABLE ACTIVEX COMPONENTS

Creating and Using ActiveX Documents

The ActiveX document allows you to bring the power of Visual Basic to the Internet or your own intranet. An ActiveX document is a Visual Basic application that utilizes Microsoft Internet Explorer (version 3 or above) as an application container. ActiveX documents allow you to create portable versions of your application that can be used on laptops, at remote offices, or even from your home. Everything runs from your browser. However, an

ActiveX document is not a Web page. It is its own application. In addition, users can navigate between ActiveX documents and Web pages seamlessly through their browser.

When you design your application, you can use ActiveX documents on the front end to serve as the interface and ActiveX DLLs on the back end to do the processing.

To make the ActiveX document shown in the beginning of the skill, follow these steps:

1. Start a new project by selecting File ➤ New Project. Select ActiveX Document EXE from the Project Wizard.
2. In the Properties window, set the Name property of UserDocument1 to **docMain**.
3. Add a drive control to the upper-left corner of docMain. Place its upper-left corner on grid line away from the top and left sides. Stretch the control so it is about 2 inches wide.
4. Add a directory list control to docMain, one grid line below the drive control. Stretch it so it is the same width as the drive control. Stretch it vertically so its bottom edge is about half-way down the document.
5. Add a file list control below the directory list control. Stretch it the same width as the directory list, and stretch it down to one grid line above the bottom edge of docMain.
6. Now, add a picture box control to the document. Place it one grid line to the right of the edge of the drive control. Stretch it so its right edge is one grid line away from the right edge of the document. Drag the bottom of the picture box so its bottom edge is even with the bottom edge of the file list control. Your document should look similar to Figure 14.3.

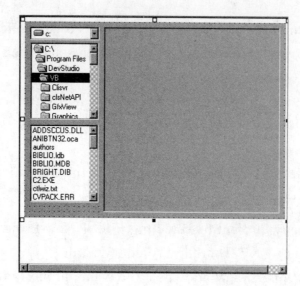

FIGURE 14.3: ACTIVEX DOCUMENT AT DESIGN TIME

7. Double-click on the drive control to open the Code window.

8. Add the following code to the Change event of Drive1:

```
Private Sub Drive1_Change()
  'Synchronize Directory with drive control
  Dir1.Path = Drive1.Drive
End Sub
```

9. Add the following code to the Change event of Dir1:

```
Private Sub Dir1_Change()
  'Synchronize files with directory control
  File1.Path = Dir1.Path
End Sub
```

10. Add this code to the Click event of File1:

```
Private Sub File1_Click()
  'Show the graphic
  picGraphic.Picture = LoadPicture(Dir1.Path & _
     "\" & File1.filename)
End Sub
```

Unlike forms, you initialize ActiveX documents in the Initialize event. You can place code in this event to prepare the document before it is displayed.

11. We only want to view bitmap graphics for now. Add the following code to the Initialize event of the UserDocument object (docMain):

```
Private Sub UserDocument_Initialize()
 'Show only BMP files
 File1.Pattern = "*.bmp"
End Sub
```

12. Add the last bit of code, listed below, to the Resize event of the UserDocument object:

```
Private Sub UserDocument_Resize()
 'Resize File List
 File1.Height = (ScaleHeight - File1.Top)

 'Resize Graphic Window
 picGraphic.Height = ScaleHeight
 picGraphic.Width = (ScaleWidth - picGraphic.Left)
End Sub
```

The above code is responsible for making everything on the document look neat. Whenever you resize the browser, the document will resize itself. The code in the Resize event will stretch the Picture Box control to fit the document. In addition, it will vertically stretch the File List control to be flush with the bottom of the document.

13. Run the project by selecting Run ➤ Start or by pressing F5. Notice that the document is not visible while it is running. That is because you need to view the document from within Internet Explorer.

You have now completed your first ActiveX document. This program is a simple graphics viewer that runs in the browser. Now let's see the document work.

1. Start Internet Explorer by selecting it from the Start button on the Taskbar.

2. From the File menu, select Open.

3. From the Open dialog box, click the Browse button to select the ActiveX document file.

4. Select docMain.vbd from your Visual Basic directory and click the OK button.

5. If you have the Visual Basic CD in the drive, select the appropriate drive from the drive control on the document.

6. Using the drive and directory list controls, open the \VB\Graphics\Bitmaps\Assorted directory.

7. Click on any of the files in the file list box to view it in the Picture Box (see Figure 14.4).

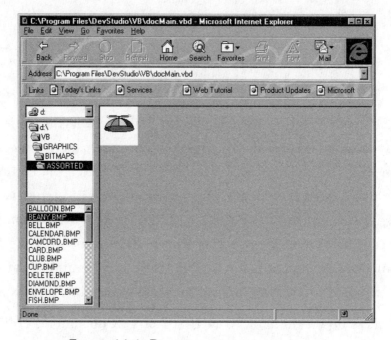

FIGURE 14.4: RUNNING THE GRAPHICS VIEWER

That's it for your first ActiveX document control. You can enhance this application or create your own. As time passes, you will see more and more ActiveX documents appearing on the Internet as well as intranets around the world. The possibilities are endless.

Note

To learn more about creating ActiveX documents, search the Visual Basic Help Topics for "ActiveX document".

Creating and Using ActiveX Controls

The ActiveX control is a custom control you create that can be added to the Toolbox and used in your applications. This type of control can then be used in other Visual Basic projects as well as other ActiveX compliant programs such as Microsoft Excel. These controls can also be embedded and distributed through HTML Web pages.

To create an ActiveX control, start a new project and select ActiveX Control as the project type (see Figure 14.5).

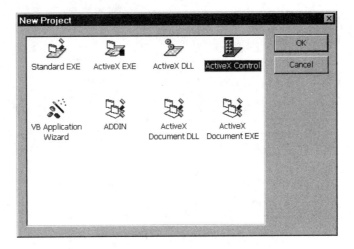

FIGURE 14.5: CREATING AN ACTIVEX CONTROL

Next you must create the interface and let the wizard finish the work for you. Let's build a simple button control so you can see how its done:

1. Start a new project. Select ActiveX Control as the project type.
2. From the Toolbox, right-click and select Components from the pop-up menu.

3. From the Controls tab on the Components dialog box, select Sheridan 3D Controls to add them to your project (see Figure 14.6). After you have selected the controls, click the OK button.

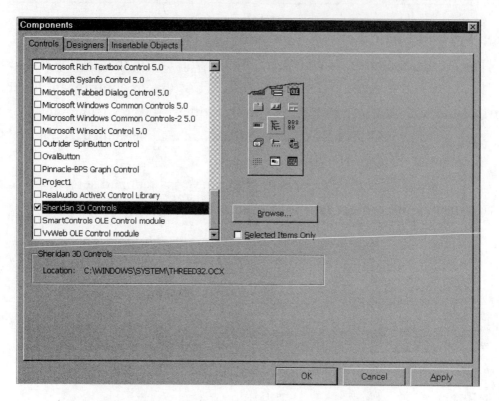

FIGURE 14.6: ADDING THE SHERIDAN 3D CONTROLS

4. From the Toolbox, add a SSCommand button to the control designer. Position it so it is flush with the top-left corner of the control container.

5. Set the button's Name property to **ctlExitButton**.

6. Now double-click on (Custom) properties in the Properties window to bring up the Property Pages for the button.

7. On the General tab of the Property Pages dialog box, set the Caption property to **E&xit** and the AutoSize property to **2 - Adjust Button Size to Picture** (see Figure14.7).

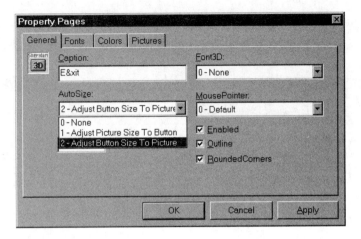

FIGURE 14.7: SETTING THE BUTTON'S PROPERTIES

8. From the Pictures tab, change the Property Name list to Picture. Now click the Browse button. Select the MsgBox01.Ico icon from the \Graphics\Icons\Computer subdirectory. The Property Pages dialog box should look like Figure 14.8. Click the OK button to close the dialog box.

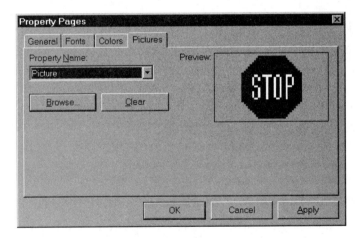

FIGURE 14.8: ADDING A GRAPHIC

9. Resize the container control (the grey, flat, form-like area that the button is sitting on) so it is the same size as the button, as in Figure 14.9.

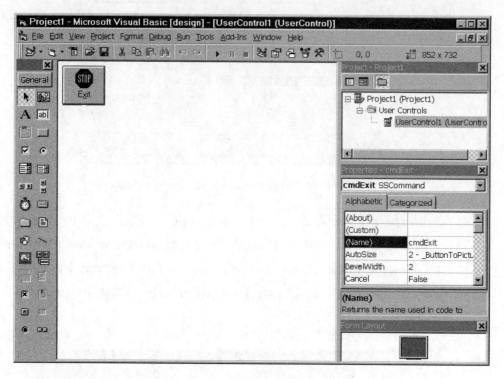

FIGURE 14.9: THE CUSTOM BUTTON CONTROL

Adding the Code

Now you are finished with the interface to the control. The next step is to code it. You will use the ActiveX Control Interface Wizard to accomplish this:

1. Select Add-Ins ➤ Add-In Manager... from the menu. This will bring up a dialog box similar to the Components dialog box in the previous exercise.

2. Check the box next to VB ActiveX Control Interface Wizard, as in Figure 14.10, and click the OK button to close the dialog box. The wizard has now been added to the IDE.

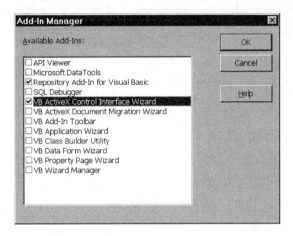

FIGURE 14.10: ADDING THE CONTROL INTERFACE WIZARD TO THE IDE

3. Next, select Add-Ins ➤ ActiveX Control Interface Wizard... from the menu to start the wizard (see Figure 14.11).

4. When the Introduction dialog box appears, read it and click the Next button.

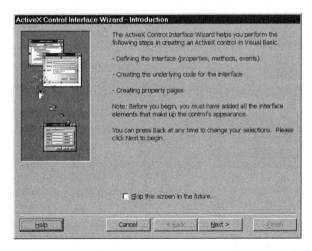

FIGURE 14.11: STARTING THE ACTIVEX CONTROL INTERFACE WIZARD

In the next step you determine which properties, methods, and events your control will need. If you think of your control as any other control, and picture its properties in the Properties window, you can get an idea of what your control will need. This button is very simple, so you only need a few properties and only one event.

5. Remove all of the items from the Selected Names list except for those listed in Figure 14.12. Your object should have Caption, Enabled, Font, and Font3D properties and one Click event. You will need to add the Caption and Font3D properties from the Available Names list. When all looks good click the next button.

6. The next dialog box will ask to create custom members. Since we have none, just click the Next button to move to the next step.

FIGURE 14.12: SELECTING THE BUTTON'S PROPERTIES

7. Now you need to map out the control's properties to the properties of its components: Click on the Caption property and map it to the Exit

button by selecting **cmdExit** from the Control drop-down list. The Member property should change to Caption (see Figure 14.13).

8. Click on the Click property and map it to the Exit button's Click event.

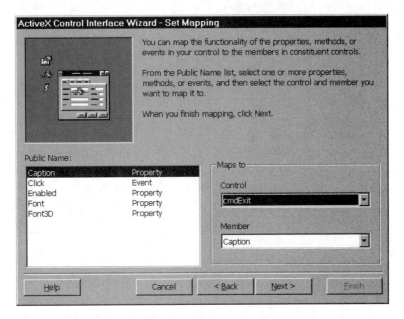

FIGURE 14.13: MAPPING THE CONTROL'S PROPERTIES AND EVENTS

9. Map your control's Enabled property to the Exit button's Enabled property.

10. Map the Font property to the Exit button's Font property.

11. Finally, map the Font3D property to the Exit button's Font3D property.

The next frame of the wizard will ask you if you want to view a summary report (see Figure 14.14). This report contains important information on how to utilize your control when it is finished. If you want to view the report, check the check box. If you do not want to view it, clear the check box.

12. Click the Finish button.

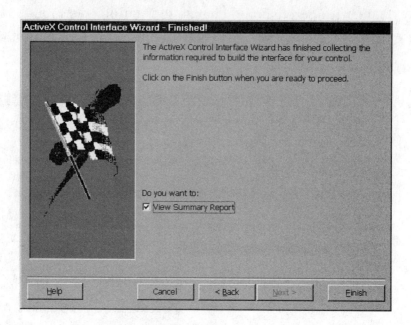

FIGURE 14.14: FINISHING THE CONTROL

You have just created your first ActiveX control. Although it seemed like a lot of steps for such a simple control, you will get used to it, and with practice you will be quickly creating ActiveX controls of your own.

You can compile this object to make a portable OCX control, or you can use it in its uncompiled form in the IDE. All you need to do is to close the object designer. It will automatically add itself to the Toolbox, where you can add it to a form in another project. In its compiled state, you can embed it into a Web document as well.

Creating and Using ActiveX DLLs

The ActiveX DLLs replace the components formerly known as OCXs. These components are especially useful when they are linked to databases and run on servers. These DLLs can be called from your browser or your custom Visual Basic front-end. In Skill 9 you created a very simple ActiveX DLL that displays several dialog boxes. But if you haven't looked at Skill 9, here is an overview of how to create an ActiveX DLL.

To create an ActiveX DLL you follow these simple steps:

1. Start a new project.
2. Select ActiveX DLL as the project type from the Project Wizard (see Figure 14.15).

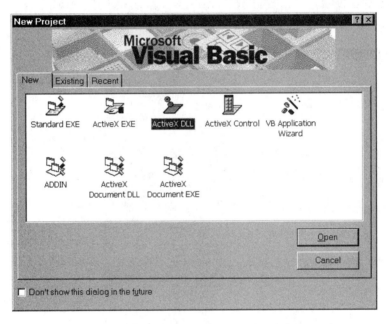

FIGURE 14.15: SELECTING THE ACTIVEX DLL PROJECT

3. Right-click on the Project Explorer to add a code module to your project. Select Add ➤ Module from the pop-up menu.
4. Select Module from the Add Module dialog box.
5. In the code module, create a Sub_Main() procedure. This will be your entry point to the DLL.
6. Define the necessary properties and methods for your class object. Add any forms and objects that are required as well.
7. Set the classes Instancing property to **5 - MultiUse**.

8. Open the Project Properties dialog box by right-clicking on the project name in the Project Explorer. Set the Startup Object to Sub_Main.

9. Set the project name and description appropriately.

10. Compile the project as an ActiveX DLL by selecting Make filename.dll, where filename is the name of your project (see Figure 14.16).

Once the DLL is compiled, you can access it through the References Window in Visual Basic. Once an object is derived from the DLL, you can call its properties and methods just like any other object.

FIGURE 14.16: COMPILING THE DLL

You can easily modify any class object in your Visual Basic projects to be their own stand-alone DLLs or custom controls. Which form you decide to create is dependent upon the design of your project. If you have not done so, please see Skill 13. It teaches you the basics of object-oriented programming

(OOP). This will help you to better understand class design and creation, which will in-turn help you to create great controls.

You can use ActiveX to exploit the features of the Internet and help you build robust client-server and Web-based applications from Visual Basic. ActiveX allows you to create your own custom controls that can be added to Visual Basic's Toolbox as well as be embedded in HTML documents. With a good understanding of OOP, client-server development, and the World Wide Web, you can create your own ActiveX controls to utilize the Internet as the foundation of your application.

Summary of Skills Acquired

Now you can...

- ☑ understand the role of ActiveX in software development
- ☑ understand and create ActiveX documents
- ☑ understand and create ActiveX controls
- ☑ understand and create ActiveX DLLs

SKILL
15

Using DLLs and the Windows API

Featuring

- ❑ Introducing Dynamic Link Libraries (DLLs)
- ❑ Understanding DLL calling conventions
- ❑ Using the API Viewer
- ❑ Using the API in your application
- ❑ Adding an application to the System Tray

Introducing Dynamic Link Libraries (DLLs)

Once in a while you'll want to accomplish something that's quite simply beyond the capabilities of Visual Basic—or at least requires some very convoluted code. In such circumstances you have three options:

- You can write the code in a language such as C and call the routines from Visual Basic.
- You can drive another application through OLE Automation.
- You can make use of existing libraries of routines that make up the Windows API.

In this skill, we'll be talking about the last option, because it is beyond the scope of this book to go into the details of C and C++ programming. OLE

Automation is also better left for when you have a good grasp of the Visual Basic fundamentals.

To access the Windows API, you link your programs to *dynamic-link libraries*, or DLLs. DLLs are components of applications that provide several functions in a file that can be linked to and used by a program when it is run. The functions are not built into your application. This is extremely useful if you want to reuse someone's code or you want your program to be smaller. Windows works in much the same way. It consists of several programs (called applets) and many DLLs that these applets use over and over. An example is the Open/Save File dialog boxes you use when opening or saving documents. Have you ever noticed they all look the same? Well, that's because they are. The dialog box is called from a DLL, so it can be used in many programs.

Many new programmers think of the Windows API as a great "black box" that is difficult to understand and use. In reality, the API is a set of functions that reside in many DLLs on your hard disk. Many of these DLLs can be found in the \Windows\System subdirectory. The most recent version of the API is the Win32 API. It contains functions that are all 32-bit functions. There are also APIs for 16-bit Windows as well as many third-party products. Just think of an API as a function in a DLL with documentation that you can use to access the function.

DLL Calling Conventions

Calling DLLs can get quite complex (especially if you're unfamiliar with C language data types), but fortunately the DLLs that make up the Windows API are well documented, and the code to declare them is provided with Visual Basic. You must declare a DLL before you can call it.

You tell Visual Basic how to access the DLL by declaring a procedure and specifying the appropriate parameters. Once this is done, you can let your program call the actual function in your code. Visual Basic will then know how to pass information to the DLL and return information based on the declaration that you created. The Windows API is a very powerful and useful set of functions, but it is also very volatile. One mismatched parameter type can cause your program to hiccup, stop, or even crash your whole system. This is especially bad if you don't save your work often. A system crash is the most likely result of a bad DLL calling convention.

Caution

When working with DLLs, save your work before every test run. If the DLL is called improperly, you could crash the computer and lose your work!

The first step to accessing the Windows API is to determine which API function you want to use. Once you determine the name of the function, you must link it to your program. You do this by declaring it with the Declare statement. For example:

```
Private Declare Function sndPlaySound Lib "winmm.dll" _
Alias "sndPlaySoundA" (ByVal lpszSoundName As String, _
ByVal uFlags As Long) As Long
```

This command may look complicated, but actually it is fairly easy to understand once you are familiar with DLL calling conventions. What it does is call the sndPlaySound API, which plays a WAV file. Let's dissect the declaration to understand better what it actually does.

Understanding DLL Calling Conventions

There are several similarities between declaration statements for the various APIs. Let's look at each of these so you can better understand what is actually happening.

Setting the API's Scope

The scope of the API function is determined just like it is for any procedures you write in Visual Basic. You can use the Public keyword to make the function available to the entire application, or use the Private keyword to make the function available only to the calling form.

In the previous declaration the Private statement makes the API function local to the module it is in. This is just like creating a private function of your own as discussed in Skill 4. You will not actually create the function, but you call it from your code just like any other function.

Declaring the DLL

The Declare Function statements tell Visual Basic to link to the sndPlaySound function that resides within the winmm.dll to your application. The keyword Alias specifies the name of the function as it is referenced in the DLL itself. The Alias keyword is used for compatibility between the standard 16-bit Windows API and the Win32 API.

Understanding Parameter Types

Parameters can be specified by value and by reference. If you pass a variable by value, using the ByVal keyword, you pass the actual contents of the variable to the function. When you pass it by reference, using the keyword ByRef, the function looks for the location in memory that the variable is stored, and gets the value from there. This is used for compatibility with C and C++ because most of the API is written in those languages.

After the Alias statement, you specify the parameter list that the function expects to see when it is called. We pass two parameters by value (ByVal). The two parameters are lpszSoundName and uFlags. The parameter lpszSoundName is a string variable that specifies the fully qualified path and file name of a .WAV file. The parameter uFlags is used to pass special handling parameters to the function. Don't worry about the prefixes *lpsz* and *u*.

These are naming conventions commonly used in C and C++. Finally, the function returns a long integer to notify you if the function is successful.

Using the Return Code

The last statement of the declaration sets the return type. Because many of the APIs perform functions that you cannot see, they return a code to your program to indicate whether the function succeeded or failed, and why. This is important for you to know because as you work with the API your program will depend on the functions within it. If an API fails for whatever reason, and your application doesn't check the return code before it continues running, the program will possibly introduce a bug and crash.

This brings up another interesting point: you can code your own functions to set return codes for your program and others to utilize. This is good practice because it keeps you application communicating with its components. When you are programming, never assume that a procedure worked, but always check the return code if possible. This helps minimize the chances of your application going haywire due to a variable being set improperly, or not being set at all.

The Windows API is similar to the functions and sub procedures you create in your own applications but with one difference: the code is already written for you. Your only responsibility is to ensure that the API declaration is valid and you only use the proper variable types to move data to and from the API. If you are careless with these, you could very easily crash your program, or even worse, hang your system.

The API Viewer

Now that you understand the basics of DLL declaration, I want to show you a shortcut. Visual Basic ships with a utility called the API Viewer (see Figure 15.1).

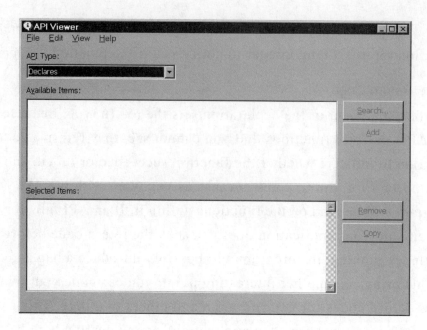

FIGURE 15.1: THE API VIEWER

The API Viewer is a browser and a file that contains most of the function declarations, variable types, and constant declarations that make up the Windows API. The viewer allows you to quickly search for the function you want to call and supplies you with the appropriate statements to include in your application.

To use the API Viewer, follow these steps:

1. From your Start menu run the API Text Viewer, which is in your Visual Basic program group.

2. In the API Viewer click File ➤ Load Text File.

3. Select Win32.api and click Open. The API Viewer will tell you that it can run faster if it converts the file to a database (see Figure 15.2).

Tip

The API Viewer will load the APIs faster if you convert the text file into a database. If you plan to make extensive use of the API, convert it to a database.

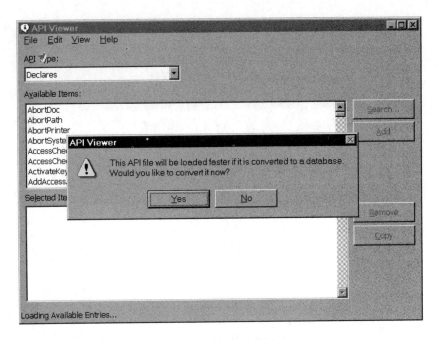

FIGURE 15.2: CONVERTING THE API LIST TO A DATABASE

4. Answer Yes to convert the file into a database.

5. After the list has been converted to a database, select Declares in the
    API Type list box at the top of the Viewer.

You can scroll down the list, although it is quite long. This is not the
entire Windows API, but it is a good subset and offers almost everything you
could ask for. You can type the letters of the API you are looking for and as
you type the list will scroll to it.

6. Scroll to the sndPlaySound function. When it is highlighted, click the
    Add button to copy the declaration to the Selected Items list (see
    Figure 15.3).

7. After the function declaration is added, click the Copy button. This
    will copy the declaration to the clipboard for you.

8. Close the API Viewer.

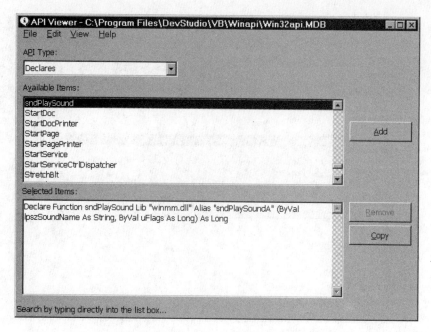

FIGURE 15.3: THE SNDPLAYSOUND DECLARATION

Using the API in Your Applications

You now know how to use the API Viewer to retrieve the declarations you need for your programs. Now let's look at integrating the declarations with your applications. We will continue where we left off with our previous example:

1. In Visual Basic, start a new project. If the Project Wizard appears, select Standard EXE2.

2. Double-click on Form1 in the Project Explorer to open up the Code window.

3. Go to the (General)(Declarations) section and select Edit ➤ Paste. Your Code window should look similar to Figure 15.4.

4. Insert the keyword Private in front of the Declare statement.

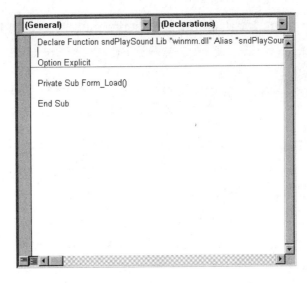

FIGURE 15.4: THE API DECLARATION IN THE CODE WINDOW

Usually, API declarations should go into their own code module. However, you can place them in a form or a class by prefixing the Declare statement with a Private keyword. If you do not do this, you will receive an error message.

5. Next, add the following code to the Form_Load() procedure of Form1:

```
Private Sub Form_Load()
 Dim filename As String
 Dim rc As Long

 filename = "c:\windows\media\tada.wav"
 rc = sndPlaySound(filename, 1)
End Sub
```

Note

You may need to change the filename parameter to point to another .WAV file on your computer. The path used above is just an example. Also notice that the return code (rc) is dimensioned as a long integer (Dim rc As Long). This must match the exact return type specified in the API declaration. The filename and the flags parameters must match as well. I set the flags parameter to 1 for this example.

6. If everything looks good, then save the project and run it.

Caution

Always save your project before you run it if you are using the Windows API. One mismatched parameter can cause your whole system to crash. If you did not save your work, then it will be lost as well.

If you have a sound card installed and the volume turned up, then you should have heard the infamous "Ta-da!" sound. You can experiment by changing the filename parameter to play different sounds. As you develop your applications, you can use this API to spice them up. Maybe audio prompts are in order. If you are creating a screen saver or a video game, then sounds are practically a must.

Modifying the API Function

You can write your own functions to call API functions as well. These functions are called *wrappers* because you wrap code inside your function. If you want to turn off the sound, you can put the API function in your own wrapper so you can selectively turn the sound off and on. For example:

```
Public Sub PlayWav(filename as string, soundon as Boolean)
  Dim rc as long
  If soundon = True Then
    rc=sndPlaySound(filename, 1)
  End If
End Sub
```

This is a useful procedure to add to your code library. You could possibly encapsulate it in your own WAV file class if you want to. The important thing to remember is to give your users the option of having the sound on or off. While many like to have sound, the novelty can get old. When you allow the user to turn the sound on and off, you can capture this value and pass it to the PlayWav procedure. You can also disable sound if the user does not have multimedia installed on their system (although highly unlikely).

Adding an Application to the System Tray

Some applications written for Windows allow themselves to be placed within the System Tray. The System Tray is the recessed box that sits on the right side of the Taskbar (shown here). Applications that monitor devices or run on schedules are often placed here when they run. Your system will most likely have a clock indicating the computer's time and possibly a speaker icon for your volume control.

Visual Basic comes with a sample program that you can compile to and ActiveX control. You can use this control in your applications to place them in the System Tray.

Creating the SysTray Control

Before you can use ActiveX control in your application, you should compile it and store it in the \System sub-directory of the Windows directory. To build the control, follow these steps:

1. Open the Systrayc.vbp project in the \Tools\UNSUPPORTED\SYSTEM TRAY ICON\Control directory on the Visual Basic CD.

2. In the Project Explorer, open the Modules folder and double-click on mSysTray to open the code module in the Code window.

Examine the (Global)(Declarations) section of the file. You will notice several API declarations including CallWindowProc, GetWindowLong, and Shell_NotifyIcon (see Figure 15.5). These APIs, along with others, are used to place an icon in the System Tray. We won't go into the details of how the functions work, but you can browse the source code and read the comments to see what makes the control work.

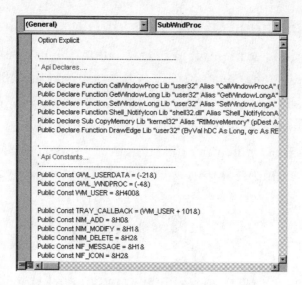

FIGURE 15.5: SYSTRAY API DECLARATIONS

3. Select File ➤ Make Systray.ocx.

4. From the Make Project dialog box, set the Save In field to the \System subdirectory of the directory you have Windows installed on your hard disk. This will be C:\Windows\System on most systems.

5. Click the OK button to compile the control.

The SysTray control is now ready for use in your own applications.

Using the SysTray Control

Now that you have created the SysTray control you can add it to your own applications just like any other controls. To try this out, let's create a simple program launcher that you can use to start some useful Windows utilities. Follow these steps:

1. Start a new project by selecting File ➤ New Project. Select Standard EXE from the New Project dialog box.

2. Once the project is created, change the Name property of Form1 to frmMain.

3.   Right-click on the Toolbox and select Components... from the pop-up menu.

4.   Click the check box next to C:\Windows\System\SysTray.ocx to add the cSysTray control to your Toolbox. Click the OK button.

5.   Place the cSysTray control on frmMain and set its Name property to clsSysTray.

6.   In the Properties window, set the InTray property to True and set the TrayTip property to Application Launcher.

7.   Click on frmMain to make it the active control. Select Tools ➤ Menu Editor... to open the Menu Editor dialog box.

8.   Create a menu by setting the Caption property to &Apps. Set the Name property to mnuApp. Click the Next button.

9.   Click the right arrow button to create menu items.

10. Create the following menu items:

Caption	Name
C&alculator	mnuAppCalc
&Explorer	mnuAppExplorer
&Notepad	mnuAppNotepad
-	mnuAppSep1
&Close	mnuAppClose

11. Your menu should look similar to Figure 15.6. Click the OK button to close the Menu Editor.

12. Double-click frmMain to open its Code window.

13. Add the following code to the Load event of the form:

```
Private Sub Form_Load()
 Me.Hide
End Sub
```

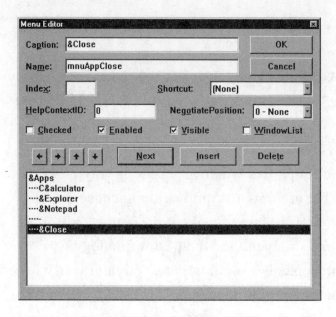

14. Open the MouseDown event of clsSysTray and add the following code:

```
Private Sub clsSysTray_MouseDown(Button As Integer, Id As Long)
  If Button = 2 Then
    PopupMenu mnuApp
  End If
End Sub
```

15. Add the following to the Click event of mnuAppCalc:

```
Private Sub mnuAppCalc_Click()
 Dim rc As Double
 rc = Shell("calc.exe", vbNormalFocus)
End Sub
```

16. Add the following to the Click event of mnuAppExplorer:

```
Private Sub mnuAppExplorer_Click()
 Dim rc As Double
 rc = Shell("explorer.exe", vbNormalFocus)
End Sub
```

17. Add the following to the Click event of mnuAppNotepad:

```
Private Sub mnuAppNotepad_Click()
 Dim rc As Double
 rc = Shell("notepad.exe", vbNormalFocus)
End Sub
```

18. Add the following to the Click event of mnuAppClose:

```
Private Sub mnuAppClose_Click()
 Unload Me
 Set frmMain = Nothing
End Sub
```

19. Finally, save and run your project.

You should see a small toaster icon in your System Tray. If you rest the mouse pointer over it for a couple of seconds, you will see a tool tip that says "Application Launcher." When you right-click on the icon you are presented with a pop-up menu that lets you select an application to launch (see Figure 15.7).

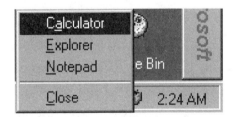

FIGURE 15.7: THE APPLICATION LAUNCHER

You can modify this program to include your favourite and most used applications, or even link it to a database or ASCII file so you can customize the applications that appear on your menu. You should now have enough experience with Visual Basic 5 to take this application and make it as powerful as you like.

Tip

System Tray applications usually offer a pop-up menu that allows the user to perform some action with the program. At a minimum you should give the user the option to close the application. If you want to show a form or dialog box, place a Show method in the MouseDblClick event of clsSysTray.

Looking to the Future

We have not even scratched the surface of what the Windows API can do. Here is a small list of interesting things you can do with the Win32API:

- Make forms "float" by remaining on top of the other forms
- Call network functions using the WNet functions
- Create a video capture application using the AVICap functions

There is no limit to what you can do when you put the right tools together with a little bit of imagination. Unfortunately the entire Win32 API would fill volumes of text, so it is impractical to attempt to cover all of what you should know about it. Inevitably, as you develop applications and become more proficient in Visual Basic, you will learn more about its limitations. When you do, start searching the API. You can create almost any program using Visual Basic and the Win32 API.

Finally, go out and get yourself a good book documenting the Windows API. Although the API Viewer gives you the declarations for the API, it does nothing to explain the parameters that the API functions require. A good API book will explain these APIs and their parameters. It is a good investment, and if you plan to do any serious development, you will need one eventually.

Tip

Get a good book that documents the Windows API. You will be using it before you know it.

Now that you have learned the basics of Visual Basic, start playing with the sample applications included on the Visual Basic CD. In addition, start creating your own programs. Before you know it, you'll be a Visual Basic pro.

Summary of Skills Acquired

Now you can...

- ☑ use the API Viewer to retrieve API declarations
- ☑ properly declare a procedure in a DLL
- ☑ use the API in your applications

INDEX

■ ■

Note to reader: First-level entries are in bold. Page numbers in **bold** indicate the principal discussion of a topic or the definition of a term. Page numbers in *italic* indicate illustrations.

Symbols

& (ampersands)
  displaying in labels, 90-91
  making captions into shortcut keys with, 34, 77
' (apostrophes) in code comments, 266–267
* (asterisks)
  in database tables, 239
  as default password characters, 83
  in filtering files, 220
$ (dollar signs) as Help file footnote markers, 306–307, *306*
- (minus signs) for signing integers, 190
+ (plus signs)
  as Help file footnote markers, 306–308, *306*
  for signing integers, 190
() (parentheses) for calling Function procedures, 159
 # signs as Help file footnote markers, 305–307, *306*
" " (quotation marks) for setting string properties in code, 53, 154–155

A

About dialog box
  adding Easter eggs to, 295–297, *296*, *297*
  overview of, 73, *73*
Access databases, 224, 227–229, 253
access keys. *See* shortcut keys
accessing. *See also* opening; storing and
    retrieving data
  ASCII files, **205–223**
    adding nonprintable ASCII characters to
    code, 187
    ASCII tables, **187**
    in binary access mode, 214–223, *215*, *221*
    in random access mode, 211–214, *213*
    in sequential access mode, 208–210, *208*, *209*
  database tables, 225–229
  Windows API, 387
Activate form event, 57–59
ActiveX, **363–383**
  controls, **373–380**
    coding control interfaces, 376–380, *376–380*
    creating control interfaces, 373–376,
    374–376
    creating SysTray control, 395–400
    overview of, 373
  defined, **363**

documents, **368–373**
  creating, *364*, 368–371, *370*
  defined, **368–369**
  viewing, 371–372, *372*
  overview of, 2, 161–162, 363–365, 383
  project templates, 367–368, *368*
  security requirements, **365–367**
    digital signatures, 365
    progressive downloading, 367
    run-time licensing, 366
    scripting and, 365–366
ActiveX Components dialog box, 336, *337*
ActiveX Control Interface Wizard, 376–380, *376–380*
ActiveX DLLs, 161–162, 380–383, *381–382*. *See also* DLLs
adding
  applications to System Tray, 395–400, *395*, *396*, *398*, *399*
  captions to forms, 18
  comments to code, 266–267
  controls to Toolbox, 22–23
  data controls to databases, 225–227
  drag-and-drop with mouse events, 292–295, *293*, *294*
  fields to database tables, 237–238, *237*, 249–253
  footnotes to Help topics, 305–308, *306*
  graphics to command buttons, 82
  icons to forms, 20, 48
  Internet controls to Toolbox, 22, 143
  lines of code to procedures, 51–53, *52*, *54*
  MDI forms with Form Wizard, 70–74, *71*, *73*
  nonprintable ASCII characters to code, 187
  procedures to code modules, 150–152, *150*
  to toolbars
    buttons, 178, *179*
    code, 181–182
    icons, 179–181, *180–181*
    menu items, 12
Advanced tab in Options dialog box, 31–32
ampersands (&)
  displaying in labels, 90–91
  making captions into shortcut keys with, 34, 77

anchors, 23
API Viewer, **389–394**. *See also* Microsoft Windows API
  converting files to databases, 390–391, *392*
  defined, **390**, *390*
  integrating declarations with applications, 392–394, *393*
  loading, 390
  retrieving declarations from, 391, *391*
apostrophes (') in code comments, 266–267
applets, Hello World! applet, 32–37, *33*, *35*, *36*
Application Launcher program example, 396–399, *398*, *399*
applications. *See also* ActiveX; compiling and distributing projects; projects
  adding to System Tray, 395–400, *395*, *396*
  document-centric applications, 65
  installing sample applications, 25–26
  integrating declarations with in API Viewer, 392–394, *393*
  linking Help files to, 318–322, *321*
arrays, **199–202**. *See also* variables
  declaring, 199–201
  dynamic arrays, 201–202
  example, 199–201
  overview of, 184, 199
ASCII files, **205–223**. *See also* storing and retrieving data
  adding nonprintable ASCII characters to code, 187
  ASCII tables, **187**
  in binary access mode, 214–223, *215*, *221*
  in random access mode, 211–214, *213*
  in sequential mode, 208–210, *208*, *209*
asterisks (*)
  in database tables, 239
  as default password characters, 83
  in filtering files, 220

B

BackColor form property, 19, 44
background colours in forms, 19, 44
binary access mode ASCII files, 214–223, *215*, *221*
boolean value properties
  changing, 16
  in database tables, 247
  defined, **16**, **185**, **192**
  overview of, 192–193
borders
  BorderStyle form property, 16–17, 44–46
  defined, **40**, *40*
bugs
  fixing with Print method, 256–260, *259*, 265
  Windows API and, 387, 389, 394
build numbers for projects, 325–326
buttons, **76–82**, **93–97**
  adding graphics to command buttons, 82
  adding to toolbars, 178, *179*
  command buttons, **76–82**
    adding graphics to, 82
    events of, 79
    methods of, 79
    overview of, 75–76
    properties for, 77–78
    testing, 80–82, *80*
  in forms, *40*, **41–42**
  moving on toolbars, 11–12
  option buttons, **93–97**
    events of, 94–96
    frames and, 103–104
    methods of, 96–97, *97*
    in Options dialog box, 96–97, *97*
    overview of, 93
    properties for, 93–94
  on Standard toolbar, 10–11, *10*
  on Toolbox, 21, *21. See also* controls
bytes, **185–187**, *186*, 187–188

C

caches, **366–367**
calculating area of circles example, 202–204, *203*, 204
calculating cube roots example, 155–160, *156–159*
calling API functions with wrappers, 394
calling conventions for DLLs, 386–389
Caption Bars
  creating clocks on, 126–128, *127*
  flickering in, 127–128
Caption property, **51–55**, **152–155**. *See also* strings; text
  adding captions to forms, 18
  captions defined, 40–41, *40*
  changing form captions example, 51–55, *52*, *54*, *55*
  changing through code, 152–155, *153–155*
  hiding form captions, 41, 45
  making captions into shortcut keys, 34, 77
CBF (code behind forms), **150**
CD-ROM, Visual Basic 5
  Help Workshop on, 300, *300*
  icons on, 48
  SysTray sample application on, 395–400
centring forms, 48–49
changing. *See also* resizing
  boolean value properties, 16
  Caption property with code, 152–155, *153–155*
  form background colours, 19, 44
  form captions example, 51–55, *52*, *54*, *55*
check boxes, **97–103**
  dimmed check boxes, 97–98, *98*
  events of, 99
  example, 100–103
  frames and, 103–104
  methods of, 99–100, *100*
  overview of, 97–98, *98*
  properties for, 98–99
  testing, 99–100, *100*
checking return codes of API functions, 389
child forms, **65**

Chr$() function for adding nonprintable ASCII characters to code, 187

circles, calculating area of example, 202–204, *203*, 204

class modules, 161–165. *See also* code modules; objects
creating, 354–357
creating interfaces for, 358–361, *359*, *361*
methods in, 163, 165
overview of, 161–162, 165
Private and Public keywords in, 163–165
procedures in, 161–163
properties in, 164–165

Click events
for command buttons, 79
DblClick mouse event, 288
for menus, 171–172
for mouse, 287
right-clicking on objects, 14

Close buttons in forms, *40*, **42**

closing databases, 234

code, 51–55, 256–260, 263–271. *See also* procedures
adding comments to, 266–267
adding lines of, 51–53, *52*, *54*
adding nonprintable ASCII characters to, 187
adding to toolbars, 181–182
CBF (code behind forms), **150**
changing Caption property with, 152–155, *153–155*
changing in form captions example, 51–55, *52*, *54*, *55*
checking return codes of API functions, 389
code libraries, **146**
Code window, 24–25, *24*
coding ActiveX controls, 376–380, *376–380*
debugging with Print method, 256–260, *259*, 265
deciphering code listings, 270–271
deciphering for MDI forms, 69–70
For...Next example, 199–201, *200*
If-Then-Else examples, 52–53
native code, 330–331
P-code, 330–331

printing, **263–271**
adding comments to, 266–267
deciphering, 270–271
overview of, 263, *263*
setting options for, 264–266
viewing results of, 267–270
scripting and, 365–366
setting string properties in code with quotation marks (" "), 53, 154–155

code modules, 145–165
adding procedures to, 150–152, *150*
class modules, **161–165**
methods in, 163, 165
overview of, 161–162, 165
Private and Public keywords in, 163–165
procedures in, 161–163
properties in, 164–165
creating, 147–149, 160–161, *161*
creating Function procedures in, 155–160, *156–159*
creating library directories for, 146
defined, **145–146**
overview of, 145–146
passing parameters to functions and procedures in, 152–155, *153–155*
printing, 264, 266
Private and Public Sub procedures in, 148–152, *149*, *150*, 161
retrieving, 146–147
wrappers
calling API functions with, 394
creating, 192–193
defined, **276–277**

colours
changing in form backgrounds, 19, 44
for text, 46–47
viewing Color Palette, 19

columns. *See also* fields in database tables
multiple columns in list boxes, 106–107
resizing, 240

combo boxes, 112–118. *See also* list boxes; text boxes
data-bound (DBCombo) boxes, 112, 115
drop-down combo boxes, 100, **113**

drop-down list boxes, 112, **114**
  events of, 114
  example, 116–118
  versus list boxes, 112, 116, *116*
  methods of, 115–116, *116*
  overview of, 112
  properties for, 113–114
  simple combo boxes, 112, **113**
command buttons, 76–82
  adding graphics to, 82
  events of, 79
  methods of, 79
  overview of, 75–76
  properties for, 77–78
  testing, 80–82, *80*
**comma-separated values (CSV) list of ASCII
  files, 205–206**, *206*
comments added to code, 266–267
compiling and distributing projects, 323–343.
    See also projects
    overview of, 323–324, 342
    setting compiler options, 330–333
    setting project options, 323–330
    with Setup Wizard, **334–342**
      compiling projects, 334–335, *334, 335*
      compressing files, *340*, 341
      distribution options, 336–338, *336–338*
      saving templates, 339–341, *339*
      scanning for viruses, 341–342, *341*
compressing files with Setup Wizard, *340*, 341
constants. *See also* variables
  Const keyword for declaring constants, 203
  data types for, 185
  declaring, 203
  defined, **202–203**
  example, 203–204, *203, 204*
contained forms, 65
contents files in Help, 302–304, *301, 302*
Control Interface Wizard, 376–380, *376–380*
Control menus in forms
  defined, *40*, **41**
  hiding, 45–46
ControlBox form property, 45–46

controls, 75–144
  ActiveX controls, **363–383**
    coding control interfaces, 376–380, *376–380*
    creating control interfaces, 373–376, *374–376*
    creating SysTray control, 395–400
    overview of, 373
  check boxes, **97–103**
    dimmed check boxes, 97–98, *98*
    events of, 99
    example, 100–103
    frames and, 103–104
    methods of, 99–100, *100*
    overview of, 97–98, *98*
    properties for, 98–99
    testing, 99–100, *100*
  combo boxes, **112–118**
    data-bound boxes, 112, 115
    drop-down combo boxes, 112, **113**
    drop-down list boxes, 112, **114**
    events of, 114
    example, 116–118
    versus list boxes, 112, 116, *116*
    methods of, 115–116, *116*
    overview of, 112
    properties for, 113–114
    simple combo boxes, 112, **113**
  command buttons, **76–82**
    adding graphics to, 82
    events of, 79
    methods of, 79
    overview of, 75–76
    properties for, 77–78
    testing, 80–82, *80*
  creating SysTray control, 395–396, *396*
  data controls, **224–229**
    accessing databases with, 224–225
    adding, 225–227
    properties for, 227–229, *228*
  data-bound controls, 112, 115
  defined, **21**, *21*
  directory list boxes, **135–136, 140–142**
    events of, 136
    example, 140–142, *141*

methods of, 136
overview of, 135, *137*
properties for, 135–136
drive list boxes, **133–135, 140–142**
    events of, 134
    example, 140–142, *141*
    methods of, 135
    overview of, 133, *137*
    properties for, 133–134
file list boxes, **136–142**
    events of, 139–140
    example, 140–142, *141*
    methods of, 140
    overview of, 136–137, *137*
    properties for, 137–139
frames, **103–105**
    check boxes and, 103–104
    events of, 104–105
    methods of, 105, *105*
    option buttons and, 103–104
    properties for, 104
images, **118–121**
    events of, 119
    example, 120–121
    methods of, 119–120
    overview of, 118
    versus picture boxes, 118, 121
    properties for, 118–119
labels, **88–93**
    displaying ampersands (&) in, 90–91
    events of, 91–92
    example, 92–93, *93*
    methods of, 92
    overview of, 88
    properties for, 90–91
    shortcut keys for, 89–90
list boxes, **106–112**
    versus combo boxes, 112, 116, *116*
    events of, 109
    examples, 110–112, 116–118
    methods of, 109–110
    multiple columns in, 107
    overview of, 106
    properties for, 106–108

menu controls, 168–169, 265
option buttons, **93–97**
    events of, 94–96
    frames and, 103–104
    methods of, 96–97, *77*
    in Options dialog box, 96–97, *97*
    overview of, 93
    properties for, 93–94
overview of, 75–76, *76*
picture boxes, **121–125**
    events of, 123–124
    versus images, 118, 121
    methods of, 124–125
    overview of, 121–122
    properties for, 122–123
printing code of, 263–271
printing lists of properties for, 265
sample application of forms and, 149–150, *149*
scroll bars, **128–133**
    events of, 130–131
    example, 131–133, *132*
    flickering in, 129
    methods of, 131
    overview of, 128–129
    properties for, 129–130
    scroll boxes in, 130
text boxes, **82–88**
    events of, 84
    methods of, 84–85
    overview of, 82
    properties for, 82–84
    testing, 85–87, *86, 89*
timers, **125–128**
    creating Caption Bar clocks, 126–128, *127*
    event of, 126
    properties for, 125–126
Toolbox of
    adding controls to, 22
    adding Internet controls to, 22, 143–144
    control buttons on, 21, *21*
    removing controls from, 22–23
converting files to databases in API Viewer,
    390–391, *392*
copyrighting projects, 327

counter fields in database tables, 244–245

crashes, **system**, Windows API and, 387, 389, 394

creating

ActiveX controls, 373–376, *374–376*

ActiveX DLLs, 161–162, 380–383, *381–382*

ActiveX documents, *364*, 368–371, *370*

Application Launcher program, 396–399, *398, 399*

Caption Bar clocks, 126–128, *127*

code libraries, 146

code modules, 147–149, 160–161, *161*

database tables, 234–236

databases with Visual Data Manager, 224, *224, 232–234, 234,* 253–254

Easter eggs, 295–297, *296, 297*

encryption programs, 214–223, *215, 221*

floating toolbars, 17

Function procedures, 155–160, *156–159*

Hello World! applet, 32–37, *33, 35, 36*

interfaces for objects class, 358–361, *359, 361*

logon forms, 196–198, *196*

MDI forms, 65–67, *66, 67*

menus, 172–175, *175*

menus in Application Launcher example, 396–399, *398, 399*

objects class, 354–357

SysTray control, 395–396, *396*

toolbars, 177–178, *178*

wrapper functions, 192–193

Crystal Reports Pro, 260–262, *261–263*, 270

CSV (comma-separated values) list of ASCII files, **205–206**, *206*

cube root calculation example, 155–160, *156–159*

currency fields in database tables, 247

customizing. *See also* setting options

MDI forms, 67–68, *69*

toolbars, 11–12

D

data. *See also* files; storing and retrieving data

Dynamic Data Exchange (DDE), **85**

editing in dynasets, 232

entering and editing in database tables, 238–240

data controls, **224–229**

accessing databases with, 224–225

adding, 225–227

properties for, 227–229, *228*

data types for variables, **184–193**. *See also* variables

booleans, 192–193

bytes, 185–187, *186*

and constants, 185

integers, 190–191, *191*

overview of, 184–185

strings, 187–188, *188*

variants, 193–194

databases, **224–254**

converting files to in API Viewer, 390–391, *392*

creating with Visual Data Manager, 224, *224, 232–234, 234,* 253–254

data controls, **224–229**

accessing databases with, 224–225

adding, 225–227

properties for, 227–229, *228*

database queries

creating, 240–243, *241, 242*

defined, **229–230**

overview of, 231–232

database tables, **229–240**

adding fields to, 237–238, *237,* 249–253

counter fields in, 244–245

creating, 234–236

currency fields in, 247

date/time fields in, 248

defining properties of, 236–237, *236*

editing data in, 232, 238–240

entering data into, 238–240

memo fields in, 247–248

number fields in, 245–246

overview of, 229–230

primary keys in, 243–244
Yes/No fields in, 247
indexes in, **229**, 250–251
Microsoft Access databases, 224, 227–229, 253
opening and closing, 234
overview of, 229, 253–254
data-bound controls, 112, 115
date/time fields in database tables, 248
DBCombo boxes, 112, 115
DblClick mouse event, 288
DBList boxes, 115
DDE (Dynamic Data Exchange), **85**
Deactivate form event, 56, 59, 61
debugging code
option for, 332
with Print method, 256–260, *259*, 265
deciphering code
in code listings, 270–271
for MDI forms, 69–70
declaring, **194–201**
API functions, 386–389
arrays, 199–201
constants, 203
retrieving declarations from API Viewer, **389–394**
variables, **194–199**
forcing declarations, 189–190, *190*
local variables, 194, 198–199
module-level variables, 194–195, *194*
overview of, 27–28
public variables, 195–198, *196*
static variables, 198–199, 201–202
deleting. *See* removing
delimited ASCII files, **205–206**, *206*
design environment. *See* integrated development environment
design time, **15**
dialog boxes, **273–286**
custom dialog boxes, 276–278
error message dialog boxes, 280, 285, *285*
input dialog boxes, 275–276
login dialog boxes, 280–281, 285–286, *286*
message dialog boxes, 273–275
overview of, 278–279, 286

testing, 281–283, *282*, *283*
Yes/No dialog boxes, 279–280, 284, *284*
digital signatures in ActiveX, 351
Dim (dimension) keyword
declaring arrays with, 199–201
declaring local variables with, 194, 198–199
static variables and, 198–199
dimmed check boxes, 97–98, *98*
directories of code libraries, 146
directory list boxes, **135–136**. *See also* list boxes
events of, 136
example, 140–142, *141*
methods of, 136
overview of, 135, *137*
properties for, 135–136
displaying ampersands (&) in labels, 90–91
DLLs (dynamic link libraries), **380–383**, **385–389**. *See also* Microsoft Windows API
ActiveX DLLs, 161–162, 380–383, *381*, *382*
calling conventions for, 386–389
overview of, 385–386
docking windows, **30**
documents, **64–70**, **368–373**
ActiveX documents, **368–373**
creating, *364*, 368–371, *370*
defined, **368–369**
viewing, 371–372, *372*
defined, **40**
document-centric applications, **65**
multiple document interface forms, **64–70**
adding with Form Wizard, 70–74, *71*, *73*
creating, 65–67, *66*, 67
customizing, 67–68, *69*
deciphering code of, 69–70
overview of, 64–65, *64*
dollar signs ($) as Help file footnote markers, 306–307, *306*
downloading, progressive, 367
drag-and-drop
adding with mouse events, 292–295, *293*, *294*
DragDrop events
for forms, 59–60
for mouse, 288–289
example, 11–12

DragOver mouse event, 289
drive list boxes, 133–135. *See also* list boxes
  events of, 134
  example, 140–142, *141*
  methods of, 135
  overview of, 133, *137*
  properties for, 133–134
drop-down combo boxes, 112, **113**
drop-down list boxes, 112, **114**
dynamic arrays, 201–202
Dynamic Data Exchange (DDE), **85**
dynamic link libraries (DLLs). *See* DLLs
dynasets, 231–232, 243

E

editing
  in Code Window, 24–25, *24*
  data in database tables, 238–240
  data in dynasets, 232
  setting options for, 27–29
Editor tab in Options dialog box, 27–29, *27*,
  189–190, *190*
encapsulation of objects, 352–353
encryption programs example, 214–223, *215*,
  221
entering data into database tables, 238–240
enumerated lists, **16–17**
Environment tab in Options dialog box, 30–31,
  30
error message dialog boxes, 280, 285, *285*
event-driven operating systems, **55**
events. *See also* procedures
  of check boxes, 99
  Click events
    for command buttons, 79
    DblClick mouse event, 288
    for menus, 171–172
    for mouse, 287
    right-clicking on objects, 13–14
  of combo boxes, 114
  of command buttons, 79
  defined, **55**

of directory list boxes, 136
of drive list boxes, 134
of file list boxes, 139–140
form events, **55–63**
  Activate, 57–59
  Deactivate, 56, 59, 61
  DragDrop, 59–60
  GotFocus, 58
  Help with, 57
  Initialize, 58
  Load, 57–58, 60–61
  overview of, 55–58, *56*
  printing lists of, 266
  Resize, 61–62
  Unload, 61–63
of frames, 104–105
of images, 119
of labels, 91–92
of list boxes, 109
mouse events, **287–297**
  adding drag-and-drop with, 292–295, *293*,
  294
  Click, 13–14, 79, 171–172, 287
  creating and finding Easter eggs with, 295–
  297, *296*, *297*
  DblClick, 288
  DragDrop, 288–289
  DragOver, 289
  MouseDown, 290–291
  MouseMove, 287, 291
  MouseUp, 79, 291–292
  overview of, 287
of option buttons, 94–96
of picture boxes, 123–124
of scroll bars, 130–131
of text boxes, 84
of timers, 126
examples
  accessing tables in databases, 225–227
  Application Launcher program, 396–399, *398*,
  399
  arrays, 199–201
  byte variables, 185–187
  calculating area of circles, 202–204, *203*, *204*

calculating cube roots, 155–160, *156–159*

changing Hello captions to Bye, 51–55, *52, 54, 55*

check boxes, 100–103

combo boxes, 116–118

constants, 203–204, *203, 204*

creating Caption Bar clocks, 126–128, *127*

creating encryption programs, 214–223, *215, 221*

creating wrapper functions, 192–193

data controls, 225–227

determining scope of variables, 194–198, *194*

directory list boxes, 140–142, *141*

drag-and-drop, 11–12

For…Next code loops, 199–201, *200*

GetBalance method, 163

If-Then-Else code loops, 52–53

images, 120–121

integer variables, 190–191

labels, 92–93, *93*

list boxes, 110–112, 116–118

peanut butter and jelly check boxes, 100–103

scroll bars, 131–133, *132*

searching files, 140–142, *141*, 192–193

string variables, 188–189

F

F1 function key for accessing Help

for form events and methods, 57

for form properties, 43

setting up, 321

fields in database tables

adding, 237–238, *237*, 249–253

counter fields, 244–255

currency fields, 247

date/time fields, 248

defined, **230**

memo fields, 247–248

number fields, 245–246

Yes/No fields, 247

file extensions, .VBP, 13

file list boxes, **136–142**. *See also* list boxes

events of, 139–140

example, 140–142, *141*

methods of, 140

overview of, 136–137, *137*

properties for, 137–139

files. *See also* databases; Help files

ASCII files, **205–223**. *See also* storing and retrieving data

adding nonprintable ASCII characters to code, 187

ASCII tables, **187**

in binary access mode, 214–223, *215, 221*

in random access mode, 211–214, *213*

in sequential mode, 208–210, *208, 209*

compressing with Setup Wizard, *340*, 341

converting to databases in API Viewer, 390–391, *392*

file name properties, 20

searching files examples, 140–142, *141*, 178–179

finding Easter eggs, 295–297, *296, 297*

fixing bugs

option for, 332

with Print method, 256–260, *259*, 265

flickering

in Caption Bars, 127–128

in scroll bars, 129

floating toolbars, 17

footnotes in Help topics, 305–308, *306*

For…Next code loop example, 199–201, *200*

ForeColor form property, 46–47

form modules

creating, 160

defined, **150**

printing details on, 264–265

Format function, 128

forms, 39–74

adding captions to, 18

adding icons to, 20, 48

centring, 48–49

changing background colours of, 19, 44

changing form captions example, 51–55, *52, 54, 55*

colouring text in, 46–47
components of, 40–42
creating logon forms, 196–198, *198*
defined, **13**, **39–40**
Form Designer workspace, 23
form events, **48–55**. *See also* events
    Activate, 57–59
    Deactivate, 56, 59, 61
    DragDrop, 59–60
    GotFocus, 58
    Help with, 57
    Initialize, 58
    Load, 57–58, 60–61
    overview of, 55–58, *56*
    printing lists of, 266
    Resize, 61–62
    Unload, 61–63
Form Layout window, 20–21, *21*
form properties, **42–55**. *See also* properties
    BackColor, 19, 44
    BorderStyle, 17, 44–46
    Caption, 40–41, 45, 51–55, *52*, *54–55*. *See also* Caption property
    ControlBox, 45–46
    ForeColor, 46–47
    Height, 47–48, 51
    Help with, 43
    Icon, 20, 48
    Left, 48–49
    MaxButton, 45–46, 49
    MinButton, 45–46, 49
    Name, 50
    overview of, 42–43, 51
    printing lists of, 265
    ScaleMode, 50
    ShowInTaskbar, 50
    size properties, 20, 23, 47–51, 61–62
    text colour properties, 46–47
    Top, 49
    Width, 47–48, 51
    WindowState, 51
Form Wizard, 62–64, *63*, *65*
hiding captions on, 35, 39
hiding from Taskbar, 44

methods for, 50, 56
multiple document interface (MDI) forms, **64–70**
    adding with Form Wizard, 70–74, *71*, *73*
    creating, 65–67, *66–67*
    customizing, 67–68, *69*
    deciphering code of, 69–70
    overview of, 64–65, *64*
naming, 50
printing code for, 263–271
printing to, 256, 264–265
renaming, 18
resizing, 20, 23, 47–51, 61–62
startup options, 51
frames, 103–105
    check boxes and, 103–104
    defined, **103–104**
    events of, 104–105
    methods of, 105, *105*
    option buttons and, 103–104
    properties for, 103–104
function keys. *See* shortcut keys
functions. *See also* Microsoft Windows API; procedures
    API functions
        calling with wrappers, 394
        checking return codes of, 389
        declaring, 386–389
        passing parameters to, 386–389
        for SysTray control, 395–396, *396*
    Chr$() function, 187
    creating Function procedures, 155–160, *156–159*
    F1 function key for accessing Help, 43, 57, 321
    Format function, 128
    passing parameters to, 152–155, *153–155*
    wrapper functions
        calling API functions with, 394
        creating, 192–193
        defined, **276–277**

G

General tab in Options dialog box, 29-30
GetBalance method example, 163
global variables, 195–198
GotFocus form event, 58–59
Graphical User Interfaces (GUIs), **176**
graphics on command buttons, 82
greyed check boxes, 97–98, *98*

H

handles, **207**
Height form property, 47–48, 51
Hello World! applet, 32–37, *33, 35,* 36
Help via F1 function key
    for form events and methods, 57
    for form properties, 43
    setting up, 321
Help files, **299–322**
    adding topic footnotes to, 305–308, *306*
    creating, **299–318**
        contents files, 302–304, *301, 302*
        overview of, 301
        project files, 313–318, *313–317*
        requirements for, 300
        topic files, 305–312, *306*
    linking to applications, 318–322, *321*
    overview of, 299
    setting up F1 key for accessing, 321
    testing, 317–318
hexadecimal value properties, 19
hiding
    Control menus in forms, 45–46
    form captions, 40–41, 45
    forms from Taskbar, 50
    New Project dialog box, 6–7, *6*
    Project Wizard, 31
    text, 47
hot keys. *See* shortcut keys

I

icons. *See also* images; picture boxes
    adding to forms, 20, 48
    adding to toolbars, 179–181, *180, 181*
    Icon form property, 20, 48
    pencil icons in database tables, 239
    for projects, 326
    on Visual Basic 5 CD-ROM, 48
    yellow smiley face icons, 20
IDE. *See* integrated development environment
If-Then-Else code loop examples, 52–53
images, **118–121**. *See also* icons; picture boxes
    events of, 119
    example, 120–121
    methods of, 119–120
    overview of, 118
    versus picture boxes, 118, 121
    properties for, 118–119
Immediate windows, viewing bugs in, 257–260, *259*
indexes in databases, **229**, 250–251
inheritance of objects, 351–352
Initialize form event, 58–59
input dialog boxes, 275–276
installing sample applications, 25–26
integers, **185**, **190**, 190–191, *191. See also* numbers
integrated development environment (IDE), **8–23**. *See also* interfaces
    components, 8–9, *8*
    Form Designer, 23
    Form Layout window, 20–21, *21*
    Project Explorer window, 8, 9, 12–13, *13*
    Properties window, 14–20, *14*
    setting options for, 26–32, *27, 30*
    Standard toolbar, 10–12, *10*
    Toolbox, 21–23, *21,* 143
interfaces, **64–70**, **373–380**. *See also* integrated development environment
    ActiveX control interfaces, **373–380**
        coding, 376–380, *376–380*
        creating, 373–376, *374–376*

creating for objects class, 358–361, *359, 361*
defined, **9**
Graphical User Interfaces (GUIs), **176**
multiple document interface forms, **64–70**
  adding with Form Wizard, 70–74, *71, 73*
  creating, 65–67, *66–67*
  customizing, 67–68, *69*
  deciphering code of, 69–70
  overview of, 64–65, *64*

Internet
  accessing with ActiveX, 363–367, 383
  adding Internet controls to Toolbox, 22, 143

K

keyboard shortcuts. *See* shortcut keys
keys, primary keys in database tables, 243–244
keywords, **163–165, 195–202**
  declaring constants with Const keyword, 203
  Dim (dimension) keyword, **198–201**
    declaring arrays with, 200–201
    declaring local variables with, 194, 198–199
    static variables and, 198–199
  Private keyword, **163–165**
    in class modules, 163–165
    declaring module-level variables with, 194–195, *194*
  Public keyword, **163–165, 195–198**
    in class modules, 163–165
    declaring arrays with, 200
    declaring constants with, 203
    declaring public variables with, 195–198, *196*

L

labels, **88–93**
  displaying ampersands (&) in, 90–91
  events of, 91–92
  example, 92–93, *33*
  methods of, 92
  overview of, 88
  properties for, 90–91
  shortcut keys for, 89–90

Left form property, 48–49
libraries, **385–389**
  code libraries, 146
  DLLs (dynamic link libraries), **380–383, 385–389**. *See also* Microsoft Windows API
    ActiveX DLLs, 161–162, 380–383, *381, 382*
    calling conventions for, 386–389
    overview of, 385–386
list boxes, **106–112**. *See also* combo boxes
  versus combo boxes, 112, 116, *116*
  directory list boxes, **135–136, 140–142**
    events of, 136
    example, 140–142, *141*
    methods of, 136
    overview of, 135, *137*
    properties for, 135–136
  drive list boxes, **133–135, 140–142**
    events of, 134
    example, 140–142, *141*
    methods of, 135
    overview of, 133, *137*
    properties for, 133–134
  events of, 109
  examples, 110–112, 116–118
  file list boxes, **136–142**
    events of, 139–140
    example, 140–142, *141*
    methods of, 140
    overview of, 136–137, *137*
    properties for, 137–139
  methods of, 109–110
  multiple columns in, 107
  overview of, 106
  properties for, 106–108
Load form event, 57–58, 60–61
loading API Viewer, 390
local variables declaring, 194, 198–199
login dialog boxes creating, 280–281, 285–286, *286*
logon forms, 196–198, *196*

M

machine code, 330–331
MaxButton form properties, 45–46, 49
Maximize/Restore buttons on forms, defined, *40*,
    41–42, 49
MDI forms. *See* multiple document interface
    (MDI) forms
memo fields in database tables, 247–248
memory, 183–184
menus, **167–177**. *See also* toolbars
    adding menu items to toolbars, 12
    Click event for, 171–172
    Control menus in forms, *40*, **41**, 45–46
    controls for, 168–169, 265
    creating in Application Launcher example,
        396–399, *398*, *399*
    creating with Menu Editor, *169*, 172–175, *175*
    methods for, 172
    overview of, 167–169, *167*, 182
    properties for, 169–171
    removing menu items from toolbars, 12
    shortcut keys for, 170–171
    standardizing, 176–177
message dialog boxes, 273–275
methods
    of check boxes, 99–100, *100*
    in class modules, 163, 165
    of combo boxes, 115–116, *116*
    of command buttons, 79
    defined, **63–64**
    of directory list boxes, 136
    of drive list boxes, 135
    of file list boxes, 140
    for forms, 57, 63–64
    of frames, 105, *105*
    Help for, 57
    of images, 119–120
    of labels, 92
    of list boxes, 109–110
    for menus, 172
    of objects, 350–351, *351*
    of option buttons, 96–97, *97*
    of picture boxes, 124–125

    Print method, 256–260, *259*
    PrintForm method, 260
    of scroll bars, 131
    of text boxes, 84–85
Microsoft Access databases, 224, 227–229, 253
Microsoft Active Platform. *See* ActiveX
Microsoft Help Workshop. *See* Help files
Microsoft Windows API, **385–401**
    accessing, 387
    API functions
        calling with wrappers, 394
        checking return codes of, 389
        declaring, 386–389
        passing parameters to, 386–389
        for SysTray control, 395–396, *396*
    API Viewer, **389–394**
        converting files to databases, 390–391, *392*
        defined, **390**, *390*
        integrating declarations with applications,
            392–394, *393*
        loading, 390
        retrieving declarations from, 391, *391*
    defined, **386**
    DLLs and, 385–389
    overview of, 385–386, 400
    system crashes and, 387, 389, 394
    Win32 API, 386, 388, 400
MinButton form properties, 45–46, 49
Minimize buttons on forms, *40*, **41–42**
minus signs (-) for signing integers, 190
modal forms, 72–73
module-level variables, 194–195, *194*
modules. *See* code modules; form modules;
    standard modules
most recently used (MRU) projects, 8
mouse events, **287–297**
    adding drag-and-drop with, 292–295, *293*, *294*
    Click
        for command buttons, 79
        for menus, 171–172
        overview of, 287
        right-clicking on objects, 14
    creating and finding Easter eggs with, 295–297,
        296, *297*

DblClick, 288
DragDrop, 288–289
DragOver, 289
MouseDown, 290–291
MouseMove, 287, 291
MouseUp, 79, 291–292
overview of, 287
moving toolbar buttons, 11–12
MRU (most recently used) projects, 8
multiple columns in list boxes, 106–107
multiple document interface (MDI) forms, **64–
70**. *See also* forms
adding with Form Wizard, 70–74, *71*, *73*
creating, 65–67, *66–67*
customizing, 67–68, *69*
deciphering code of, 69–70
overview of, 64–65, *64*
multiple projects, opening, 25–26

N

naming
file name properties, 20
forms, 50
Name property for forms, 18, 50
naming conventions, 50
renaming forms, 18
native code, 330–331
New Project dialog box, 6–8, *6*
numbers. *See also* integers
build numbers for projects, 325–326
number fields in database tables, 245–246
version and revision numbers for projects, 325–
326

O

object-oriented programming (OOP), **161**, **345–
346**, 345–361
objects, **349–361**. *See also* class modules
creating interfaces for, 358–361, *359*, *361*
creating objects class, 354–357

defined, **14**, **345–346**
encapsulation of, 352–353
inheritance of, 351–352
methods of, 350–351, *351*
overview of, 349
polymorphism of, 353–354, *354*
printing code of, 263–271
properties of, 349–350, *350*
OCXs. *See* ActiveX
opening. *See also* accessing
databases, 234
multiple projects, 25–26
option buttons, **93–97**
events of, 94–96
frames and, 103–104
methods of, 96–97, *97*
in Options dialog box, 96–97, *97*
overview of, 93
properties for, 93–94
options. *See* properties; setting options
Options dialog box, **26–32**
Advanced tab, 31–32
Docking tab, 30
Editor Format tab, 29
Editor tab, 27–29, *27*, 189–190, *190*
Environment tab, 30–31, *30*
General tab, 29–30
option buttons in, 96–97, *97*
overview of, 26, *27*
**Options dialog box in Help Compiler
Workshop**, 313–314, *314*

P

parameters
passing to API functions, 386–389
passing to functions and procedures, 152–155,
153–155
parent container windows, **64–65**, *64*
parentheses () for calling Function procedures,
159
PasswordChar property for text boxes, 83
passwords as variables, 197–198

P-code, 330–331
pencil icons in database tables, 239
picture boxes, **121–125**. *See also* icons; images
   events of, 123–124
   versus images, 118, 121
   methods of, 124–125
   overview of, 121–122
   properties for, 122–123
plus signs (+)
   as Help file footnote markers, 306–308, *306*
   for signing integers, 190
polymorphism of objects, 353–354, *354*
predefined value properties, 16–17
primary keys in database tables, 243–244
Print dialog box, 263–267, *263*
printing, **255–271**
   code, **263–271**
      adding comments to, 266–267
      deciphering, 270–271
      overview of, 263, *263*
      setting options for, 264–266
      viewing results of, 267–270
   debugging code with Print method, 256–260, *259*, 265
   overview of, 255–256
   PrintForm method, 260
   reports with Crystal Reports Pro, 260–262, *261–263*, 270
Private keyword
   in class modules, 163–165
   declaring module-level variables with, 194–195, *194*
Private Sub procedures, 148–152, *148*, *150*, 161
procedures. *See also* code; events; functions
   adding lines to, 51–53, *52*, *54*
   adding to code modules, 150–152, *150*
   in class modules, 161–163
   creating Function procedures, 155–160, *155–159*
   passing parameters to, 152–155, *153–155*
   Private and Public Sub procedures, 148–152, *149*, *150*, 161

programs. *See also* applications
   creating Application Launcher example, 396–399, *398*, *399*
   creating encryption programs, 214–223, *215*, *221*
   Crystal Reports Pro, 260–262, *261–263*, 270
   object-oriented programming (OOP), **345–361**
      benefits of, 346, 354
      defined, **161**, **345–346**
      overview of, 345–348
progressive downloading, 367
projects, **313–318**, **323–330**. *See also* ActiveX; applications; compiling and distributing projects
   checking parameters passed to, 328–330
   copyrighting, 327
   icons for, 326
   most recently used (MRU) projects, 8
   names for, 326, 328
   opening multiple projects, 25–26
   Project Explorer window, 8, 9, 12–13, *13*
   project files in Help, 313–318, *313–317*
   Project Wizard
      hiding, 31
      overview of, 6–8, *7*
      removing templates from, 31
   revision numbers for, 325–326
   setting options for, 323–330
   templates for, 6–7, *6*, 367–368, *368*
   version information on, 326–328
   version numbers for, 325–326
properties, **14–20**, **42–55**, **262–271**. *See also* setting options
   boolean value properties
      changing, 16
      in database tables, 247
      defined, **16**, **185**, **192**
      overview of, 192–193
   Caption property, **51–55**, **152–155**
      adding captions to forms, 18
      captions defined, 40–41, *40*
      changing form captions example, 51–55, *52*, *54*, *55*
      changing through code, 152–155, *153–155*

hiding form captions, 40–41, 45
making captions into shortcut keys, 34, 77
for check boxes, 98–99
in class modules, 164–165
for combo boxes, 113–114
for command buttons, 77–78
for data controls, 227–229, *228*
for database tables, 236–237, *236*
defined, **14–15**
for directory list boxes, 135–136
for drive list boxes, 133–134
for file list boxes, 137–139
file name properties, 20
form properties, **42–55**
    BackColor, 19, 44
    BorderStyle, 16–17, 44–46
    Caption, 40–41, 45, 51–55, *52, 54, 55. See also* Caption property
    ControlBox, 45–46
    ForeColor, 46–47
    Height, 47–48, 51
    Help with, 43
    Icon, 20, 48
    Left, 48–49
    MaxButton, 45–46, 49
    MinButton, 45–46, 49
    Name, 18, 50
    overview of, 42–43, 51
    printing lists of, 265
    ScaleMode, 50
    ShowInTaskbar, 50
    size properties, 20, 23, 47–51, 61–62
    text colour properties, 46–47
    Top, 49
    Width, 47–48, 51
    WindowState, 51
for frames, 104
hexadecimal value properties, 19
for images, 118–119
for labels, 90–91
for list boxes, 106–108
for menus, 169–171
of objects, 349–350, *350*
for option buttons, 93–94

for picture boxes, 122–123
predefined value properties, 16–17
printing code of, 263–271
for printing reports with Crystal Reports Pro, 262, *263*
Properties window, **14–20**, *14*
for scroll bars, 129–130
string value properties
    overview of, 18
    setting in code with quotation marks (" "), 53, 154–155
for text boxes, 82–84
for timers, 125–126
Public keyword
in class modules, 163–165
declaring arrays with, 200
declaring constants with, 203
declaring public variables with, 195–198, *196*
Public Sub procedures, 148–152, *149, 150,* 161
public variables, 195–198, *196*

Q

queries, **229–232, 240–243**. *See also* databases
creating, 240–243, *241, 242*
defined, **229–230**
overview of, 231–232
quotation marks (" ") for setting string properties in code, 53, 154–155

R

random access mode ASCII files, 211–214, *213*
records
defined, **211, 229**
primary keys for, 243–244
removing
controls from Toolbox, 22–23
menu items from toolbars, 12
templates from Project Wizard window, 31
renaming forms, 18. *See also* naming
Report Wizard in Crystal Reports Pro, 260–261, *261*

reports printing with Crystal Reports Pro, 260–262, *261–263*, 270
resizing
  columns, 240
  forms, 20, 23, 47–51, 61–62
  preventing users from, 49, 62
  Resize form event, 61–62
retrieving code modules, 146–147. *See also* storing and retrieving data
return codes of API functions, 389
revision numbers for projects, 325–326
right-clicking on objects, 14. *See also* Click events
rows. *See* records
run-time, 15
run-time licensing in ActiveX, 366

S

sample applications
  of forms and controls, 149–150, *149*
  installing, 25–26
  SysTray, 395–400
  VB Terminal, 323–333
saving
  project templates with Setup Wizard, 339–341, *339*
  setting options for, *30*, 31
ScaleMode form property, 50
scanning for viruses with Setup Wizard, 341–342, *341*
scripting and ActiveX, 365–366
scroll bars, 128–133
  events of, 130–131
  example, 131–133, *132*
  flickering in, 129
  methods of, 131
  overview of, 128–129
  properties for, 129–130
  scroll boxes in, 130
searching files examples, 140–142, *141*, 192–193

security requirements, ActiveX, 365–367
  digital signatures, 365
  progressive downloading, 367
  run-time licensing, 366
  scripting and, 365–366
sequential access mode ASCII files, 208–210, *208*, *209*
setting options. *See also* customizing; properties
  for compiling projects, 330–333
  for editing, 27–29
  for IDEs, 26–32, *27*, *30*
  for printing, 264–266
  for saving, *30*, 31
setting string properties in code with quotation marks (" "), 53, 154–155
setting up F1 function key for Help access, 321
Setup Wizard, 334–342. *See also* compiling and distributing projects
  compiling projects, 334–335, *334*, *335*
  compressing project files, *340*, 341
  project distribution options, 336–338, *336–338*
  saving project templates, 339–341, *339*
  scanning projects for viruses, 341–342, *341*
shortcut keys
  F1 key for accessing Help
    for form events and methods, 57
    for form properties, 43
    setting up, 321
  for labels, 89–90
  making captions into, 34, 77
  for menus, 170–171
  primary keys in database tables, 243–244
  right-clicking on objects, 14
  standardizing, 176–177
ShowInTaskbar form property, 50
simple combo boxes, 112, **113**
sizing forms, 20, 23, 47–51, 61–62. *See also* resizing
smiley face icons, 20
standard modules. *See also* code modules
  creating, 160–161
  printing, 264
Standard toolbar, 10–12, *10*
startup options for forms, 51

statements. *See* keywords
static variables, 198–199, 201–202
storing and retrieving data, 205–254
in ASCII files, **205–223**
adding nonprintable ASCII characters to
code, 187
ASCII tables, **187**
in binary access mode, 214–223, *215*, *221*
in random access mode, 211–214, *213*
in sequential access mode, 208–210, *208*, *209*
data controls in, **224–229**
accessing databases with, 224–225
adding, 225–227
properties for, 227–229, *228*
database queries
creating, 240–243, *241*, *242*
defined, **229–230**
overview of, 231–232
in database tables, **229–240**
adding fields to, 237–238, *237*, 249–253
counter fields in, 244–245
creating, 234–236
currency fields in, 247
date/time fields in, 248
defining properties of, 236–237, *236*
editing data in, 232, 238–240
entering data into, 238–240
memo fields in, 247–248
number fields in, 245–246
overview of, 229–230
primary keys in, 243–244
Yes/No fields in, 247
in databases, **224–254**
creating with Visual Data Manager, 224, *224*,
232–234, *234*, 253–254
indexes in, **229**, 250–251
opening and closing, 234
overview of, 229, 253–254
strings. *See also* Caption property; text
defined, **18**, **185**, **187–188**
overview of, 187–190, *188*
setting in code with quotation marks (" "), 53,
154–155
string value properties, 18

Structured Query Language (SQL). *See* queries
Sub procedures, Private and Public, 148–152,
149, *150*, 161
switches, 176
system crashes and Windows API, 387, 389, 394
system modal forms, 72–73
System Tray on Taskbar, 395–400
adding applications to, 395–400, *395*, *396*
creating SysTray control for, 395–396, *396*
defined, **395**
hiding forms in, 50

T

tables. *See* databases
Taskbar System Tray, 395–400
adding applications to, 395–400, *395*, *396*
creating SysTray control for, 395–396, *396*
defined, **395**
hiding forms in, 50
templates. *See also* ActiveX
ActiveX project templates, 367–368, *368*
removing from Project Wizard window, 31
saving templates of setup programs, 339–341,
339
Visual Basic 5 project templates, 6–7, *6*
testing
check boxes, 99–100, *100*
command buttons, 80–82, *80*
dialog boxes, 281–283, *282*, *283*
Help files, 317–318
text boxes, 85–87, *86*, *89*
text. *See also* Caption property; strings
colouring, 46–47
hiding, 47
text boxes, 82–88. *See also* combo boxes
events of, 84
methods of, 84–85
overview of, 82
properties for, 82–84
testing, 85–87, *86*, *89*
time/date fields in database tables, 248

timers, 125–128
    creating Caption Bar clocks, 126–128, *127*
    event of, 126
    properties for, 125–126
title bars, *40*, **41**
tool tips, 10
tool windows, 17
toolbars, 177–182. *See also* menus
    adding buttons to, 178, *179*
    adding code to, 181–182
    adding icons to, 179–181, *180*, *181*
    adding menu items to, 12
    creating, 177–178, *178*
    floating toolbars, 17
    moving buttons on, 11–12
    overview of, 167–168, *167*, 182
    removing menu items from, 12
    standardizing, 177
Toolbox. *See also* controls
    adding controls to, 22–23
    adding Internet controls to, 22, 143
    buttons on, 21, *21*
    removing controls from, 22–23
Top form property, 48–49
topic files in Help, 305–312, *306*
twips, 47

U

Unload form event, 61–63

V

variables, 183–204
    arrays, **199–202**
        declaring, 199–201
        dynamic arrays, 201–202
        example, 199–201
        overview of, 184, 199
    constants and, **202–204**
        data types for, 185
        declaring, 203

    defined, **202–203**
        example, 203–204, *203*, *204*
    data types for, **184–193**
        booleans, 192–193
        bytes, 185–187, *186*
        integers, 190–191, *191*
        overview of, 184–185
        strings, 187–188, *188*
        variants, 193–194
    declaring, **194–201**
        local variables, 194, 198–199
        module-level variables, 194–195, *194*
        overview of, 27–28
        public variables, 195–198, *196*
        static variables, 198–199, 201–202
    defined, **184–185**
    memory and, 183–184
    passwords as, 197–198
    variants and, **185**, **193–194**
VB Terminal sample application, 323–333
.VBP file extension, 13
version numbers for projects, 325–326
viewing. *See also* accessing; opening
    ActiveX documents, 371–372, *372*
    code listings, 267–270
    Color Palettes, 19
virus scanning with Setup Wizard, 341–342, *341*
Visual Basic 5, 5–37
    CD-ROM
        Help Workshop on, 300, *300*
        icons on, 48
        SysTray sample application on, 395–400
    Code window, 24–25, *24*
    creating Hello World! applet, 32–37, *33*, *35*, *36*
    integrated development environment (IDE),
        8–23
        components, 8–9, *8*
        Form Designer, 23
        Form Layout window, 20–21, *21*
        Project Explorer window, *8*, *9*, 12–13, *13*
        Properties window, 14–20, *14*
        setting options for, 26–32, *27*, *30*
        Standard toolbar, 10–12, *10*
        Toolbox, 21–23, *21*, 143

opening multiple projects in, 25–26
overview of, 5–8, *6*
sample applications
   of forms and controls, 149–150, *149*
   installing, 25–26
   SysTray, 395–400
   VB Terminal, 323–333
Visual Data Manager for creating databases,
   224, *224*, 232–234, *234*, 253–254

W

Width form property, 47–48, 51
Win32 API, 386, 388, 400. *See also* Microsoft
   Windows API
**Window Properties dialog box in Help
   Compiler Workshop**, 314–315, *315*
windows
   Code window, 24–25, *24*
   docking, **30**
   Form Layout window, 20–21, *21*
   Immediate windows, 257–260, *259*
   parent container windows, **64–65**, *64*
   Project Explorer window, *8*, 9, 12–13, *13*
   Project Wizard window, 6–7, *6*, 31
   Properties window, 14–20, *14*
   tool windows, 17
   window lists, **68**
   WindowState form property, 51
Wizards
   ActiveX Control Interface Wizard, 376–380,
     376–380
   Form Wizard, 70–74, *71*, *73*
   Project Wizard
     hiding, 31
     overview of, 6–8, *7*
     removing templates from, 31
   Report Wizard, 260–261, *261*
   Setup Wizard, **334–342**
     compiling projects, 334–335, *334*, *335*
     compressing project files, *340*, 341
     project distribution options, 336–338, *336–338*

saving project templates, 339–341, *339*
scanning projects for viruses, 341–342, *341*
World Wide Web
   accessing with ActiveX, 363–367, 383
   adding Internet controls to Toolbox, 22, 143
wrapper functions
   calling API functions with, 394
   creating, 192–193
   defined, **276–277**

Y

yellow smiley face icons, 20
Yes/No dialog boxes, 279–280, 284, *284*
Yes/No fields in database tables, 247

NOTES

NOTES

NOTES

NOTES

NOTES

NOTES

NOTES

NOTES

SERIES TITLES

■ ■

The Complete Guide series of comprehensive books provide all you need to know for a total solution. Titles available for:

Java 1-874029-48-2	Payroll using Sage, etc 1-874029-24-5
Visual Basic 5 1-874029-64-4	Quicken 5 - UK 1-874029-55-5
Visual Basic 4 1-874029-36-9	Quicken UK using V4 1-874029-38-5
	Sage Sterling/Windows 1-874029-34-2

In easy steps series is developed for time-sensitive people who want results fast. It is designed for quick, easy and effortless learning. Titles available for:

Access 1-874029-57-1	PagePlus 1-874029-49-0
CompuServe UK 1-874029-33-4	PowerPoint 1-874029-63-6
CorelDRAW 1-874029-72-5	Publisher 1-874029-56-3
Excel 1-874029-69-5	Quicken UK 1-874029-71-7
FrontPage 1-874029-60-1	Sage Instant Accntg. 1-874029-44-X
HTML 1-874029-46-6	Sage Sterling for Win. 1-874029-43-1
Internet Explorer 1-874029-58-X	SmarSuite (97) 1-874029-67-9
Internet UK 1-874029-73-3	Upgrading Your PC 1-874029-76-8
Microsoft Money UK 1-874029-61-X	Visual Basic 1-874029-74-1
Microsoft Office 97 1-874029-66-0	Visual J++ 1-874029-75-X
Microsoft Works 1-874029-41-5	Windows 95 1-874029-28-8
Netscape Navigator 1-874029-47-4	Word 97 1-874029-68-7
PageMaker 1-874029-35-0	WordPerfect 1-874029-59-8

These books are available from your local bookshop now, or in case of difficulty, contact Computer Step at:

Southfield Road . Southam
Warwickshire CV33 OFB . England

Tel: 01926 817999
Fax: 01926 817005

http://www.computerstep.com